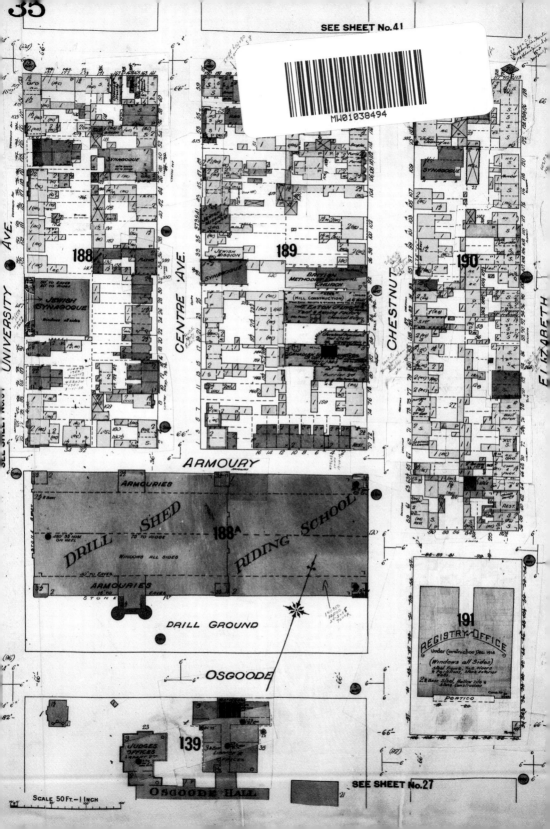

Gilded and transfer-printed ceramic plate with Blue Willow pattern, inspired by Chinese hand-painted ceramics and landscape designs. Popular in the late nineteenth and twentieth centuries.

# THE WARD UNCOVERED
## THE ARCHAEOLOGY OF EVERYDAY LIFE

*edited by*

**HOLLY MARTELLE, MICHAEL McCLELLAND,
TATUM TAYLOR, and JOHN LORINC**

COACH HOUSE BOOKS, TORONTO

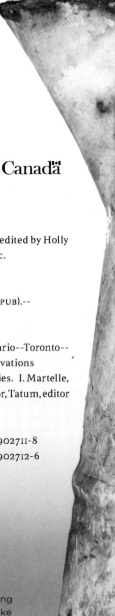

  Canadä

LIBRARY AND ARCHIVES CANADA CATALOGUING IN PUBLICATION

The Ward uncovered : the archaeology of everyday life / edited by Holly Martelle, Michael McClelland, Tatum Taylor, and John Lorinc.

Issued in print and electronic formats.
ISBN 978-1-55245-369-8 (softcover).--ISBN 978-1-77056-559-3 (EPUB).--
ISBN 978-1-77056-560-9 (PDF)

1. Ward (Toronto, Ont.)--History. 2. Neighborhoods--Ontario--Toronto--History. 3. Immigrants--Ontario--Toronto--History. 4. Excavations (Archaeology)--Ontario--Toronto. 5. Toronto (Ont.)--Antiquities. I. Martelle, Holly, 1969-, editor II. McClelland, Michael, 1951-, editor III. Taylor, Tatum, editor IV. Lorinc, John, 1963-, editor

FC3097.52.W274 2018          971.3'541          C2018-902711-8
                                                C2018-902712-6

Tin enamelled pitcher, early twentieth century. Popular among working-class families and in transient worker settlements like railway and lumber camps.

*In memory of*
*Stephen A. Otto*

# CONTENTS

Chestnut Street and Armoury,
looking northwest, 1972.

# PREFACE

HON. JEAN AUGUSTINE

IT WAS THE end of a busy day at my office, at the intersection of Bay and Dundas Streets. The phone rang and I was alerted to a dig taking place on 'my' parking lot.

How could that happen? What was going on? I thought, *We must get down there. The community must be alerted! Let's meet at Chestnut and Centre Avenue where there is an opening in the tall plywood fence that surrounds the block.* So we did, with all the official partners from the City of Toronto and Infrastructure Ontario.

This archaeological dig, with its fascinating array of findings, offered evidence of the area as a multicultural and immigrant reception site. The archaeologists had stripped away the layers of asphalt and debris to reveal the outlines of homes, artisan shops, a synagogue and early city mission, as well as the sturdy foundations of Toronto's first British Methodist Episcopal Church, which, I learned, had once been the heart and soul of African Canadian life in this unique district.

The dig exposed some of our city's earliest roots and gave me a peek into early Black life in Toronto. It also disclosed industrial activities, homes established by generations of hopeful newcomers and the businesses they conducted there. Layers of soil contained artifacts evocative not only of early African Canadian life, but also of successive waves of immigrants from Eastern Europe, Italy, China, and a host of places whose hardy and intrepid emigrants helped build our city.

As we gingerly walked around the dig, I was amazed to realize that, until then, so little attention had been paid to the place where so many strong and vibrant communities had begun life in our city.

After all, we parked our cars on this concrete surface and went about our business downtown.

Who thought of what was beneath our feet?

I did know that by the mid-nineteenth century, a substantial proportion of Toronto's population was made up of African American immigrants and refugees who were engaged in a variety of activities and occupations, and that the area north and east of Osgoode Hall was the first working-class suburb in Toronto. But did it register with me? Here was the evidence spread out before me now.

There was something awesome about the fact that I, an immigrant from the Caribbean who arrived in Toronto in 1960, would have an affinity for the neighbourhood and a connection with the area of the dig without knowing its incredible history.

In my early years in Toronto, all the activities of newly formed Caribbean organizations took place at the Chestnut Street Holiday Inn, with its large banquet hall and a kitchen willing to prepare Caribbean cuisine. We parked on that very lot. Saturday and Sunday outings brought us to Chinese restaurants in the area. We gave little thought to this downtown neighbourhood and its relevant history.

This archaeological project has provided us with the opportunity to understand the history of the area known as St. John's Ward. The following personal accounts, journalistic essays, and academic chapters will highlight the broader questions of immigration, early settlement, and life and activities, all of which mark the beginning of the strong and vibrant multicultural mosaic that Toronto is today.

Imitation Staffordshire dog figurine. Although the figurine's form is similar to authentic and expensive Staffordshire ceramics, the dull and sloppy paint job indicates a cheap reproduction.

Luxurious press-glass whale oil lamp. A rare find on an Ontario archaeological site, especially in a working-class neighbourhood.

Nail polish bottle. Widely circulated images of The Ward depicted dishevelled working-class mothers in dirty kitchens. Such small luxuries offer an interesting juxtaposition.

Department of Health
series: 'Slum interior –
13 Centre Avenue.'
August 28, 1914.

DEPT. OF HEALTH No 323

28 1914 13 CENTRE AVE

# INTRODUCTION: THE OBJECT IS THE SUBJECT

JOHN LORINC & TATUM TAYLOR

THE OFFICE WORKERS were the first to notice the curious scene far below their windows: unusually high construction hoardings, a cross-hatching of test trenches, and, finally, the footings of a building emerging from the asphalt, like an apparition.

Throughout early 2015, this tableau – the early phases of an extensive year-long archaeological dig – developed quietly on a piece of real estate that few downtowners thought twice about. The 1.6-acre parking lot – bounded by Centre Avenue, Chestnut Street, and Armoury Street – had sat there for years, flanked by commercial buildings, the blank side of an adjacent hotel, a University of Toronto student residence, and the 361 University Avenue courthouse.

Surface lots in recent years have become increasingly scarce due to the voracity of Toronto's development boom. Yet this one lingered, distinguished only by its continued existence. It's safe to assume that few of the lot's customers or the pedestrians who cut across it had ever paused to imagine what lay beneath the asphalt.

That dig, the subject of this anthology, has proven to be a dramatic moment in the history of a city that doesn't do an especially good job of remembering its past. Dramatic, because the excavation – commissioned by Infrastructure Ontario (10) and completed by London, Ontario-based Timmins Martelle Heritage Consultants – ranks as one of the largest urban archaeological projects ever carried out in Canada. Its scale rivals vast digs in locations such as New York City's Five Points, in lower Manhattan.

The excavation yielded between 300,000 and 500,000 artifacts, ranging from a 2,000-year-old Onondaga projectile point to mid-twentieth-century commercial signs.

Together, these artifacts offer unprecedented insights into the complex and multi-layered stories of an immigrant neighbourhood that existed, in various forms, on that unprepossessing block from the 1840s until the 1988 demolition of the site's final structure – a brick church at 94 Chestnut Avenue that traced its roots to a c. 1842 wood-frame chapel established there by formerly enslaved African Americans.

The block itself occupied a corner of St. John's Ward, a.k.a. The Ward, an area bordered by Queen, College, Yonge, and University. This part of the city began to develop from the 1830s onwards as a modest working-class neighbourhood consisting of small cottages, taverns, shops, and even a few bowling alleys. Decades before The Ward became shorthand for squalor in turn-of-the-century Toronto, this community had begun to accommodate waves of newcomers arriving to the city.

During the 1840s and 1850s, St. John's Ward, but especially streets such as Centre, Chestnut, Elizabeth, and Agnes, became home to hundreds of African Americans fleeing slavery via the Underground Railroad. The area also served as a landing point, along with many other parts of the city, for thousands of Irish migrants fleeing the devastating potato famine.[1] By the 1880s, Italian labourers began migrating to Toronto, settling in a cluster of rooming houses and small shops around Edward and Chestnut Streets, just north of the bus station.

By the mid-1890s, The Ward saw the arrival of thousands of Eastern European Jews fleeing brutal pogroms. After the area's Jewish population had decamped to Kensington Market, the neighbourhood in the 1920s rapidly evolved into a hub of Chinese settlement.

The district became infamous for its overcrowded conditions. Cluttered backyards were lined with reeking outdoor privies. Meanwhile, a small army of social reformers fanned out across The Ward, looking for converts, juvenile delinquents, and bootleggers.

Soon after the end of World War II, however, city officials voted to raze the community, embarking on a prolonged process of land expropriation to make space for a new city hall. This exercise in slum clearance closed out a long period of stigmatization directed at The Ward's generations of residents, whose languages, customs, cultural habits, religions, and commercial practices were intolerably alien in a city that saw itself as more British than the British.

The city block that eventually became the Armory Street dig can be seen as a microcosm of a microcosm – a tiny piece of Toronto that was both unremarkable and yet rich in the sort of social history that has often been overlooked in the narratives of our civic past.

The Ward in the mid-nineteenth century was known for its rowdy taverns and incidents of street crime. In 1858, a house on Sayer Street (later Chestnut) just north of Osgoode Hall was the scene of a violent gang rape: fifteen men attacked Mary Hunt and Ellen Rogers, who likely ran a brothel. During the highly publicized trial, the two women courageously insisted that the fact they were prostitutes didn't mean the accused should go free – a view of justice sharply at odds with prevailing attitudes.[2]

Through the second half of the nineteenth century, with more immigrants moving into the area, the residential properties on Centre

JOHN LORINC & TATUM TAYLOR

and Chestnut became denser, with an accumulation of rear houses and privies. As the block became increasingly industrial, some of these dwellings were replaced with factories.

After the turn of the century, a handful of small synagogues opened along Centre and Chestnut Streets, including one, Shaarei Tzedec, that set up shop in an old foundry. Directly behind it sat the stately British Methodist Episcopal Church, on Chestnut – the Black church that had grown out of the c. 1842 wood-frame chapel.

By the 1910s, a pair of brick-and-beam factories, each four storeys high with numerous tenants, had gone up on Chestnut Street north of Armoury. One, located directly south of the BME Church, was leased during World War II by Eaton's for its tents and awnings operation. These warehouses, which wouldn't be out of place on Spadina today, loomed over Chestnut until they were demolished in the late 1950s.

The block's population and demographics mirrored that of the broader Ward – labourers, merchants, tradespeople, and many immigrant families struggling to establish a toehold – and a future – in a foreign place. At various times, the residents were Black, Irish, Jewish, and also British; only the ethnic mixing was a constant.

Some led ordinary lives filled with the usual joys and sorrows, hardships and opportunities. Many others, however, found themselves caught up in the cross-currents of broader historical dramas that originated in faraway places but left imprints on this seemingly undistinguished city block.

The survival of these stories and the accompanying archaeological evidence represent an almost impossible coincidence. If the property had been developed earlier, all those objects would have been sent to landfill or dumped in the lake. If former property owners had made different investment choices, the parking lot itself may never have been assembled. If the ground hadn't been quite so waterlogged, much of the evidence would have decomposed. And if the province had identified another space for the new provincial courthouse that is going up on the site, the lot could have ended up in the hands of a private developer that might have been far less willing than 10 to make a serious investment in archaeology and heritage preservation.[3]

Instead, the stars and planets aligned to preserve this uniquely rich trove of Toronto's immigration history, which is no small outcome in a city region that has become home to a larger proportion of foreign-born residents than any other metropolitan area in the world.

T HE ARMOURY STREET DIG lifted the asphalt veil from the remains of a century that had settled into layers of damp soil. For years, shoe leather had rested alongside ceramics; dolls and dentures had lain beneath lines of cars; and the lives that once animated these interred objects had faded from urban awareness. With the site's excavation in 2015, however, one point became clear: this was not a burial but rather a decades-long hibernation. Now that we've coaxed these past belongings back to life, they're challenging popular notions of what it means to be an artifact.

As this excavation – and others like it – has demonstrated, archaeology can elevate everyday objects to a realm that should not belong only to Egyptian tombs and Grecian urns. This discipline investigates ancient pottery as readily as twentieth-century eating habits and privy lore. Viewed even more broadly, archival photographs and texts can be artifacts; perhaps memories, too, can be seen as artifacts, provided we find ways to capture them. The act of sifting and studying all this material reveals new insights into our ancestors' lives. It also raises questions about our relationships with time and the physical world: what do we – as individuals, families, and communities – carry with us, either purposefully or unknowingly, as we move through generations? And what traces do we leave behind?

In contemporary Toronto, as in many cities, the objects we don't keep often wind up in distant landfills – which became a common form of waste management in the mid-nineteenth century – or recycling plants, or perhaps on the shelves of second-hand shops. One person's garbage is another's vintage bargain.

Torontonians might be surprised to learn that the Leslie Street Spit, a beloved recreational area and 'urban wilderness' not far from downtown, is essentially a public memorial to decades of rubbish that turns out to be far more varied than most people realize.

JOHN LORINC & TATUM TAYLOR

From 1959 until 2016, the Toronto Harbour Commission (later the Toronto Port Authority) constructed this artificial peninsular landmass through the systematic dumping of lake dredgeate and construction detritus. In the heyday of Toronto's mid-century urban growth and redevelopment, the city began adding the rubble of urban projects – from fragments of the demolished Temple Building, one of Toronto's first skyscrapers, to excavated dirt from new subway tunnels – onto the spit, stretching it farther into Lake Ontario.

In 2013, Heidy Schopf, a heritage specialist, and Jennifer Foster, an urban ecology professor, documented the discoveries made when archaeologists applied their fieldwork and research methodology to the Leslie Spit. This process produced startling revelations about the spit's composition. Amid the shores of crushed rock and lake-lapped bricks, the team identified domestic artifacts, from teacups to eyeglasses. Their findings suggested that lax dumping controls in the 1960s allowed entire households within demolished housing projects to be deposited on the spit.

The everyday objects among the building debris recall a period when the city took a tabula rasa approach to urban renewal, redeveloping entire low-income neighbourhoods dismissed as slums. This was the same phenomenon that brought about The Ward's demise. On the Armoury Street site, similar everyday objects were sealed beneath a busy parking lot; some of these objects will now end up in public exhibits. The tension between trash and treasure reflects many perspectives and shifts in social values, and it plays out in more spaces than we may realize.

In the world of archaeology, artifacts can act as protagonists. As we edited this anthology, we often encountered sentences where the objects were the subjects, inverting traditional rules of storytelling. In fact, archaeological theorists have debated concepts such as 'object agency' – essentially, that objects carry social meaning and represent the people who valued them – and 'object biography,' the process of following an item's life from origin to end point.[4] But beyond academic discourse, we can ponder these ideas in our daily interactions with our belongings. Consider what each object in your living room says about you, or the journey on which you send your kitchen waste when you throw it away. What will these ordinary things tell future archaeologists who find them decades or centuries from now?

Early Torontonians – as they broke that dish, lost those dice, cast liquor bottles into the privy – could not have conceived of the archaeologists' glee at finding them again. They could not have anticipated our handling these mundane items with care and photographing them with awe. They surely could not have fathomed the existence of this book, or the possibility that their old, rusted teapot might end up displayed in a public space.

Excavated artifacts contribute to an understanding of heritage that combines fact and emotion, science and imagination. When added to a historical narrative, archaeology can confront or correct existing perceptions and long-standing biases. For example, starting in the late nineteenth century, depictions of The Ward in civic documents and popular media shaped public opinion, constructing an image of the area as a slum. In reality, this neighbourhood was far more complex. The Armoury Street Dig uncovered a pair of silk stockings, collections of pipes and fine china, a glass bottle still crimson with nail polish – all luxury items that reflect a lesser-known side of life in The Ward. Ongoing study of the hundreds of thousands of artifacts will continue to yield new information for years to come.

Through the organization of this book's sections, we have suggested a journey of discovery that reflects the process of archaeology. With each section, we dig a bit deeper, exploring the layers that comprised The Ward. Beginning with an understanding of the site's evolution, we move to unearthing remnants of daily life, and consider some of the industries that produced those items. We then delve into the underlying cultural activities and social forces that were at play on this site, as well as the individual lives of a cross-section of nearby residents. Finally, we contemplate the field of archaeology, which is the foundation of this anthology, and the role it can play in enriching our public spaces.

A nearly vanished neighbourhood does not have defined edges and weight; we can't set it like an object in our palms and hold it up to the light. We can only know The Ward – as we try to grasp more of its infinite facets – through the images, stories, and artifacts we have uncovered.

JOHN LORINC & TATUM TAYLOR

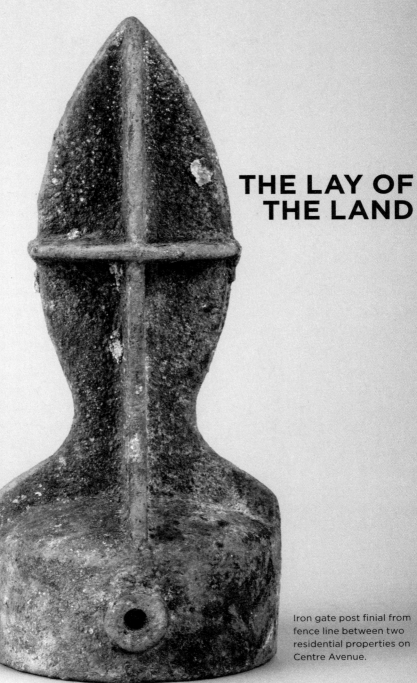

# THE LAY OF
# THE LAND

Iron gate post finial from
fence line between two
residential properties on
Centre Avenue.

# PARK LOT 11

## JOHN LORINC

THE ORIGINAL COLONIAL owner of the one-hundred-acre strip of real estate that included what eventually became the site of the Armoury Street Dig was a Boston-born lawyer named William Dummer Powell, who had fled post-Revolutionary America in 1776. Powell settled in Montreal, but eventually landed judicial postings in Detroit (still part of the British Empire) and Niagara-on-the-Lake after ingratiating himself with Upper Canada's first lieutenant-governor, John Graves Simcoe.

In the early 1790s, Simcoe and his surveyors carved up the future city into several north-south 'park lots,' which were 'granted' to officers and elites in his ambit, Powell among them. In later years, Powell became Upper Canada's third chief justice, yet he was also known as a 'malcontent' who picked fights with prominent members of the colony's tight-knit ruling class. Perhaps most notably, he fought an 1822 proposal to restore the Town of York's name to the original Toronto, and then, in 1834, complained strenuously about the decision to incorporate the City of Toronto, warning about the risk of giving the vote to its 'miserable Inhabitants.'[1]

As for Park Lot 11, a skinny rectangle that extended from Lot Street (Queen) to where Bloor Street is today, Powell held it for only a few years. As he didn't actually live in York/Toronto, the powers that be decided it would be best if the property – a strip of forests, creek beds, and swamps – became the asset of someone local. Indeed, that ribbon of fallow land – today it extends from Queen to Bloor, and Chestnut to University, encompassing Osgoode Hall, Sick Kids, the Toronto General Hospital, the MARS Discovery District, half of Queen's Park, and Victoria College – changed hands three more times between 1797 and 1828.

ALL THOSE EIGHTEENTH- and nineteenth-century colonial real estate deals, of course, occur very late in the long narrative of this piece of land, not at the beginning.

Over a period of many decades, archaeologists have identified Indigenous artifacts and settlements across the Toronto region dating back 12,000 years, to the end of the last ice age.

There was clear evidence of Iroquoian use of Toronto's central waterfront area prior to early French contact, notes the Stage 1 archaeological report on the parking-lot excavation:

> When European explorers and missionaries arrived in Ontario in the 17th century, the Huron-Wendat no longer inhabited the lakeshore and instead occupied a vast area between Lake Simcoe and Georgian Bay. By 1650, many Wendat had fled their 17th century homeland due to the onset of epidemic disease and increasing raids by Five Nations Iroquois groups who had established an increasing presence on Lake Ontario ... It was the Mississaugas [Ojibwa] who had settled the area by the time the British arrived in the late 18th century and from whom the Crown secured land for settlement.[2]

(Ongoing conflicts between the Mississaugas and the Iroquois confederacy that began in the late 1860s eventually led to a series of peace treaties, which resulted in Mississauga control over the territory between Lake Huron and Lake Ontario and beyond.[3])

The archaeological evidence of Indigenous occupation is extensive, and indeed represents the bulk of archaeological work carried out in southern Ontario. As Ron Williamson writes in *Toronto: A Short Illustrated History of Its First 12,000 Years*, dozens of 10,000- to 11,000-year-old artifacts have been found along the old Lake Iroquois shoreline, which is skirted by Davenport Road, an ancient Indigenous trail. Elsewhere across the region, archaeological consultants, construction crews, and individuals have encountered a wide array of Indigenous artifacts produced over a vast period of time, including ceramic-effigy pipes, projectile points, scrapers, engraving tools, jewellery, and various vessels.

Numerous large Huron-Wendat villages consisting of clusters of longhouses have been located along the Humber, Don, West Duffins Creek, and the Rouge, as well as other Greater Toronto river systems. The concentration of Seneca artifacts is so dense in the Teiaiagon settlement area on the Toronto Carrying Place portage route up to Georgian Bay (now known as Etobicoke's Baby Point neighbourhood, on the eastern banks of the Humber) that it has been formally designated an archaeologically significant area, with special rules for anyone doing construction.

In several locations, archaeologists have been brought in to investigate Huron-Wendat ossuaries and cemeteries discovered by construction crews, including, in 1997, an extensive burial site filled with the bones of eighty-seven individuals. It was situated at the base of a new light standard erected at the edge of a soccer field near Leslie Street and Highway 401 that was built atop a thirteenth-century village.

'Aboriginal leaders have viewed the disturbance to this sacred site as an immense act of disrespect that could have been avoided by proper planning in advance of development,' Williamson writes. 'Under the direction of the closest Iroquoian-speaking band, the Six Nations Council of Oshweken, Ontario, the ossuary was completely excavated and the remains re-interred in another location nearby.'[4]

On September 23, 1787, just six years before that land grant to William Dummer Powell, officials representing the British Crown completed an ambiguous deal with the Mississauga leadership to acquire a swath of more than 100,000 hectares of land, extending forty-four kilometres north from Lake Ontario, in exchange for £1,700 – a deal that came to be known as the Toronto Purchase. (The price included '2,000 gun flints, 24 brass kettles, 10 dozen mirrors, 2 dozen laced hats, a bale of flowered flannel, and 96 gallons of rum.'[5]) The original map of the acquisition, as well as the terms, were so murky that the surrender had to be clarified in 1805, by which point Lot 11 – a tiny sliver of the whole purchase – was the property of the widow of a high-ranking colonial official who had owned it since 1797.[6]

That piece of land would be flipped a few more times over the next two decades, and it's not difficult to understand why. According to

various historic maps of York/Toronto created in the early nineteenth century, the city didn't extend above Lot Street, which meant that Lot II, and indeed the rest of the park lots granted by the colonial administrators, were nothing more than lines on a map. After all, the area north of that original concession road consisted mainly of forests and river courses, including one that meandered south from what is now the University of Toronto and then cut east, traversing Lot II on its way to the Don.

James Cane's Map of City and Liberties, 1842.

In other words, Lot II's realizable commercial value, circa the late 1820s, was still highly theoretical, awaiting that watershed moment when Toronto had grown enough to spill across its original northern boundary. It would take a keen-eyed young Attorney General named John Beverley Robinson to begin the process of transforming Lot II into a lucrative development opportunity.

# CHIEF JUSTICE ROBINSON'S PLAN
GUYLAINE PÉTRIN

IN 1828, JOHN BEVERLEY ROBINSON, a powerful jurist, member of the Legislative Assembly of Upper Canada, and United Empire Loyalist, sold ten acres, the south part of Lot 11, to the Law Society of Upper Canada for the building of Osgoode Hall. At the time, the area was primarily countryside, outside of the city limits. But by 1833, 'Macaulaytown,' on the north side of Lot Street (now Queen Street West) between Yonge Street and Osgoode Hall, had become a growing suburb. Lots were small and affordable, and they provided a place where new-comers (predominantly from the British Isles and Ireland) could build small cottages.

As Toronto continued to expand, and the area between Yonge and Osgoode Hall filled, there was a need for more affordable housing for the skilled immigrants contributing to the city's growth. Like today, these new arrivals dreamed of owning their own homes.

Born in 1791 in Lower Canada, the son of Virginia United Empire Loyalist Christopher Robinson, John Beverley Robinson was a lawyer, politician, and later chief justice of Upper Canada. He was described as the 'bone and sinew' of the Family Compact, as the colony's ruling elite was known – a man esteemed and relied on by a succession of lieutenant-governors of Upper Canada. When he was nominated to the bench in 1829, Robinson had to leave his lucrative private law practice, which meant he relied more heavily on his real estate holdings for his income. He owned quite a lot of property in the Toronto area as well as in Simcoe County.

In 1840, Robinson, by then chief justice, decided it was time to create his own little subdivision on that mostly undeveloped strip of land he

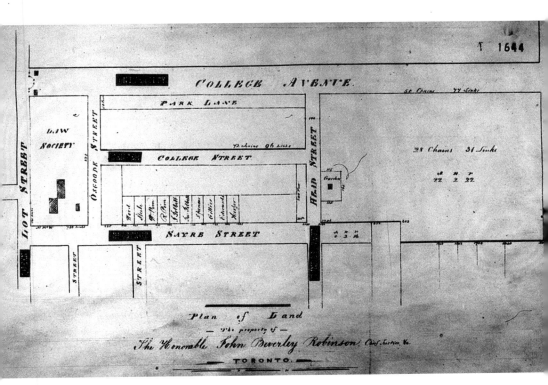

Chief Justice Robinson's property.

owned north of Osgoode Hall, immediately west of Macaulaytown. He produced a plan for a subdivision between Sayer Street (later Chestnut Street), named in honour of his mother's maiden name, and what is now University Avenue. A new road, to be named Centre Street, was to divide the subdivision into two blocks. Most lots were twenty feet wide by 120 feet deep – long and narrow, reflecting the fact that Toronto real estate taxes were assessed based on street frontage.

Robinson offered the lots at an affordable rate. Leases were for twenty-one years, at five pounds' rent per year (equivalent to about $3,100 in 2018), payable in two installments. There was also an option to buy the lot outright at a cost of two pounds per foot of frontage, so a lot that was twenty feet wide would cost forty pounds, payable in four equal payments of ten pounds per year.

Under Robinson's terms, the deed for the lot would only be registered once the lot had been paid in full. If payments were not made on time, the agreement would be deemed void and the lot would be sold to another buyer. This explains why so many of these properties do not appear in the land registry office books until many years later.

While some defaulted on their payments, others transferred their leases and their improvements to other owners. Some of the leases signed by John Beverley Robinson can be found in the Archives of Ontario, among his other business papers. The Archives also holds two maps of the area – one a simple drawing showing the various lots being leased, with the names of the proposed leaseholders; and a more formal plan, prepared for Robinson by surveyor Charles Rankin, that gives an idea of which lots were first leased and by whom. The Robinson papers at the Archives of Ontario also contain correspondence about this subdivision, including an agreement transferring the land to his son James Lukin Robinson in 1847.

As an example, these maps and leases show that Lot 12, on the west side of Sayer Street, the future location of the British Methodist Episcopal Church, was first leased to a man named Samuel Hamilton in July 1841. But this agreement became void because Hamilton did not pay the rent. As a result, the lot was again available, and Robinson then sold it to five local Black men on March 18, 1842, for forty pounds, as the location for a Methodist Meeting House.

As Robinson affirmed on the record of the transaction, 'I hereby agree to sell to John Hooper, William Handy, Noah Brooks, Charles Davis and William Harny, as trustees for the African Methodist Episcopal Church Lot number twelve on the West side of Sayer Street adjoining to John Hooper's lot for the sum of forty pounds of which ten pounds has been this day paid to me.' The remaining three payments were made to Robinson, and the deed to the lot was formally registered in January 1845.

While Robinson owned the lots until they were fully paid, the leaseholder was responsible for building any dwelling or structure on the property, and also for paying the taxes. The lease agreement further stated that if the leaseholders did not renew, they could move their dwelling at the end of the term.

The first people who took advantage of these small lots were the carpenters, masons, and builders who started constructing small cottages for themselves, and also as rental units. At first, each lot had only

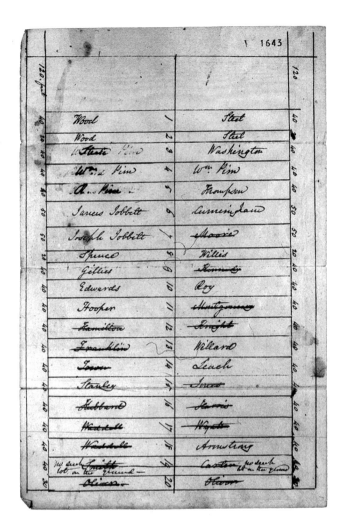

A list of names of lot leases.

one house on it. But eventually more houses were built on these lots, including rear houses, as the small shacks in the backyards were known. Originally, this area north of Queen Street was part of St. Patrick's Ward. By 1853, a decade before Robinson's death, the population in the area between Yonge Street and University Avenue had become so dense that a new electoral district was created. It would be called St. John's Ward.

# DOING JUSTICE TO THE COURTHOUSE SITE

TATUM TAYLOR

THE ARCHAEOLOGICAL DISCOVERIES beneath the Armoury Street parking lot directly resulted from a development project led by Infrastructure Ontario, a provincial agency that manages and develops government property, on behalf of the Ministry of the Attorney General. The new Toronto courthouse at 11 Centre Avenue brings together a number of the Ontario Courts of Justice that were operating for many years in different facilities across the city. Because of the site preparations for this project, we have gained access to a remarkable hidden repository of The Ward's history.

That a courthouse would be the catalyst for these discoveries seems somehow appropriate. In a sense, the artifacts would never have found their way to this particular location had it not been for Sir John Beverley Robinson, the chief justice of Upper Canada and then Canada West from 1829 to 1862.

Throughout his tenure as chief justice, Robinson lived in a mansion near the intersection of John and Richmond Streets, and his family owned portions of the surrounding park lots. Shortly after his appointment to the bench, he sold a piece of his family's land holdings to the Law Society of Upper Canada for the construction of Osgoode Hall, completed in 1832. Just north of this legal hub, he developed a subdivision in the early 1840s that would later become part of St. John's Ward. The site of the new Toronto courthouse sits on his former landholdings.

As a colonial official and then a jurist, Robinson's legal work shaped the early provincial government. Among many realms of influence, his law-making helped to establish Upper Canada's identity as a haven for

formerly enslaved Blacks who had fled the United States. His legacy in relation to early Black Canadians is not without controversy, however. For example, he agreed to the extraditions of certain former slaves accused of crimes such as murder. But in 1833, the year when the British parliament voted to ban slavery throughout the empire, he led the drafting of the Fugitive Offenders Act, a formalized extradition agreement between Upper Canada and the United States. Robinson's approach to this legislation ensured that Blacks who had fled slavery were not immediately turned away upon reaching Canada.

Rendering of the New Toronto Courthouse. Renzo Piano Building Workshop/ Infrastructure Ontario.

As archaeologist and historian Karolyn Smardz Frost writes in *I've Got a Home in Glory Land*, 'It is not overstating the case to say that the Underground Railroad could not have found its main terminus in Canada had it not been for legal decisions made by John Beverley Robinson.'

As it happened, many Black residents settled on the parcels of land Robinson was selling – real estate that, some 160 years later, would become the new Toronto courthouse site. Freedom-seekers such as Cecelia

Holmes (see page 202) established their homes on this site, as did abolitionists such as Francis G. Simpson (see page 208). The British Methodist Episcopal Church that once stood here was founded by Black Canadians who had arrived via the Underground Railroad.

Robinson drafted the Fugitive Offenders Act, as Frost points out, at the prompting of his colleague James Buchanan Macaulay. One of the three judges for the Court of King's Bench, Macaulay had questioned the approach to extradition between Upper Canada and the United States, encouraging Robinson to formalize it and thereby provide a degree of security to formerly enslaved Blacks. Like Robinson, Macaulay owned a family estate at the western edge of Toronto. He had subdivided his land in the 1830s to form Macaulaytown, which sat on land now occupied by Old City Hall and Nathan Phillips Square. Many of these lots were also purchased by members of Toronto's early Black community. Macaulay's story provides an additional layer of judicial affiliations to this area of the city: his working-class suburb became the core of St. John's Ward.

Beyond coincidence, the rise of a courthouse on the parking-lot site in The Ward is also, perhaps, ironic. After all, a temple of justice will stand on land that was once home to marginalized communities that had been systemically oppressed by the forces of law and order, and not only in the United States.

The site's former residents would have been all too aware of the presence of police and judicial officials. Besides the fact that these residents were living only blocks away from Osgoode Hall, Toronto's city courts in 1900 moved from the York County Court House, at Church and Adelaide Streets, to the newly constructed City Hall, which loomed over The Ward's southeast corner. Local inhabitants would have been brought before these courts for a wide range of infractions. During the second half of the nineteenth century and well into the twentieth, Toronto's police regulated public order through a complicated system of bylaws, often to the detriment of low-income, newcomer communities. Police imposed extensive social constraints through the establishment and enforcement of liquor licence controls, laws limiting alcohol consumption and prostitution, commercial

Osgoode Hall, Toronto C.W.

bylaws and licence regulations that unequally affected the working classes, and the severe

Stereoview photograph of Osgoode Hall c. 1860s.

Sabbath laws that prohibited many activities on Sundays. While the role of the police evolved to become less concerned with regulating public morality, law enforcement arguably continues to unevenly target particular social and racial groups to this day.

We have a moral imperative to acknowledge that the new Toronto courthouse will spatially coincide with the memories of communities that continue to struggle with equality under the law. Following this logic, of course, the development of a courthouse on any Indigenous land must encourage us to consider truth and reconciliation, and address the historic and ongoing injustices experienced by Indigenous peoples. At this particular courthouse, the site's judicial associations run deep, and the new building will gather these threads and manifest connections between past and present. The excavation conducted prior to the building's construction uncovered a century of buried objects – tangible reminders of the marginalized Canadians who once lived there. Within this context, the new Toronto courthouse represents an opportunity and obligation to serve as a beacon of justice for all.

**DAILY LIFE**

51   NOV· 25 1913

# THE PRIVIES

HOLLY MARTELLE

THE OUTHOUSE, THE 'necessary,' the 'fortress of solitude' – these are all names for the historical archaeologist's fantasy: the privy. There are few types of archaeological features that bring as much joy and excitement to the archaeologist as the privy, the early settler's receptacle for human waste. While most people would be repulsed by the thought of excavating these putrid-smelling deposits, archaeologists take great delight in hefting shovelfuls of goopy night soil, oozing with artifacts and other evidential tidbits of past human life.

The Armoury Street Dig uncovered over forty privies, an incredible number for a single archaeological excavation. Why so many? First, the large number of outhouses reflects the density of residential settlement in this working-class neighbourhood. By the late nineteenth century, the demand for toilets on each property multiplied, as residents infilled rear yards with additional dwellings, and multiple families and tenants crowded into single-family quarters. Second, prior to the twentieth century, the city lacked a formal system of municipal waste removal and required landowners or tenants to build and maintain their own exterior 'facilities.' With such heavy traffic, fecal matter would quickly pile up, filling the rank receptacle. In such an undesirable circumstance, an occupant had two choices. A scavenger could be hired to clean out the privy and take away the excrement – usually late at night to spare the public the unpleasant experience of encountering the cartloads of fragrant, unsightly waste – or else the occupant

Left: privy in The Ward. November 25, 1913. City officials extensively documented unsanitary conditions in 'slum' housing.

would close the teeming privy and expeditiously dig a new chamber elsewhere. Fortunately for archaeologists, when the tin-clad or wood-planked outhouses were subsequently moved and a new privy dug, the old chamber was simply closed off and left in place. At the Armoury Street Dig, the privy vaults were dug very deep into the ground (some over a metre or more). This contributed to their remarkable preservation by protecting them from the higher surface disturbances that created the parking lot.

Producing thousands of objects, the privies were some of the most information-generating and artifact-rich features on the site, owing both to the nature of their construction and the human behaviours involved in their use.

The majority of privy pits at the site were lined with wood planks that acted like cribbing by protecting the contents of the pit, discouraging it from caving in. The planks were laid horizontally or vertically and supported with interior corner braces. Many of the earliest privies were 'one-holers,' about a metre by a metre and just large enough for a single seat. They were not very deep and do not appear to have been used for a significant amount of time. Many others were at least twice the size. Some of these 'two-holers' had double chambers with remnants of central partitions left in place, and featured drainpipes that flushed the liquid contents away and allowed for a longer duration of use before cleaning. Although more rare, expedient toilets were fashioned from barrels sunk deeply in the ground. They served their purpose just as well as the more carefully built wood-lined vaults, but required minimal effort and cost.

Spanning several metres, the site's longest privy existed behind the circa 1895 Standard Foundry building, eventually converted into the Shaarei Tzedec synagogue (see pages 173–177). Detailed analysis of its structure and contents revealed that it was originally a two-holer that was dug into by a later privy in the early twentieth century. This privy, as well as several others, had been impacted by the construction of a 1940s-era cinder-block auto garage and warehouse used by the Pearl Furniture Company, the last occupant of the late-nineteenth-century foundry building.

HOLLY MARTELLE

As the turn of the twentieth century brought a growing appreciation for the link between poor sanitary conditions and disease, it became common in urban contexts to line privy pits with more substantial materials, such as brick, cinder block,

and cement, to offer a more watertight seal and discourage the leaking of liquid contents into the ground. However, we didn't find evidence of this trend in the Armoury Street Dig, because either the working-class occupants lacked the funds for more expensive materials, or they found the traditional wood vaults equally suitable. While many late-nineteenth and early-twentieth-century privies at the site bore remnants of sturdier superstructures fashioned from these more solid materials, the underlying chambers continued to be lined in wood.

The effectiveness of the wood lining of the nineteenth- and twentieth-century privies was evident during the archaeological excavations. Both the lining and the heavy, nearly impenetrable clay surrounding it served to hold in the contents of chambers and, combined with the high water table at the site, ensured the deposits remained liquefied

THE PRIVIES

through time. The sealed, wet conditions created an anaerobic environment conducive to a high level of organic preservation, safeguarding the privy frame and its organic contents from significant decay. This allowed for the recovery of items rarely observed archaeologically, including over seventy complete shoes, boots, slippers, hats, and woven garments, as well as rare wooden objects, such as briar and burl wood pipes and children's playthings, the whittled bust of a doll or marionette representing one of the most spectacular of these finds.

Figuratively speaking, to the archaeologist, privy deposits are both liquid and solid gold. A privy pit is a treasure trove of evidence about the past. Much can be learned from both the fecal matter itself and the objects deposited in privies as trash. The excrement from the privies on the Armoury Block site contained small bits of food (seeds, bone, etc.) that speak to diet, the availability and preference for specific food types, and the seasonality of privy use. We anticipate that it also contains microscopic indicators of disease and health issues, making it a valuable source of information to test early-twentieth-century political claims of poor sanitary conditions in The Ward. In some of the most fascinating studies of archaeologically derived privy soils, scientists have been able to identify the remains or eggs of various parasites that can live within or on the human body – ringworm, tapeworm, whipworm, thorny-headed worms, and lice – many derived from contaminated soils and water. They are thus able to measure the health and welfare of historic populations and identify common ailments, some of which are also reflected in the medical paraphernalia (bottles, syringes) recovered from privies. We retrieved many small medicinal vials from the privies at the site, some containing potent deworming medications like Doctor McLane's American Worm Specific and B. A. Fahnestock's Vermifuge. These treatments would have been administered in sweetened water and used to combat common parasitic infections that affected both children and adults from all sectors of nineteenth-century society.

Other privy treasures included standard trash, such as kitchen waste (food containers, peach pits, oyster shells, chestnuts, coconut fragments, animal bones, etc., and the occasional complete rotten egg), broken items (ceramic dishes, glass tableware, window-pane fragments, lanterns, wash basins, and chamber pots), and beverage bottles. Outside of a formal municipal system of garbage collection, everyday garbage was deposited in the loo, safely out of the reach of children, animals, and vermin. As the field of 'garbology' has shown, most notably through the popular work of University of Arizona archaeologist Dr. William Rathje and his Tucson Garbage Project, a person's waste provides insight into fundamental aspects of behaviour and belief systems; it can represent consumer and disposal behaviours that directly link to wealth, status, and ethnic background. Further, privy trash can help archaeologists distinguish between what people profess to do, reflected by social ideals and expectations, and what people actually do, their real behaviour. For example, Irish matron Annie Whalen, who lived at 15 Centre Avenue (pages 219–223), was regularly under suspicion by police for running a bootlegging operation, a claim she adamantly denied publicly and in court. The high number of alcohol bottles retrieved from the privy in Annie's backyard suggest she was less than truthful to police. Not only that, but glass beer steins and other items could signify she operated a tavern or brothel from her house.

Accidental losses – coins that had fallen out of trouser pockets, clay pipes that slipped away from the lips of smokers, and buttons tugged loose from undergarments – also made their way into the loo, as occasionally did children's toys and cherished possessions. The loss of a religious medallion or rosary inlay, which we found in a privy at 13 Centre Avenue, would surely have been heartbreaking. More incidental inclusions in night-soil deposits are newspaper and textile fragments that served the same purpose as modern-day toilet tissue and female sanitary products.

We commonly find bottles in the privy, especially those that held beer, wine, spirits, or so-called 'medicinal' tonics, some of which were also highly addictive, containing traces of alcohol, opiates, and cocaine. As its name suggests, the privy was an inherently private and secluded place where socially questionable or embarrassing acts could take place without fear of discovery, and where the damning evidence could be safely discarded, cloaked by excrement and hidden away from a scornful wife, critical husband, or reprimanding parent.

# A FINE KETTLE OF FISH

HOLLY MARTELLE

THE ARCHAEOLOGICAL STUDY of foodways focuses on the cultural, social, and economic rules or circumstances that guide food choices and behaviours. Foodways include all aspects of food acquisition, preparation, serving, and consumption. But studying foodways based on remnant archaeological bits can be a muddled state of affairs. Most often, archaeologists find only small pieces of the culinary puzzle, leading us to fit together the bigger picture of *food*, with all of its cultural, social, and economic ingredients, from multiple lines of direct and indirect evidence.

The best recipe mixes science, mathematics, anthropology, cultural history, household economics, and an understanding of local and global markets, with all of the archaeological fixings – food remnants, food and condiment containers, serving dishes, eating utensils, beverage bottles, and the like. Once sprinkled with supplementary information from archival records – such as photographs, cookbooks, grocery-store

inventories, guides on gardening and butchery – the full foodways picture is ready for thoughtful digestion.

The Armoury Street Dig generated extensive food-related data sets. The reconstruction of foodways in this nineteenth- and early-twentieth-century immigrant neighbourhood starts with our examination of direct evidence of food consumption – that is, the physical remains of food such as peach pits, eggshells, T-bones, raspberry seeds, and fish scales. Most often, we found these artifacts in the form of human excrement or kitchen waste in privies. Food remains are the focus of two subspecialties: zooarchaeology (the study of animal-related or 'faunal' remains) and paleobotany (the study of plant remains), both of which apply knowledge and methodologies from the biological sciences to the study of archaeological materials.

Technical experts first sort, count, and identify the remains, noting any important modifications that might reflect cultural behaviours, including food-processing techniques. In faunal analysis, the species, age, and sex of an animal are recorded, along with the portion of the body represented and the location of any cut marks or fractures. By such analysis, zooarchaeologists can establish whether people of the past were eating wild or domestic species, what meat cuts they preferred, what butchery practices they used, and whether they were raising animals for other purposes (to provide eggs, milk, wool, and so on). The patterns that emerge in the data speak to past food choices, which reflect a variety of factors, including location (urban vs. rural),

An oyster shell and chestnuts. Oysters were a common nineteenth- and early-twentieth-century specialty and tavern food in early Toronto, arriving at the dockyards in barrels.

species availability (year-round vs. seasonal), economic standing or class, ethnicity, familial needs, and personal preference.

But foods consumed in the past don't always make it onto the archaeologist's analytical plate. In fact, many foods, like leafy vegetables, boneless cuts of meat, and gelatinous desserts, leave no physical traces. Others experience different degrees of decomposition; some survive only as fragments and may only be visible at the microscopic level. For this reason, the most abundant and visible remains will tell only part of the overall *food* story. At the Armoury Street Dig, robust and macroscopic animal remains were plentiful and confirmed that typical nineteenth-century meats (beef, pig, lamb) were the mainstays of the diet. On the other hand, smaller and more fragile elements, like chicken and fish, were often fragmentary and less frequent, even though they may have ended up in the soup pot just as often. Consider, too, that two staples of the nineteenth-century Irish immigrant diet – fish and potatoes – left few obvious traces on the site. While a less visible presence of fish on the site at first begged the question of whether residents had abandoned the Old World tradition of eating fish on Fridays, the thousands of microscopic fishbones derived from fine-mesh water screening and privy soil flotation verified that the Irish folk on the site were indeed good Catholics!

When we calculate the importance of less archaeologically abundant foodstuffs to the immigrant diet, we must consider several other factors: varying waste-disposal practices, reuse of food waste for fuel, raw materials, pet and livestock feed, site of consumption, overall cost, availability, and seasonality. Take oysters, for example. Oyster shells never appeared in large quantities in the Armoury Street Dig. By the first part of the nineteenth century, shellfish was regularly shipped in barrels from the eastern seaboard and generally available to most interior centres. In Toronto, records and archival photographs suggest that local grocers and butchers imported oysters as seasonal delicacies. The low frequency of oysters at the site could reflect market factors (minimal to infrequent availability), cost (perhaps working-class folk in The Ward couldn't afford them), cultural or religious restrictions on consumption, reuse of shells for buttons and tools, or general distaste. Alternatively,

HOLLY MARTELLE

since oysters were also standard nineteenth-century tavern fare, people in The Ward might have consumed them somewhere other than the family dinner table.

Wood-lined privy, Lot 9, Centre Avenue, 2015.

The archaeological remains from the Armoury Street Dig appear to conform to an urban subsistence pattern. An abundance of beverage bottles, food and condiment containers, minimal variety in plant remains, low frequency of game animals and non-meat bones, and presence of non-local foods indicate that residents acquired the majority of their food from retail sources. The animal-bone sample is dominated by leg and rib bones representing standard butchered cuts of meat, whereas the most common botanical remains – peanut, chestnut, walnut, and almond shells, peach and cherry pits, and pumpkin seeds – signify standard market produce. The prevalence of pickle and sauce containers as well as soda-water bottles proves that folks were making regular visits to the grocer, while the plethora of milk bottles indicates local dairies were also making regular deliveries. The occasional occurrence of coconut shells demonstrates that even more global foodstuffs were available to immigrant families.

The site's food remains also contain atypical finds, speaking to other food behaviours that, although tricky to verify, might inform how we understand the poverty, hardship, and industry of The Ward's working-class and immigrant folk. The notion that working-class families were eking out a living is certainly supported by some food evidence that reflects the purchase of cheap cuts of meat (especially flanks), the use of less palatable meats for soups and stews, and the consumption of older chickens, sheep, and pigs when times were tough. The fact that privies were teeming with chestnuts, a 'poor people's food,' could suggest that struggling families were using them as meat and wheat-flour substitutes in soups and in making bread, as was common in Old World poverty-stricken communities. As in other low-income districts in London, England, and in the New World, roasted chestnuts were also a popular street food or snack, sold by vendors pushing wheeled carts throughout the neighbourhood. But not all of the food remains from the site speak to poverty. Archaeological remnants of clams and beefsteak signify that more expensive foodstuffs were at least periodic indulgences.

We've also found evidence of the industriousness of immigrant and working-class families in The Ward who found ways to feed their loved ones independently of Toronto retailers. An unusual privy find of deer antlers hints that hunting also put food on the table. As with fishing, it would have been a quick and inexpensive way for struggling and newly arrived families to fill the frying pan, especially in the mid-nineteenth-century, when the emergent community was on the fringe of wilderness at the outskirts of town. Homegrown and home-raised foods supplemented more costly market-purchased items to feed growing families more cheaply. That the bones of roosters and hens appear archaeologic-ally, alongside sheep of varying ages, suggests households were keeping some livestock on-site, at least until later in the nineteenth century, when this congestion of rear yards with additional dwellings made this less possible. While the occurrence of seeds and pits from standard market fruits indicates that families made regular trips to the market, both the archaeological prevalence of terracotta pots and twentieth-century photographs show that folks were utilizing kitchen gardens, even in cramped surroundings. Residents also used crockery and mason jars to take advantage of cheaper, seasonal produce, storing it for tougher times and to eat in the winter, when paid work could be scarce.

HOLLY MARTELLE

Archival and archaeological evidence also suggests that many foods were useful beyond the belly. For such industrious and frugal folk, food choices involved consideration of how to make use of non-consumable leftovers. Many archaeological specimens show evidence of being boiled or cracked open to collect marrow and fat that could be used to produce soap, tallow for candles, lantern fuel, and medicinal products. We know that people crafted deer antlers into awls and handles for knives and utensils, and fashioned simple buttons and fasteners from discarded shells and the flat rib bones of mammals. In times when supplies of scrap lumber were low, a family could use bone waste to fuel the woodstove, the only source of heat in their small, drafty home. Waste not, want not.

Throughout human existence, eating has always been more than just a form of nourishment. Just as The Ward's foodways reflected the cultural, social, and economic behaviours of working-class immigrants, our current culinary choices say a lot about us. For example, fast food as a cultural construct speaks to societal and individual values, prioritizing time and cost efficiency above health and family togetherness. Since foodways are intimately linked to individual and shared identities, this field of inquiry encourages us to consider what our food behaviours say about us today. A century from now, how will archaeologists interpret our lives based on the food waste *we* leave behind?

Deer antlers. A complete rack is an unusual find on an urban site.

# YOU ARE HOW YOU EAT

TOM PORAWSKI

A FTER ALMOST A year of digging at the Armoury Street parking lot, our team recovered thousands of animal bones – remnants of meals that had been discarded in outdoor privies, basements, and backyard refuse or garbage pits across the site. In fact, when the excavation wrapped up, on a cold and dreary day in December 2015, standing on that lot, backfilling just underway, I became incredibly excited about what we were going to learn about the immigrants who used to live here, based on the table scraps we had unearthed.

As zooarchaeologists – a sub-field that focuses on the study of animal bones from archaeological sites – we look at other people's leftovers with great enthusiasm. The sort of food remains we found under that parking lot isn't like the trash we produce today. Few of us have time to raise or butcher our own food. We generally bring our meat home wrapped in plastic, often deboned, and ready for the oven or pan, with little food processing required. These days, in a commercially driven market, where animals are sourced from outside the city, fewer of us know exactly where or what part of the animal our food comes from.

Just as our own leftovers can shed interesting information about our own food habits, historical food remains can reveal how previous generations obtained, prepared, ate, and discarded food, and integrated it with the other aspects of their lives. These food clues hint at a broader network of choices made regarding food that were affected by environment and availability, individual preference, social and economic status, religion, ethnicity, and so forth. By seeking to understand how these choices are preserved in the animal-bone collection, and whether they can be recognized, zooarchaeologists can recon- struct aspects of past food habits that teach us about people's lives.

In the first half of the nineteenth century, Toronto's residents could purchase live animals, wholesale cuts, barrels of salted meats, and imported foods from one of three public markets across the city. Because most dwellings at the time had open back lots, many people also kept chickens, pigs, sheep, and even dairy cows.

By the 1860s, butcher shops began dotting the city's streets, helping to feed a rapidly expanding population. In neighbourhoods like The Ward, property owners began building rear houses in their backyards, making it less practical to keep cows, pigs, and sheep. Many, however, continued to keep chickens, whose populations peaked in the early twentieth century.

Throughout the nineteenth century, in many cities, butchers gener- ally sold meat that came from animals that had just reached an optimal weight – a mass they attain just prior to skeletal maturity. The timing of the sale was about cost-effectiveness: farmers understood it made no sense to waste money feeding an animal that wasn't going to get bigger. Consequently, a bone collection made up of mostly juvenile or sub- adult-aged animals typically reflects a focus on commercially available food products. By contrast, a collection containing some really young (premature death) and some mature (mom and dad) animals, may sug- gest occupants were raising animals on-site.

Butchers often divided the meat into manageable cuts. Their tools typically included knives, an axe or a cleaver that would shear or break bones, and a saw to cut through them. The meat was rarely deboned. Substantial wholesale cuts and barrels containing preserved, salted meat provided the biggest bang for the buck. Larger meat cuts required further butchery in the kitchen. Because sanitation norms and ideas of cleanliness were different back then, many people often buried their garbage in their backyard, including leftover bones. This cycle explains why archaeologists often recover large collections of animal bones dur- ing the excavation of historical sites.

The Armoury Street parking lot was no exception. By analyzing these food scraps, we can learn a lot about what and how the residents of this neighbourhood chose to eat, and what those choices, in turn, can tell us about their lives. As we continue to analyze this extensive collection of food remains, I compared the animal-bone refuse recovered from two backyard privies once located behind adjacent residential lots, at 7 Centre Avenue (earlier privy) and 11 Centre Avenue (later privy). (These municipal addresses were once 31 and 33 Centre, but were changed after the city redeveloped the land where the 361 University Avenue courthouse now stands.)

The first house lot had a rectangular, wood-lined privy, about half a metre deep, out back. It contained 131 animal-bone fragments dating to the mid-nineteenth century. The second privy, bounded by cinder blocks at top and lined with wood below, contained 252 animal-bone fragments, with artifacts dating the deposit to the late nineteenth and early twentieth

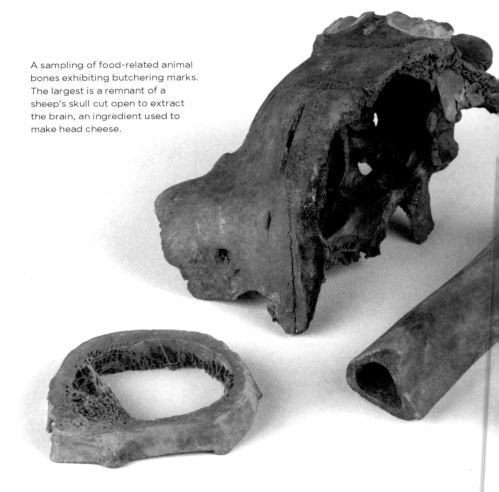

A sampling of food-related animal bones exhibiting butchering marks. The largest is a remnant of a sheep's skull cut open to extract the brain, an ingredient used to make head cheese.

centuries. Although the sample size is small, the date range provides some insight into food availability and/or consumer preferences across a lengthy span of time that saw the area develop and change substantially.

Sheep remains composed the single largest identifiable class of bones in the earlier privy, with far fewer cow and pig bones. Cuts of pork and beef were likely purchased from the local market, and included rib cuts, a hind shank, and arm roast enough to feed a large family. Also present were parts of one chicken, a freshwater mussel, and local fish, all of which added variety to the residents' diets. We observed at least seven sheep, mostly represented by skull and jaw fragments. Many displayed a range of butchery marks associated with skinning, disarticulation, and possible food processing. For example:

› cut marks present on the snout of one specimen may indicate that a butcher had removed the animal's hide with a knife;
› the back of several skulls displayed cut and shear marks suggesting skulls were severed from the neck;
› jaws were cut free from skulls using a knife and cleaver, based on the cut, shear, and impact marks left behind on several specimens; and
› several skull fragments were halved longitudinally with a cleaver, possibly to get at the brains, an integral ingredient when making head cheese, a meat jelly.

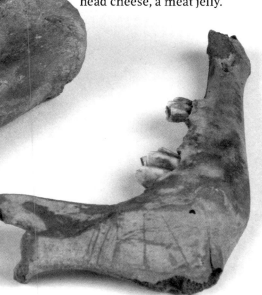

We noticed that few other parts of the sheep skeleton were recovered from the early privy. It is possible the occupants may have simply loved sheep's heads – which were traditionally consumed in Scottish households – and sought them out at the market. However, we also found both very young and fully mature skulls and jawbones, meaning the sheep may have been raised and butchered behind the home. Other parts of the animal were possibly sold or shared with neighbours and disposed of elsewhere after the meat had been consumed. It is also possible that nineteenth-century Ward residents raised sheep to produce their own wool.

As the city grew, fewer animals were kept in residential lots, and specialized butchers did more of the slaughtering and butchery. In other words, households purchased more trimmed-down meat cuts. The newer privy we studied clearly reflects this change in buying habits. It contained an almost even mix of cattle, pig, and sheep bones, all acquired from local shops. We learned the residents on this house lot favoured rib cuts from all three animals. Beef had been predominately cut into steaks, based on the thin, sawn sections of long bones we recovered. Sheep and pig, on the other hand, had been mainly served as roasts. The discarded long bones had cut and scrape marks left when the meat was removed.

This privy also contained small amounts of turkey and goose, one freshwater mussel, and catfish bones. It's possible the occupants caught the fish themselves. They may have also hunted. While it's difficult to distinguish wild and domestic bird specimens, the turkey and goose bones we found are mature adult specimens, suggesting they were wild birds. If these birds were domestic species, they would have been raised on-site or purchased commercially, and processed prior to reaching skeletal maturity. The goose bones in particular were heavily processed, perhaps by an inexperienced household butcher, suggesting geese were not raised on-site.

Most interesting is the amount of chicken recovered from this newer privy. We found bones from all parts of the body, indicating that whole chickens had been prepared for consumption on-site. As well, at least half the chickens we examined were juvenile – they were likely raised to eat or

TOM PORAWSKI

purchased from a butcher shop that sold both whole and dressed chickens. The rest of the bones came from adult chickens, which may have been kept on-site and used to produce eggs to eat or hatchlings to raise.

Both privies showcase how animal bones can be used to provide information about what people ate, how they acquired their food and processed it, and how all this changed through time. In some cases, it is possible to deduce the ethnicity and the economic status of occupants. For example, when we find larger cuts that demonstrate evidence of household butchery, or bones from animals raised on-site, we have evidence that suggests the occupants' lack of wealth. After all, it was cheaper to buy larger pieces of meat and butcher them at home than purchase retail cuts exclusively. Sometimes low-grade barrelled meat was purchased and shared to save money.

It's also worth noting that backyard animals provided other resources, such as eggs, milk, and wool – all items that people would otherwise have to purchase elsewhere. What's more, if consistently cheaper cuts of meat are found in a deposit, one might conclude that the residents could not afford to purchase higher quality or tastier meats.

We also found hints about ethnicity. Patterns of meat-cutting differ between most countries and regions, so it may be possible to deduce the ethnic background of a resident based on the types of meat being consumed, and how the animals raised on-site had been butchered.

The collection of bones we found in the earlier privy, which contained several processed sheep skulls, suggests the occupants may have been Scots, who traditionally prefer lamb. The newer privy, in turn, had a mix of domestic mammals in nearly equal proportions, with no preference for a particular animal or cut. In this assemblage, there's little evidence of a dominant ethnicity of the users of the privy. It is possible that multiple families living at this address used the same privy. By the late nineteenth and early twentieth centuries, in fact, Toronto's population had grown significantly, with crowded residential dwellings in The Ward often occupied by several Italian, Jewish, and later Chinese families. It could have been a mix of residents who created the mixed deposit we examined.

## COCONUTS IN LATRINES!

ELIZABETH DRIVER

AMONG THE THOUSANDS of food scraps retrieved during the Armoury
Street Dig, coconut shells were some of the more curious and
indeed unexpected items, given Toronto's distance from the tropical
regions where these fruits grow.

The hard, brown shell around the white coconut meat does not
decompose easily, so when archaeologists unearthed these fragments,
there was still fibre on them. Despite many years underground, they
looked as if the coconut flesh had just been eaten. This exotic food does
not fit neatly into our expectations of an archaeological dig in Ontario,
raising questions: Who was consuming the tropical coconut's delicious

meat and milk, and why? Was it a reflection of food fashion or ethnic identity? I can speculate on the story of these surprising artifacts by looking for clues in the coconut's history in Toronto and in census records.

Coconuts are the fruit of the coco or coconut palm.[1] The hard 'nut' within the thick, fibrous husk is the fruit's stone. Likely a native of the East Indies and Melanesia, the coconut palm was dispersed around the tropical world by early seafarers and traders, becoming a culinary staple in the Caribbean and the east and west coasts of Africa. The date of first cultivation in the United States is uncertain, but may be as late as the 1860s.[2]

Coconuts were well-known in Toronto from the mid-nineteenth century onward, and merchants advertised in the newspapers for both whole coconuts and processed forms as specialty items. On May 5, 1857, Toronto's Rowe and Co., at 2 Church Street, announced fresh coconuts, along with Messina and Palermo oranges, lemons, peanuts, figs, dates, and prunes, all 'just received in good order' and 'at the lowest possible cash prices.' On October 29, 1868, Bilton's, at 188 Yonge Street and 123 King Street, offered '20 sacks of Carthagena cocoanuts,' and on December 17 of the same year, '20 sacks of Carthagena and Baracoa Cocoanuts' as part of its 'splendid stock of foreign fruits for Christmas' use.' (Cartagena is a city in Colombia, on an inlet of the Caribbean Sea; Baracoa is a Cuban city.) Coconuts were such a big trade item that in 1881, 'the Cocoanut Question' threatened the federal finance minister's

Left: Tin enamelled cooking pot.
Right: Coconut shells.

reputation when it was reported that a Central American importer had fooled him into reducing the duty on coconuts. This had allowed a syndicate, controlling the sale of 20 million coconuts to North America, to greatly increase the cost for Canadian and American consumers.[3]

It is not clear whether the coconut oil that was imported free of duty at the Port of Toronto in 1864, in its 'crude, unrectified, or natural state,' was for cooking.[4] However, later in the century, desiccated coconut (the shredded and dried white meat) was available for home baking: for example, Linton's Trinidad Brand of English Desiccated Cocoanut advertised on New Year's Eve, 1887, in '1 lb. and ½ lb. fancy cannisters' by its Canadian agent, C. A. Liffiton of St. James Street;[5] and the desiccated coconut sold in 1898 by Toronto's T. Eaton Co. as a 'grocery special' for thirteen cents per pound, along with the best Italian macaroni and choice Spanish olives.[6]

Sweet baked goods can contain fresh or desiccated coconut. Almost as soon as whole coconuts hit the Toronto market, coconut treats were in fashion and for sale in stores and on hotel menus: Cocoanut Cakes from Paxon's in 1860;[7] Cocoanut Pies on the Rossin House banquet menu for over two hundred members of the St. George's Society, on St. George's Day, 1868 (listed between English Plum Pudding and Rhubarb Pies);[8] and Peanut and Cocoanut Candy, from R. Simpson, at the southwest corner of Yonge and Queen Streets, in 1894.[9]

At the same time, coconut recipes were undoubtedly also circulating among the city's home cooks, especially middle-class women who could afford to buy *The Home Cook Book,* or who knew someone with a copy. This 1877 Toronto cookbook was a bestseller for decades, and its 'tried, tested, proved' recipes included at least seventeen for coconut desserts![10] The food fashion for coconut was clearly established in mainstream Toronto society by this period, and by the 1890s coconut recipes were also appearing in newspapers.[11] Over time, coconut recipes likely also found their way into homes in The Ward.

*The Home Cook Book,* replete with trendy coconut recipes, was originally 'published for the benefit of the Hospital for Sick Children,'[12] which was first located in The Ward in 1875, in a rented house on Avenue Street (just east of the southeast corner of today's College Street and University Avenue), and has remained in The Ward almost

ELIZABETH DRIVER

continuously.[13] Founded by a ladies' committee, the hospital was 'part of a larger movement of charitable initiatives directed towards assisting, and uplifting, the urban poor' and it 'emerged from a tradition of visiting poor children in their own homes.'[14] It is not entirely fanciful to imagine the ladies enjoying coconut candy at one of their committee meetings or dispensing coconut sweetmeats to child patients.

Given The Ward's cultural makeup during the nineteenth and early twentieth centuries, it is more difficult to find a link between coconut consumption and ethnic identities from coconut-growing countries. The predominant groups settling in The Ward were Anglo-Irish (1830s–40s), an increasing Black population escaping from the United States via the Underground Railroad (1840s–60s), Italian labourers (1880s), Central and Eastern European Jews (from the 1890s), and Chinese (1910s onward). The censuses of 1861, 1871, and 1881 listed a few Ward residents from coconut-producing countries, but usually they were of English, Scottish, or Irish origin, or of indiscernible cultural roots. The 1861 census, for example, listed thirteen residents from the West Indies and three from the East Indies. The 1871 census listed one resident from Jamaica (Samuel Gibbons), but he was an Irish labourer; one resident from the East Indies (Thomas Lumsden), a Scottish gentleman; and two residents from the West Indies (Francis Duncan, John Peacock), one a Scottish finisher, and the other born in the West Indies but ethnically English.[15]

The question remains: how did this tropical food enter a home in The Ward? Did these coconut shells originate from a fruit stand, a catering service, or as a specialty item at a local grocery? Whatever the answer, that long-ago resident's mundane act – disposing of coconut shells in a backyard outhouse – has established that coconuts are part of The Ward's food history. These shells have opened up a realm of enquiry that goes far beyond the neighbourhood's boundaries.

Of course, now that Greater Toronto is the world's most culturally diverse city region, seemingly exotic produce has become more commonplace. Supermarkets, from the downtown core to the inner suburbs, stock food items that suit the cultural cravings of newcomers, and that, like the coconut, eventually become part of the everyday Canadian palate.

# DIGGING UP THE NORTH MARKET

PETER POPKIN

THE ARMOURY STREET excavation resulted in the recovery of thousands of animal bones deposited in various locations across the property. The bones described in 'You Are How You Eat' (pages 52–57) are, for the most part, the physical evidence of the foodways that existed within the City of Toronto around the turn of the twentieth century.

The concept of foodways encompasses the full range of activities that occur during the procurement, slaughter, processing, distribution, preparation, consumption, and disposal of food.[1] The final stage – disposal – may lead to the formation of discrete archaeological deposits within an urban centre. These deposits will also be influenced by past waste-disposal practices.

The Armoury Street animal-bone assemblages consist mostly of post-consumption household-refuse deposits. But to fully understand what's been thrown away, archaeologists must look to other locations, such as public markets, butcher shops, and slaughterhouses, to identify deposits representing earlier stages in the foodways process.

The City of Toronto's decision to redevelop the St. Lawrence Market North, at the northwest corner of Front and Jarvis Streets, created an excellent opportunity to conduct just such an assessment. It is the site of the earliest public market in Toronto, and was home to butchers in the city for almost a century. It is quite likely that some of the animal bones found on the Armoury Street site came from animals or cuts of meat purchased at the North Market.

The market site's history goes back to the earliest days of 'Muddy York.' In 1803, Lt.-Gov. Peter Hunter decreed that the St. Lawrence Market

North property and surrounding area was to be officially established as a 'Public Market.' By 1820, there was a one-storey wooden market

building on the property. It could house around twenty butchers. In 1831, a two-storey brick building with an open interior courtyard was constructed as the Town of York Market. All of the stalls on the ground floor, and their associated cellars, were reserved for butchers.

But a fire swept through the Town of York Market building in 1849, forcing the city to rebuild it in 1850–1851. The interior of the new North Market had a long arcade reserved for butchers and exterior areas designated for the sale of produce and poultry.

This reconstructed market served the city for several decades. But as the population and local economy surged in the 1890s, it became apparent that a new facility was needed. In 1898, the Market Commission released a report recommending the improvement of the existing north and south St. Lawrence Market buildings, based on their survey of public markets in Montreal, Boston, New York, Philadelphia, Baltimore, Washington, Cleveland, and Buffalo.[2]

In 1904, the city demolished the 1851 North Market and replaced it with a new brick-and-stone structure with a vaulting glass roof supported by iron girders. This expanded facility included a wholesale

market that had been engineered as a single large open space strad-
dling Front Street, into which farmers could drive their wagons.

While wholesale butchers still plied their wares in the 1904 North
Market, they were now accompanied by farmers, hucksters, and hay
sellers. City officials relocated the retail butchers to the new South
Market. The changes in the functions of the north and south
St. Lawrence markets at the turn of the twentieth century led to the
end of the butchers' century-long domination of the North Market.

The 1904 North Market served its purpose for another six decades
before the city demolished it in favour of a more modest structure that
was developed in 1968 as a centennial project. And for most of the fifty
years that followed, the North Market functioned as the home for the
St. Lawrence Farmers' Market.

In 2015, the City of Toronto began exploratory archaeological excavations of the St. Lawrence Market North in preparation for the
redevelopment of the property as a multi-purpose building that will
house the farmers' market, Toronto Court Services, and a large underground parking garage.

During preliminary excavations – via trenches dug into the North
Market's concrete floor – our team readily identified well-preserved
archaeological resources, such as drains and foundation walls, beneath
the structure. After the city demolished the 1968 building, we conducted
a full excavation through 2016 and 2017. Our crews recovered approximately 9,000 animal bones. As of this book's publication, the analysis
of the archaeological remains has yet to be completed, and city officials
were debating how best to conserve and publicly present the site's
archaeological resources, including the large-scale infrastructure that
remained from previous market buildings.

THE 1851-1904 NORTH Market would have been familiar to the residents of The Ward, even if they preferred to do most of their
shopping at a local butcher or to buy animal products directly from
producers.

The market offered Torontonians spectacle as well as staples, especially around Christmas. '[C]hildren who did not visit St. Lawrence

PETER POPKIN

Ceramic Russian Bear's Grease ointment jar lid. A hair tonic or conditioner. The manufacturers claimed that it could prevent greying and hair loss.

Arcade at Christmas time would have thought themselves as not only being badly used, but also cruelly disappointed,' *Telegram* publisher John Ross Robertson remarked in 1908.[3]

The December 24, 1855, edition of the *Globe*[4] reported on the St. Lawrence Market's butchers' 'grand display': 'The thousands of observing and admiring strangers who passed through the Arcade during the past few days, have carried away with them the well-grounded impression, that in no city on this continent can better meat be found than in Toronto, nor better taste displayed in exposing it to public view.'

In its December 23, 1858, edition, the *Globe*[5] noted both the large crowds as well as butcher stalls 'tastefully ornamented with ribbons and appropriate devices.' The article singled out some stalls for special praise, including that of Mr. J. Britton, at number 15: 'Mr. Britton's meat is, as usual, of the primest and richest quality. He shows a splendid heifer, fed by the late Jno. Dow, of Whitby; 30 fine sheep, fed by Mr. Isaac Howard, of Whitby; and, as the greatest novelty of the season, two fine goats, all the way from the Rocky Mountains.'

Nor did the market butchers limit themselves to stocking the usual fare (veal, pork, etc.) at these festive periods. In one story about the Christmas displays in 1873,[6] the reporter noticed a large supply of venison, four fat raccoons, and at least four black bears, one of whose grease was to be rendered for 'toilet purposes.'

Ward residents, like other Torontonians, would also have been familiar with butchery and slaughter practices in the 1851–1904 North Market, practices that had evolved in the city over several decades. For an animal to enter into the animal food distribution network, it had to be slaughtered. In the nineteenth century, animal slaughter in Toronto was, unsurprisingly, regulated. While the first municipal abattoir, located on Niagara Street, didn't open until 1914, all animal slaughter prior to that date took place at private stockyards, abattoirs, and slaughterhouses. Inevitably, unregulated home slaughter of animals would also have taken place, including in the backyards of cottages in The Ward.

Slaughterhouses and butchers' shops were very different establishments in nineteenth-century Toronto. The second bylaw written by the new city council in 1834 regulated the practice of slaughtering animals and selling meat within the city. Bylaw 173, passed on September 12, 1851, set the tone for slaughtering animals that would end up being sold at the 1851–1904 North Market: 'That no person shall butcher or slaughter for sale any ox, cow, heifer, steer, hog, calf, sheep or lamb, within the City in any case, or within the Liberties, unless his slaughter house shall be constructed in such a manner as shall prevent nuisances to the adjoining premises or neighbourhood, and that no offal or impurity shall be allowed to remain in or near such slaughter house, and no pigs shall be kept or fed by him at or near such slaughter house.' (The city at the time lay between Queen Street, Parliament Street, Peter Street, and the Lake Ontario shoreline. Surveyed areas beyond those borders were called 'liberties.')

As Toronto grew, the city also sought to expand and regulate the distribution network. On October 30, 1854, council moved to allow butchers to open shops or stalls outside of Toronto's public markets (besides St. Lawrence, the two others were the St. Patrick's Market on the north side of Queen Street, between McCaul and John Streets, and St. Andrew's Market between Richmond and Adelaide Streets and Brant and Maud Streets). Four years later, council passed another bylaw that specified that newly allowed butcher shops must be located a minimum of five hundred yards from any public market.

The rules distinguishing slaughterhouses from butcher shops were not always followed, of course. The 1886 report of the Toronto Medical Health Officer,[7] related to the inspection of slaughterhouses and butcher shops, indicated that the slaughtering of calves and sheep occasionally took place in eighteen of the 143 butcher shops inspected. This practice wasn't especially prevalent, but when it did occur, city officials didn't look well on it.

PETER POPKIN

The point is that animals were *not* being slaughtered at the 1851–1904 North Market; rather they were being slaughtered in a registered slaughterhouse, likely in the liberties, with the carcasses then transported to the North Market on carts or wagons.

The animal bones recovered during the North Market excavation, then, do not come from the slaughtering process or immediate post-slaughter carcass preparation, such as disembowelment. Instead, the bones we found represent activities that occur further down the foodways chain.

For example, North Market butchers would have selected their live animals from producers in the countryside, or from the adjacent cattle market, and arranged for their slaughter at a registered slaughterhouse prior to delivery to the North Market. The carcasses would have been carved into commercially desirable cuts of meat at the market using a variety of knives, cleavers, and saws.

Despite market regulations about keeping stalls in a 'clean and proper' state and ensuring that no 'offal, hides or tallow remain on or near the premises after eight o'clock in the morning,' the waste disposal at the market was not flawless. Occasionally, animal bones from offcuts or butchers' waste were disposed of at the North Market.

The heart of The Ward was about a fifteen-minute walk from the North Market, which was the centre of Toronto's nineteenth-century foodways system. Surrounding the North Market's butchers' stalls were produce stands, poultry stands, the Grain, Flour and Meal Market, the Hay and Straw Market, the Cattle Market, the Fish Market, and the Lower (South) St. Lawrence Market, with its fruit and vegetables. Whether residents of The Ward needed food for their table or feed for their animals, everything they required could be found at the market.

We may never know whether those sheep skulls excavated from the old wood-lined privies on Lot 7, on Centre Street, were purchased at the North Market or elsewhere. But one thing is likely: they offer evidence that someone who lived there liked to make 'jemmy,' or cooked sheep's head – a relatively common nineteenth-century dish that serves up a choice story of how those long-forgotten foodways have lain buried beneath a city preoccupied with new ones.

# A MATTER OF MENDING

MATTHEW BEAUDOIN

A JUG - WITH its pale blue, transfer-printed flowers still intact – didn't initially stand out among the large number of ceramics we'd found at the Armoury Street Dig; in fact, it wouldn't have been out of place in many archaeological collections from across the province. However, after we cleaned and analyzed the jug, its missing handle raised intriguing questions about its story. The iron rivets at the back of the vessel indicate that the previous owners decided to repair the handle when it originally broke, instead of simply throwing the jug away and getting a new one. We don't know the specific people who owned, used, and eventually discarded this artifact. But their decision to repair it gives us a unique vista to explore how people bought and used objects in The Ward.

In today's cultural and economic environment, replacing an item is usually far more straightforward than repairing it. That shift reflects the dramatically reduced cost of most manufactured goods, along with the decline of the skilled craftspeople who can fix household objects. By contrast, in the nineteenth century, this jug's owners might have repaired it themselves within the home; otherwise, in many urban areas, ceramic-repair specialists would do this work for a fee.

While we don't know who fixed this piece, we do have a sense of how they did it. After drilling holes through the vessel, they used iron rivets to reattach a handle. They might have used the original handle if it wasn't too damaged, or they might have replaced it with a handle taken from another jug or fashioned out of wood, metal, or rope. Once they had covered the rivets and holes with adhesives to create a water-tight seal, the jug would have been as good as new.

Despite their fragility, ceramic vessels are also durable, so they often make up a large portion of archaeological collections. Dishes easily break into many pieces and end up thrown away, but their fragmentary potsherds survive remarkably well within archaeological contexts. Ceramic repair has a long international history, with evidence discovered on archaeological sites from Roman-period sites throughout Europe, Iron Age sites in Scandinavia, fourteenth-century France, and fifteenth-century China. A well-known approach to repair, the practice of *kintsugi* in fifteenth-century Japan, used golden-coloured resins and glues to mend vessels, leaving beautifully lacquered scars.

North American evidence of ceramic repair is less common, but not absent. Among Indigenous communities, it has been occasionally noted on Archaic period steatite vessels, in Pueblo ceramic vessels in the southwestern United States (ca. AD 1200–1600), and on Inuit soapstone vessels from across the Arctic. Archaeologists have also found repaired ceramics on Iroquoian sites in southwestern Ontario, eighteenth-century sites along the eastern seaboard of the United States, and nineteenth-century fishing stations in Labrador.

While repair is much less common today, the reasons for mending ceramics in the past are still relatable. If we drop a dish or break a jug, we might consider repairing it if it was a costly piece, or represented sentimental connections or family histories. When the handle broke off this particular vessel, the owners might have not had the finances to buy a replacement. Or the jug could have been important to the owners as an heirloom or display piece; it's possible that this item completed a favourite set of dishes. Alternatively, the family members might have simply appreciated the floral design. We'll never know exactly why this piece was brought back to life through repair.

Yet if the owners had valued this jug so highly, how did it end up in the privy? Perhaps they eventually had the money to replace it. Alternatively, the meaning that this jug had to its owners might have changed. We can imagine, for instance, that the family member who valued this vessel had passed away and the rest of the family didn't consider it worth keeping. Whatever the reason, at some point the owners decided this jug was no longer important and threw it in a privy with the rest of their household debris. Ultimately, archaeologists many decades later excavated the pit and recovered the jug, giving it yet another life – this time as an artifact.

Printed earthenware jug with handle mends.

# CERAMICS AS NINETEENTH-CENTURY SOCIAL MEDIA

## HOLLY MARTELLE

LONG BEFORE MODERN technology and the age of the internet, ceramics functioned much like social media in transmitting messages about people, their beliefs, and aspirations. Displays of objects, whether passive or overt, public or private, were means of expressing human emotions and sensibilities – pride, loyalty, conservatism, frugality, righteousness, greed, and sorrow. In the late eighteenth century, British potters began to produce a variety of ceramic wares that both celebrated and commemorated historic people, places, and events, as well as important literary works. In their manufacture of goods, potters often sought to capitalize on consumers' emotional connection to such topics in current popular culture and socio-political life. With the production of both lavish and inexpensive wares, they appealed to a wide audience, targeting markets locally as well as globally. For example, by the mid-nineteenth century, potteries were making dishes with 'Canadian' scenes primarily for the fertile colonial market, in addition to ceramics with views of the British countryside that had local appeal and also nurtured memories of the homeland for British subjects abroad.

Two vessels recovered from the archaeological excavations at the Armoury Street Dig are commemorative wares that exemplify the use of ceramics in identity formation, social discourse, and the preservation of memory. Although each has distinct symbolism with unique social meaning, both are simple and inexpensive household objects that would have been used in an intimate, private context – a family's dinner table, an inherently social and educational setting where individual and collective identities were moulded, reified, and refashioned.

The first vessel (page 75) is a refined white earthenware pitcher commemorating the coronation of young Queen Victoria, which took place shortly after her eighteenth birthday. Although incomplete, enough of the brown transfer-printed design is present to visualize its theme. Bordered by a floral motif of thistles, roses, and clovers, a panel on the front of the vessel bears the royal crown, with the words 'VICTORIA REGINA' above and 'Proclai…e…1837… Crowned…838' (Proclaimed 20th of June 1837 Crowned 28th of June 1838). The side panels contain two busts of Victoria when she was the Duchess of York. Partially visible on the archaeological specimen, one of these is a circa 1833 copy of a drawing by Sir George Hayter, the official portrait painter for Victoria in her early years. This is one of the most popular and widely used images of young Victoria, occurring on both proclamation vessels of 1837 and memorials of her coronation in 1838. The other is a circa 1832 replica of a miniature of Victoria by Sir William Ross of the Royal Academy. This vessel well illustrates the common use by British potters of existing drawings, watercolours, and illustrations for display on ceramic pieces. In the process of transfer printing, an illustration would be etched on a copper plate that was then covered in ink. Fine tissue paper would be applied to the copper plate to absorb the painted design and then 'transferred' to a bisque ceramic before firing and glazing.

In the nineteenth century and before Confederation, the monarchy was widely popular among British subjects worldwide, and potters both exploited and encouraged nationalist sentiments through the production of ceramics celebrating various aspects of royal life – coronations, weddings, anniversaries, births, deaths, jubilees, and visits to various places across the globe. With tremendous appreciation for the obstacles their young, passionate new Queen had overcome in her ascension to the throne, British subjects excitedly anticipated Victoria's crowning. After a long line of unpopular monarchs, she inspired optimism, and Britain's hopes for the future culminated in one of the largest royal expenditures to date, a lavish ceremony costing the equivalent of $6 million today. In that period, the scale of commemoration for Victoria's

HOLLY MARTELLE

crowning rivalled that for the wedding of Prince Charles and Lady Diana in 1981, encouraging the production of a large quantity and diversity of memorabilia both practical and decorative in multiple media – from medallions, pins, pendants, postcards, and textiles to thimbles, bodkins, and other sewing apparatus. Staffordshire potteries in particular quickly took advantage of Victoria's popularity and the renewal of national pride at her coronation by commemorating the event on plates, pitchers, mugs, tankards, gravy boats, smoking pipes, and even stoneware gin flasks. Hoping that the public's exultations would influence their purchasing decisions, some potters worked so hurriedly to capitalize on the event that many of the earliest proclamation and coronation pieces shipped to the North American market actually displayed an incorrect birthdate for the Queen.

The beginning of the Victorian Era (1837–1901) illustrated on the 'Victoria Regina' vessel is only one of the Queen's life events memorialized by Staffordshire potters. In fact, John May's 1983 book *Victoria Remembered* illustrates the history of the Queen's early life (her coronation, her marriage, birth of her children, visits, and events) entirely through transfer-printed pottery. That so many of the royal commemorative pieces have survived testifies to their emotional worth, as cherished pieces and family heirlooms passed along from generation to generation, regardless of their monetary value.

Recovered in fragments, the Victoria commemorative vessel was clearly used by its owners and discarded after it was broken, thrown into a privy in the rear of a Chestnut Street lot, where it would sit in night soil for the next 150 years, until we unearthed it alongside other 1840s and 1850s wares. Despite its disposal in a privy, the fact that the pitcher predates the opening of this area for settlement hints that it must have been a valued possession, packed away in a trunk with the rest of an immigrant family's few but cherished belongings and brought to the property a few years after the coronation. The vessel is marked on the base with the initials 'R & C,' attributable to Read & Clementson, a short-lived Staffordshire pottery in existence from about 1832 to 1839. Its date of production is no earlier than the 1838 coronation and no later than 1839, the last year the pottery was in operation. The two residential lots associated with the privy that yielded this object were not settled until late in 1840 at the earliest, as reflected by indenture agreements signed by the Hon. John Beverley Robinson after he initially subdivided the land. Such artifacts of remembrance, heirlooms, and curios are not uncommon on nineteenth-century archaeological sites and testify to the personal attachments people had to material objects, especially in contexts of immigration.

Some more common Victoriana ceramics were fashioned in a familiar Staffordshire style reserved largely for commemorative and educational wares, featuring captioned illustrations surrounded by embossed and painted borders. With slightly fancier-than-normal treatment of the ceramics' brims and a focus on themes that were in vogue at the time, potters were justified in charging slightly more for their products without an equivalent investment of time, material, or labour. Perhaps the best known of these items are the 'ABC plates,' or children's plates that depicted letters of the alphabet, fairy-tale characters, and educational scenes, providing for playful learning. Others targeting adult audiences were embellished by mottos or captions with embedded moral messaging, and used to both educate the masses and enact social change.

The second commemorative vessel from the Armoury Street Dig embodies this Staffordshire tradition. It is a refined white earthenware small plate adorned with an embossed floral motif border. Central to the plate (page 159) is the printed scene 'Eliza Crosses the Ohio,' taken from Harriet Beecher Stowe's influential anti-slavery novel, *Uncle Tom's Cabin*. The origin of the engraving is not known, although it was common for potters to take illustrations directly from various versions of the novel or to produce copies, with varying degrees of artistic licence. Published in 1852, *Uncle Tom's Cabin* was an immediate success not just in America, but in Great Britain, France, and other parts of Europe. In Canada West, its popularity might have derived from both its abolitionist sentiments and the celebrity of resident Josiah Henson, founder of the Dawn Settlement and reputed inspiration for Stowe's character Uncle Tom.

Amid anti-slavery debates in Britain, Upper Canada, and the United States, Stowe's novel quickly rose to the status of cultural phenomenon,

HOLLY MARTELLE

Brown transfer-printed earthenware
pitcher commemorating the coronation
of Queen Victoria. The front reads
'VICTORIA REGINA, Proclaimed 20th of
June 1837 Crowned 28th of June 1838.'

drawing the attention of Staffordshire potters. Manufacturers produced a plethora of *Uncle Tom's Cabin*-themed memorabilia beginning in 1853, including ceramic objects reflecting the moral overtones of the book. Some of these were lavish decorative items for display in Victorian parlours, such as statuary and tapestries, intended to rouse discussion and political debate. Others were less expensive pieces, like serving platters, jugs, mugs, plates, and saucers that were both inspirational on a more personal and familial level but also utilitarian in function. The two most popular printed *Uncle Tom's Cabin* scenes on ceramic showed Eva lovingly dressing Uncle Tom with garlands of flowers, and Eliza frantically fleeing slave catchers with baby Harry after hearing news that he would be sold. Both themes incited strong emotions that spoke to core values of people all over the world and, in many cases, inspired support for the anti-slavery cause.

By the time Uncle Tom pottery appeared, Staffordshire potters already had a long history of producing ceramics with abolitionist themes. Josiah Wedgwood, one of England's most notable potters, was also a member of the Society of Friends, an organization that led the country's late-eighteenth-century anti-slavery movement. Wedgwood mass-produced a ceramic cameo bearing one of the first global abolitionist emblems – a placard depicting a kneeling African man in chains, accompanied by the anti-slavery dictum 'Am I Not a Man and a Brother?' Wedgwood's thematic cameos quickly became all the rage in abolitionist circles and were particularly popular among women who were otherwise denied the right to formally participate in political debates and organizations. As fashionable inlays for jewellery, hairpieces, and furniture, the emblematic items soon became trendy with the general public.

The two commemorative pieces from the Armoury Street Dig demonstrate that ceramics, as with most everyday items, are not simply utilitarian objects. As both decorations and calls for remembrance, nineteenth-century ceramic vessels reflected and shaped national sentiments and global causes.

# TWO EYES AND A SMILE

ABBEY FLOWER

O N A VISIT to the Armoury Street Dig one warm and sunny day in
September 2015, Holly Martelle, the consultant archaeologist
overseeing the project, excitedly approached me and placed a small
figure in my hand. The silhouette was a bit curious, but the simple facial
carving of two eyes and a smile was unmistakable. With joints for
articulated arms and legs, it looked to be a wooden doll that dated, as we
learned later, back to the mid-nineteenth century. This object made one
fact instantly clear – that life in The Ward was not all work and no play.

Before becoming a heritage specialist at Infrastructure Ontario,
advising the agency on the heritage and archaeological aspects of our
projects, I did my graduate work on the toys and play items that turn up
on digs. Typically, archaeological sites yield few artifacts relating to
children's play and pastimes. This dig, however, was different. We
recovered dozens of such objects, including miniature tea sets, person-
alized children's cups, dolls, toys, figurines, fragments of writing slates,
and a sizable collection of marbles. The site also produced a remarkable
collection of toys we'd describe today as 'educational' – items geared at
teaching the children of predominantly immigrant families living in
The Ward how to read or count.

What do all these toys, many found in over forty privy pits located
across the site, tell us about life in a neighbourhood once stigmatized
for its grinding poverty?

At one level, they convey a far more complete account of the lives of
the individuals and families who occupied this community. They tell
a story that acknowledges the pastimes that allowed Ward residents to

balance work and play. These objects also reveal how children represented a vital part of these neighbourhoods – they were not just props in official photographs used to project a particular image to the public and motivate city officials to clean up an area deemed to be slumlike. They remind us that regardless of culture or class, children will play. And more than anything else, the presence of so many learning-oriented toys suggests that the newcomer families who settled in this dense, impoverished block were invested in their children's future, and in making a better life for the next generation.

ONE OF THE COUNTLESS lessons my one-year-old son has taught me is that kids will play with anything. His favourite drum is the cookie tin he pulls out of our bottom kitchen cupboard. Indeed, every parent knows that children have a great instinct for transforming everyday functional items into toys, and this knack is perhaps especially well-developed in economically

Whittled wooden doll or marionette. When in use, this toy would have had separate arms and legs (likely also of wood) fastened to the main body with wire.

impoverished neighbourhoods. We see the captivating photo of Ward children running alongside metal hoops that likely had a different original use. When we dig up items like bicycle rims on an archaeological site, we may only see their original purpose. Yet such objects may have had a more playful secondary use.

Play is a fundamental part of life that begins in childhood and extends throughout adulthood. Yet it is often forgotten or overlooked when we try to understand the past. Historians and archaeologists frequently focus on big-ticket themes that have a clear connection to major societal shifts. Even when we seek to understand individuals' lives, we focus on occupations or aspects relating to their social and economic status. And when we look at generations within families, we ask of the children: what did they do once they grew up? Because of this focus, we create representations of the past dominated by work, religion, politics, social change, and economic status. Yet these markers don't tell the whole story.

While pastimes and play tend to be the lesser-contemplated aspects of daily life, details about these activities show us some of the more personal connections we have to those previous generations. To archaeologists and historians, the challenge in understanding the fun

Brown printed child's ceramic mug touting lessons about hard work and morality, taken from *Poor Richard's Almanack*.
Left: Bone Crown and Anchor die. Right: A variety of marbles.

and games of the past is that these activities were rarely documented with much consistency or detail in their own time. It's impossible to know whether immigrant parents in The Ward had encouraged their tots to bang on the many pots, jars, and jugs we unearthed from the Armoury site.

Other objects are less cryptic. What could more clearly embody playtime than a mid-twentieth-century rubber ball we found from the later years of The Ward? It was decorated with not only dots and lines, but also the alphabet and numbers from one through ten. Toy balls have been around for millennia, yet it's rare to find them on archaeological sites. In earlier periods, balls were made from materials – wood and leather, for example – that didn't survive well in most conditions. With industrialization, however, balls were made from rubber and then plastic, which take longer to break down. It is easy to imagine children playing with balls or marbles in the backyards and alleys of The Ward. But when a young child caught this particular rubber ball, did some adult also quiz her about the letters and numbers adorning its surface?

Another item we found was a fragment of a beautiful glass children's plate with the alphabet embossed along the rim. Similar late-nineteenth-century plates sometimes also feature text in the centre, but only this piece was recovered, so we don't know if the entire plate contained any other decorations, educational or otherwise. This alphabet plate suggests that parents in The Ward may have sought to engage their children in learning during mealtimes, a practice twenty-first-century parents can easily relate to.

Nor was the learning aspect limited to the basics. Another iconic children's artifact unearthed from this site is known as a 'Poor Richard's Almanack Mug.' These mugs combine printed scenes with sayings from *Poor Richard's Almanack*, an annual book written by Benjamin Franklin. Dating to the mid-nineteenth century, this cup is inscribed with lessons meant to teach young children the virtues of hard work and morality: 'Industry need not wish, and he that lives on hope will die fasting.' These mugs reached their peak popularity around 1860 with a series of different quotations and illustrations. Such objects reflect not only the values of one family but also early Toronto society, and possibly also the values of communities like The Ward, from a time before Confederation.

It's important to acknowledge that the need to play doesn't end when people reach adulthood. Some of the leisure-time objects and toys excavated from the site were likely used by grown-ups. Dominoes, for example, were popular from the late nineteenth century and well into the twentieth, with examples from two different sets found on the site. One set has large, chunky wooden pieces, while the other is smaller, made of bone, and more delicate.

Also uncovered was a single bone die from Crown and Anchor, a game that, like dominoes, included elements of chance and gambling. These items may serve as a reminder that civic officials, police, and social reformers of the time saw The Ward as an area of vice and ill repute. It's true that some adults like to add stakes to their pastimes, but not all will gamble away their earnings. The social aspects of these pastimes are the most telling – dice and dominoes are not played alone. In fact, such artifacts conjure up domestic scenes of several adults huddled around a domino table or a game of dice on a day off. The newcomer communities of The Ward came together through play and leisure as much as through labour.

Much of the official written record of life in The Ward, particularly in the early twentieth century, paints a two-dimensional picture dominated by caricatures of a low-income immigrant community filled with hardship. Yet the remarkable collection of toys recovered from this site helps us understand that life in The Ward included fun, education, and the sorts of keepsakes that children treasure. These artifacts dare us to ignore them, because they reveal a community with the vibrant colours of leisure, learning, and laughter.

Holding that small wooden doll in my hand made me feel like a kid again. It brought back memories of my own childhood and the toys I cherished. Looking into the featureless yet jovial face is to know the presence of the child who played with it so long ago. Through one object, we can so clearly envision her imagination and the joy she must have experienced. That day on the site was, in a sense, a little less work and a little more play.

NEW REGISTRY OFFICE SITE MAY 15 1912

SOUTH WEST COR ELIZABETH & LOUISA ST

Southwest corner, Elizabeth and Louisa, May 15, 1912. The City Hall parking permit office is now located at this spot.

# THE CIVIC ENGAGEMENT OF WARD CHILDREN

BETHANY GOOD

IN THE EARLY twentieth century, many reformers and public figures who advocated for social change in Toronto's urban core used the needs of (urban) children as their central focus. These campaigns tended to represent children as vulnerable and at risk within the growing, dirty, and dangerous city. However, as some historical sources and photographs exemplify, children were active, vital, and often very capable participants in the daily functioning of Toronto.

## SWAT THE FLY CONTEST

SOME EARLY REFORMERS actively engaged city children in efforts to improve conditions in neighbourhoods such as The Ward. For example, Dr. Charles Hastings, the Medical Officer of Health for Toronto (1909–29), in conjunction with the *Toronto Star,* initiated the Swat the Fly contest. This citywide fly-collecting competition encouraged children to become aware and help solve the problem of the spread of bacteria and disease by eliminating what public health officials considered to be the source.

Throughout the summer of 1912, children were enlisted to collect flies and bring them to city hall to be counted. The children who collected the most flies split a cash reward of two hundred dollars. Fifteen-year-old Beatrice White was the resounding winner, having collected more than half a million flies over the six-week contest.

By late August, health officials reported that the children participating in the contest had collected 3.5 million dead flies. Beatrice on her own had collected

Beatrice White with her fly traps, photographed by William James.

543,360 using traps she constructed. For her efforts, she was awarded fifty dollars. Children were central actors in this public health initiative and contributed to improving health conditions in a unique way.

## ELIZABETH NEUFELD AND ORGANIZING WARD CHILDREN

ELIZABETH NEUFELD, THE first head worker at Central Neighbourhood House on Gerrard Street in the heart of The Ward, found other means of engaging children in community social action. In the 1910s, playgrounds, along with most stores and municipal services, were closed on Sundays. As a result, children of The Ward, many of whom were Jewish and did not celebrate Sunday as their Sabbath, had only the streets as play spaces. In response, Neufeld organized weekly 'Sunday Parades.' The parades doubled as rallies, urging the city to open up the Elizabeth Street Playground on Sundays. Local children would meet and march through the streets, playing musical instruments, including pots and pans as drums. On one occasion, the parade marched to city hall, with the children demanding that the park be opened. Unfortunately, it was another decade before city council changed the Sunday park closure rules. Nevertheless, the parades were important community-building activities.

In 1912, Neufeld also made a bid to have the city approve the modification and use of an old schoolhouse on the Elizabeth Street Playground property for Central Neighbourhood House (CNH) activities. This request led other charitable organizations to demand that they, too, be given public funds to expand their facilities.

While the CNH's initial request was not successful, Neufeld a few years later once again organized the community to pressure city officials to approve a municipally generated plan to build a shelter house on the Elizabeth Street Playground property.

Though this plan was not connected to CNH, Neufeld believed the project would benefit community residents. On the day council was to debate the shelter-house proposal, Neufeld rallied two hundred neighbourhood children to march to city hall. The children met with the Board of Control, which consisted of several aldermen and the mayor. A ten-year-old, Jonny Senson, delivered a speech to the city officials:

Mr. Mayor and members of the Board of Control. We the children of the Ward are asking for a playhouse on the Elizabeth Street playground. We need a place where we can have baths, gymnasium and entertainments. Mr. Chambers (the park commissioner) said we might have it, so we thought we had better come and ask you to give it to us.

City officials soon processed the necessary documentation required to build the recreation house. As controller Jesse O. McCarthy reported, 'It was the most interesting deputation the Board had ever heard.'

### JUST KIDS SAFETY CLUB

IN 1928, CITY officials and the public were growing increasingly concerned about motor vehicle accidents involving urban children. The *Globe*, in conjunction with local community organizations, introduced a campaign to raise awareness about the dangers on city streets. Originally an offshoot of the U.S. National Safety Council, this movement was initiated by Augustus Daniels 'Ad' Carter, a Brooklyn, New York, reporter and artist who created the popular children's comic strip *Just Kids*. The Just Kids Club was started following one comic storyline in which a passing truck knocks down Mush Stebbins, a regular character, leaving him with a broken arm. A police officer at the scene asks Mush to promise to 'look both ways before crossing.'

The Just Kids Club recruited children to become members. To join, they made a pledge to cross streets safely and could participate in activities like essay and drawing competitions. The club, in turn, gave each a membership card and badges. The children could then collect a series of pins with characters associated with the club, whose motto was 'Remember to look up and down before you cross the street.'

Schools and community groups encouraged children to join and participate in the growing conversation about street safety. By October 1928, Just Kids had 275,847 members and was growing fast. Businesses and government leaders endorsed and actively promoted the expansion of the campaign. J. F. H. Wyse, the general manager of the Ontario Safety League, and P. B. LaTrobe, the secretary, visited fifty educational institutions across the province that promoted Just Kids. Between March 1928 and September 1932, the *Globe* regularly profiled children who were participating in public education activities related to the club.

T HESE THREE EXAMPLES of children's civic engagement provide a glimpse into the dramatic changes taking place in the early twentieth-century urban centres. Children and, in turn, their families were learning about germ theory through public health initiatives in which children were active participants. The increasing presence of motor vehicles on the streets led to safety education initiatives. And local settlement-house groups worked to inspire community children, especially those from immigrant families, to advocate for their needs within their neighbourhoods.

What is striking is the contrast in perspectives these reformers employed to address public health, safety, and child welfare. At once, they portrayed children as weak, vulnerable, and in need of supervision and rescue by adults. Simultaneously, however, these same advocates embraced the autonomy and independence of local children, encouraging them to take on active and independent roles within these communities.

One could further argue that this contradiction reflects the prevailing conceptions of young newcomers to Canada. There was an optimism and hopefulness associated with bringing immigrant children into the fold of a developing Canadian identity. These children embodied a resourcefulness and resilience that was promoted and celebrated. At the same time, there was also a notion that immigrant children were unruly, uncivilized, and in need of direction and supervision to properly assimilate into Canadian culture. Their participation in these three examples of civic engagement illustrates the contrasting notions about both young people and newcomers that were circulating among reformers and the general public at the time.

BETHANY GOOD

## 'JEWISH BOYS WITH HOOPS'

VID INGELEVICS

WILLIAM JAMES'S PHOTOGRAPH of three boys rolling hoops along a street in The Ward in the early twentieth century exists in multiple forms and sites. It is part of the William James lantern-slide collection at the City of Toronto Archives, captioned there as 'Jewish boys with hoops, 1910–1930.' It is found at the Toronto Public Library as a photographic print captioned 'Chestnut Street, 1922.' This version also ran in the *Globe* on August 29, 1922, to illustrate an article titled 'They All Understand the Hoop.' The *Globe* describes it as showing 'three young Canadians of three races –

Greek, Hebrew, and Polish – rolling their hoops in happy unison on Chestnut Street.' It is credited to James & Son. Lastly, as an image in the public domain, it has been chosen to virtually illustrate the Wikipedia entry on hoop rolling with the caption 'Bowling bicycle rims in Toronto, 1922.'

The fact that James, often called 'Canada's first photojournalist,' produced a lantern slide from his original negative indicates that this image had a didactic purpose and value for him beyond its saleability. Lantern slides were often projected to illustrate lectures. An uncredited 1912 photograph in the City of Toronto Archives' William James family fonds shows James at a meeting of the Canadian Photographers' Association, in which a lantern slide projector sits at the front of the room. Although we will never know what he said about this photograph, one can speculate that in a forum of avid photographers, the image's aesthetic success would likely have been a topic of discussion.

Given James's formation as a photographer in England and the popularity of the aestheticized representation of 'waifs' (street children) across a range of media and art forms in Britain and North America in the late nineteenth century, I'd like to explore this possible connection as a stylistic motivation for the hoop photo and other images by James of The Ward's children.

In 'Jewish boys with hoops' and, in fact, many other of James's Ward images, he favoured a particular photographic technique combined with relatively upbeat content that seems to counter notions of poverty as unmitigated misery, especially when it came to the representation of children.

His painterly portraits of clusters of joyful but poor Ward children contrast sharply with those of his contemporary, Arthur Goss, the city's first official photographer. Hired in 1911, Goss produced work that could be characterized as deadpan, distanced, and descriptive. While Goss often worked with a wide-angle lens with significant depth of field – meaning all or most parts of his images remained sharp – James used a longer focal length, giving a narrower field of vision and a shallower area in focus. The goal was to direct attention to his subjects through the artistic blurring of their backgrounds. Goss favoured the representation of the overall environment in his outdoor images, with children appearing as almost inadvertent subjects, while James tended to foreground the children.

The image of the three boys suggests spontaneity, but is, in fact, staged. In this sense the photo has more in common with late nineteenth- and early twentieth-century Pictorialism, a movement in which photographers sought to make their work more 'artistic' by mimicking painterly modes of representation and subjects.

Like other serious photographers of the era, James worked with a large-format camera that used individual sheets of film and was supported on a hefty wooden tripod. Due to equipment limitations and low film sensitivity at that time, action shots posed a significant technical challenge to photographers. Given the number of variables at play (including the capturing of the 'right' expressions of three children), it is quite likely that there were many unusable outtakes produced in James's pursuit of capturing the 'spontaneous' joy of young children inventing their own fun on the streets of The Ward. Careful planning and execution were necessary.

The photograph ultimately reveals James's vision of The Ward as a romanticized place filled with happy but poor – and always anonymous – street children of multiple nationalities, able to entertain themselves with the simplest of found objects. It's less clear whether James had any interest in making a critical or interpretive statement about social conditions.

Were his pictures a conscious refutation of stereotypes of poverty, or were the depictions of 'happiness' among the children a soothing rationalization, aimed at more affluent Torontonians, for the existence of atrocious living conditions in The Ward? Or was he simply striving for a pleasing aesthetic to enhance his freelance sales? Christopher Hume, in his introduction to the 1999 book *William James' Toronto Views* (which includes the Chestnut Street photograph), leans toward the latter interpretation. 'His passion was for the city,' Hume writes, 'not the eradication of evil.'

Regardless of motivation, what informed James's stylistic approach to the photography of his Ward subjects? Were there cultural and/or aesthetic influences that he might have absorbed before his arrival in Toronto?

Questions around exactly how, where, and when James learned photography are difficult to answer; existing biographies offer spotty information regarding the time before his immigration to Canada in 1906. He was born in Walsall, England, in 1866, spent some time in London and briefly North America before returning to Walsall, where he married and began his pursuit of photography. Said to be self-taught, he arrived in Toronto with his family at age forty and began his Canadian photography career soon after. Given this, it is likely he learned his craft during the 1890s, while in his thirties. The earliest images in the William James family fonds date to 1900 and reveal evidence of an already-advanced grasp of photographic technique.

James's depiction of the lives of street children had specific popular precedents that he would likely have encountered in England. One distinct genre of nineteenth-century literature and painting is devoted to the representation of the poor children, also known as 'waifs,' 'urchins,' 'ragamuffins,' and, in an especially pejorative term, 'street arabs.' To give some examples, Charles Dickens's novel *Oliver Twist* (1838) focused on the exploitation of homeless children in the early nineteenth century while, in North America, Horatio Alger published several popular novels based on rags-to-riches stories of poor children struggling to overcome adversity. In England one saw numerous painters specializing in the depiction of street children with the better known being the prolific Augustus Edwin Mulready (1844–86) and Lady Dorothy Stanley (1855–1926), whose well-known 1896 work, *His First Offence*, depicting a raggedly dressed child in court for some unidentified petty crime, is now part of the Tate Britain's collection.

In North America, transplanted British artist John George Brown (1831–1913), who specialized in depicting New York's street urchins, expressed the societal fascination with such children. His paintings served as flashpoints for growing concerns about abject poverty, criminality, and public health issues in large cities. Yet these children also became 'picturesque' subjects of artists. In Toronto, Frederic Marlett Bell-Smith (1846–1923) exhibited paintings made in 1878 of 'newsies' (newspaper boys and girls) selling papers on King Street.

Children as victims of urban poverty also constituted a thematic focus for photographers – again, as emblematic of social injustice for some and as aestheticized subjects for others. An early example, by British photographer Oscar Gustave Rejlander (1813–75), is a staged 1860 series of romantic images of a young boy he called 'Poor Jo.' Augustus Edwin Mulready blatantly copied one of Rejlander's Poor Jo photos for inclusion in his 1871 painting *Uncared For.*

Also in Britain, journalist and reformer Adolphe Smith (1846–1924) and photographer John Thomson (1837–1921) published the book *Street Life in London* in 1877, which depicted the dire poverty of London's underclass, with many of the images featuring ill-dressed, barefoot children. Thomson's style of photographing people – shallow focus with blurred backgrounds – anticipates the technique James later used in many of his photographs. By contrast, the Danish-born journalist and anti-poverty crusader Jacob Riis (1849–1914) placed his subjects against a sharp background in the striking documentary images of New York's Lower East Side published in his bestselling 1890 book, *How the Other Half Lives.*

The popular media also fed the public's appetite for images and stories of underprivileged children. For example, the *Illustrated London News* regularly published sensationalist articles accompanied by photos, including, for example, the 1846 story 'The Boys in the Streets,' which argued that 'uncontrollable and unemployable' boys should be sent to 'the colonies.' In Toronto, Central Neighbourhood House, a settlement agency that served The Ward, also published a magazine that included articles about the hardships of street children.

None of this proves decisively that James was referencing a popular, nineteenth-century genre when he went looking for subjects in The Ward. However, his work certainly reflects the proliferation of popular, artistic representations of impoverished children and 'slums.' For me, they pose an important question about the history and fate of this community: what effect did James's aestheticized and pleasing depictions of seemingly untroubled children on the streets of The Ward have on Torontonians at a time when progressive reform movements were using less romanticized photographic images in their battles for social change?

# ALL MANNER OF SHOES

## ABBEY FLOWER

FOOTWEAR – LEATHER scraps, discarded shoes, shoemaking tools, etc. – figured prominently among the thousands of objects found during the dig. A preliminary assessment, in fact, suggests the site yielded more nineteenth- and twentieth-century shoe-related artifacts – including a wide variety of complete shoe styles – than any previous archaeological dig in Canada.

The footwear-related artifacts uncovered included boots, shoes, and slippers made for and worn by men, women, and children. There is something personal and provocative about a single shoe, alone and separated from its owner. Shoes both protect our feet and make social statements. As one might expect in a neighbourhood like The Ward, several leather work-type boots were found, many repaired time and again to stretch out their useful life.

Yet some of the other shoes unearthed on the site also challenge the perception of what life was like in The Ward. These included fancy footwear, delicate slippers, and dress shoes. Like people from all social classes, the low-income residents of The Ward evidently liked putting their best foot forward.

It makes sense that this site yielded such a wealth of shoes and shoemaking items. Nearly a dozen Black, Irish, and English cobblers lived and worked here from the 1840s through 1900, making and repairing all manner of shoes. We found leather cast-offs, shoe lasts,

and partial soles on or near the lots where these cobblers lived. Francis G. Simpson, for example, was a prominent abolitionist and leader in the Black community. He lived on Chestnut Street within the Armoury Street site and was also a skilled and established cobbler. The majority of the shoes and shoemaking artifacts were found in the rear yards surrounding Simpson's home.

Typically, soles and heels, the more robust parts of footwear, are the only elements that occasionally survive when shoe material gets buried in our climate. Yet the unique conditions at the Armoury site – wet and soggy ground capped with asphalt for decades – slowed the decomposition process, which is why so much leather survived.

Consequently, this extensive assemblage, of both the final products as well as the cast-offs and manufacturing materials, offers important insights about the production process and the tradespeople who made these items. By the late nineteenth century, several trades, including shoemaking, had become more mechanized. With industrialization, the manufacturing process was shifting from the home and small businesses to large-scale factories run by companies like Eaton's.

The recovered tools and leather cast-offs show that up until this shift, cobblers in The Ward maintained their smaller-scale, handmade techniques. Newly arrived shoemakers needed portable tools they could easily carry with them as they established their new life in The Ward. Even once small community businesses were established, the artifacts suggest a focus on creating handcrafted quality items, employing traditional methods perfected over time and with skill.

Left: A man's shoe, with extra sole tacks indicating extensive repair. Right: A child's shoe.

# THE MILK BOTTLE BATTLE

SARAH B. HOOD

'HIGHLAND DAIRY LIMITED. TUBERCULIN TESTED.'
A painful, decades-long struggle is encapsulated in those few words embossed on a clear glass milk bottle recovered from the Armoury Street Dig.

Highland Dairy was founded in June 1929, and, despite the Wall Street stock crash, 'nearly trebled its business in the [next] six months.'[1] It occupied a building at 670 Ontario Street from 1931 to 1964,[2] when it was replaced by the high-rise towers of St. James Town. However, this particular dairy's history is less significant to The Ward and its residents than the second part of the bottle inscription: 'Tuberculin Tested.' The phrase evokes an earlier fight to keep Toronto children, particularly those living in crowded urban neighbourhoods like The Ward, from dying as a result of contaminated milk.

The story behind Ontario's pure-milk crusade did not begin in this community, however. In fact, the movement started outside Toronto. In 1889, Adelaide Hunter Hoodless, a Hamilton-area mother, watched helplessly as her fourteen-month-old son died from 'summer complaint' – a severe gastroenteric illness that was, at the time, a leading cause of death in young children. The condition was caused by unsanitary milk. Hoodless's biographer, Cheryl MacDonald, notes:

> Milk was delivered in open containers in Hamilton, accessible to flies and other disease carriers... [S]ome dairy farmers continued to feed their cows garbage and contaminated material, or pastured them in fields of raw sewage. Some middlemen who distributed the milk were worse yet, adding

chemicals like saltpetre, boracic acid and baking soda to the milk to make it
look fresher...[3]

Apparently motivated by the grief of her loss, Hoodless threw her-
self into a lifetime crusade to educate women about home management.
In 1897, she founded the Women's Institutes, which grew into a power-
house national network for rural women in Canada, spearheading calls
for mandatory pasteurization of milk.

A few years later, another champion rose up in the person of Charles
Hastings, an obstetrician from Markham who served as the Medical
Officer of Health for Toronto from 1910 to 1929. He fought for public
health on many fronts, but was especially passionate about milk sanitation. Like Hoodless, he had lost a daughter to typhoid-infected milk.

Before Hastings took his post with the city, Toronto's milk supply
was in bad shape, despite praiseworthy efforts by some dairies to
ensure purity. For instance, Toronto entrepreneur Walter Massey's City
Dairy was founded in 1900 specifically to distribute safe, clean milk.
The company's impressive red-brick buildings still dominate the eastern side of Spadina Circle, on the University of Toronto's St. George
campus. As historian Kevin Plummer explained on Historicist, 'The
onsite laboratory conducted 75,000 tests on the milk supply annually,
to prevent contamination.'[4]

Most milk vendors were less scrupulous. In the summer of 1908,
Toronto publisher James Acton headed a philanthropic mission to
make sure mothers in The Ward had a supply of safe milk for their
babies. He set up a depot at the Italian Evangelical Mission at 88 Edward
Street – now demolished – that distributed affordable (but not pasteurized) milk in sealed, sterilized bottles.

A *Globe* reporter who visited the depot wrote that 'the place had been
open only a short time and thirty bottles had already been given out.
Emaciated children, women with fretting babies in their arms, and
even men carrying a burden of domestic worry applied to the deacon-
ess for milk and received it gladly.'[5] The depot was so successful that
Acton's group quickly opened more, including one at the Fred Victor
Mission at Queen and Frederick.[6]

But the root problem – the prevalence of substandard milk – had not yet been addressed. In 1908, Hastings called 'the existing conditions of the clean milk problem...the most lamentable that ever confronted the medical profession.' According to Provincial Board of Health bacteriologist J. A. Amyot, 'there are eighty thousand quarts of milk consumed in Toronto daily, and if we can for the time being procure 1,000 quarts a day under ordinary Christian cleanliness it would be only a short time before we would be able to get our full supply under similar conditions.'[7]

Hastings accompanied the Hospital for Sick Children's board chair, John Ross Robertson, in the spring of 1909 to visit pasteurization facilities set up by pure-milk advocate Nathan Strauss in New York.[8] On their return, they immediately established milk stations based on the New York model: first, a temporary facility at a house at 253 Elizabeth Street, and five years later a more permanent pasteurization plant at the hospital.[9]

By fall 1909, Hastings was confident about the pace of reform. 'I believe that before next summer from fifty to seventy-five per cent of the milk sold in Toronto will be quite safe to use, and that within a year this city will have the largest supply of pure milk of any city of its size on the continent,' he told the press,[10] adding that one Toronto dairy was already pasteurizing its milk (Massey's City Dairy, which began in 1903),[11] and others were considering it.

In May 1911, Hastings championed a bylaw to regulate safe food handling. The *Globe* gives a clue to The Ward's living conditions in pointing out that '[p]robably the clause...that will cause the most trouble in "The Ward" is the following: – "No room in which meat, poultry, game, flesh, fish, fruit or milk are kept for sale shall be used for domestic purposes...."'[12] This comment suggests it was common for people to sell food out of their homes; the crackdown might have resulted in depriving some of a source of income while it curtailed food-borne illness.

In 1914, Toronto became the first Canadian municipality to legislate mandatory pasteurization, but health officials recognized that they needed to do more for children in The Ward. 'In their dingy lodgings in the Ward and other slum districts, where they breathe a murky

Glass milk bottle marked
'Highland Dairy Limited.
Tuberculin Tested.'

atmosphere of dust and foul air, these unfortunate little children have scant chances of getting a fair start in life,' a *Globe* reporter dramatically observed.

In a bid to reduce infant mortality, the City Health Department ran free ferry trips to the islands on every summer weekday that year, beginning in July, and handed out a bottle of pasteurized milk from the hospital plant to every child. For the inaugural cruise on the *Island Queen* (which Hastings attended), '[t]he Bay street wharf was crowded with upwards of 200 tired, anxious mothers, each having in their charge one or more pale-faced babies.' Many came from The Ward, others from elsewhere in the city.

As Hastings had predicted, over the following decade the quality of Toronto's milk went from being a civic disgrace to a matter of justifiable pride. In April 1921, the Canadian Public Health Association (with Hastings on its executive board) launched a week-long children's milk promotion campaign.[13] 'It is not a campaign for cleaner and purer milk,' noted an approving editorial in the *Toronto Daily Star*. 'That, fortunately, is not necessary in this city. Nowhere is the quality and the cleanliness of the supply more jealously guarded.'[14]

The project was carried out with creative zeal that would do credit to a viral social-media campaign of this century, with a widely advertised children's poster competition, 'I Drink Milk' buttons, blotters shaped like 'Mr. Milk Bottle,' a milk fountain, costumed milk mascots, milk-slogan slides in movie theatres, and the idea of the path to health as the 'Milky Way.'[15] Milk sales boomed.

While other areas still struggled with dirty milk, Toronto residents were now protected from what had once been a deadly risk to every child. The Hospital for Sick Children's pasteurization plant continued to operate until 1928, at which point the pure-milk battle had largely been won.[16] By the time Highland Dairy was founded in 1929, the landscape had changed; crusaders like Hoodless (who had died in 1910) and Hastings (who would die early in 1931) could rest easy, because they had ensured that no one else would have to experience the tragedy they endured in losing a child to contaminated milk.

# THE SELTZER BOTTLE'S JOURNEY

NICOLE BRANDON

OTTLE AFTER BOTTLE came out of the soil during the Armoury Street Dig. In total, we excavated dozens of soda-water bottles, representing a good number of the over two hundred soda-water manufacturers in Toronto from the late nineteenth century into the twentieth century. Primarily dated after 1880, most of these bottles were glass, adorned by moulded labels identifying the company that sold them. But one water bottle was not like the others. It was ceramic instead of glass, and it was not local – not by a long shot.

This surprising find (see page 103) had a label reading *Selters* in a circle, followed by *Herzogthum Nassau,* which is German for 'Duchy of Nassau.' Selters water was the ancestral Eve of soda water, and the ceramic bottle was the predecessor of all the glass bottles recovered from The Ward. The origin of this particular ceramic bottle dates back centuries to the Rhine Valley of Germany, where a stoneware ceramic industry thrived and endures today.

In a tradition going back generations, the bottle was hand-thrown by a potter in the Rhine, and once contained carbonated mineral water from a world-renowned spring in Selters, Germany. This water represents the origin of carbonated beverages as we know them today. Eventually discarded in Toronto, 6,000 kilometres from its origins, the bottle we discovered represents a journey rooted in Canada's colonial history. From the seventeenth-century fishing colonies of Canada's eastern shores to the urban streets of nineteenth-century Toronto, Rhenish stoneware found a place in our homes. Few other artifacts claim such a distinction.

Apart from clay tobacco pipes, Rhenish stoneware was the most global artifact of the sixteenth to eighteenth centuries, according to archaeologist David Gaimster, a leading expert on these goods. Other archaeologists have confirmed this assertion by digging up potsherds of Rhenish stoneware, both on land and under the sea, all over the world. We have found evidence of Rhenish stoneware at a wide range of sites: palaces, taverns, humble cottages, and sunken ships whose voyages between the Old World and the New were cut short by weather.

In the sixteenth century, Rhenish stoneware was a unique commodity in continental Europe, and more so in England. Ceramic as a material was just beginning to gain popularity, slowly replacing wood on the dining tables of the masses. Stoneware, though, was special even within the larger ceramic family. Stoneware is non-porous – it does not require glaze to make it impermeable to most liquids. Consequently it found its niche as a liquid container, in particular as the perfect receptacle for alcoholic beverages, which at the time were part of the daily diet.

Numerous potting centres emerged along the Rhine River, mostly in present-day Germany. The Rhine Valley provided ample wood for the kilns and the right clays needed for stoneware production. Potteries churned out vessels by the hundreds, then thousands, then tens of thousands, as Rhenish stoneware became an indispensable commodity in Germany, Belgium, the Netherlands, and England. The English market for Rhenish stoneware grew during the sixteenth century, peaking in the seventeenth century.

Rhenish stoneware had a monopoly on bottles for a very long while. The glass wine bottle did not yet exist, and English ceramicists had no idea how to manufacture stoneware. So England imported Rhenish stoneware by the literal boatload. Wherever the English went, their commodities went with them – the English landscape is peppered with potsherds of Rhenish stoneware, as are English colonies from the seventeenth and eighteenth centuries.

The top seller in the seventeenth century was a globular bottle with a face known as the Bartmann bottle.[1] It was the king of bottles, so successful that English potters longed to replicate and capitalize on it. By

NICOLE BRANDON

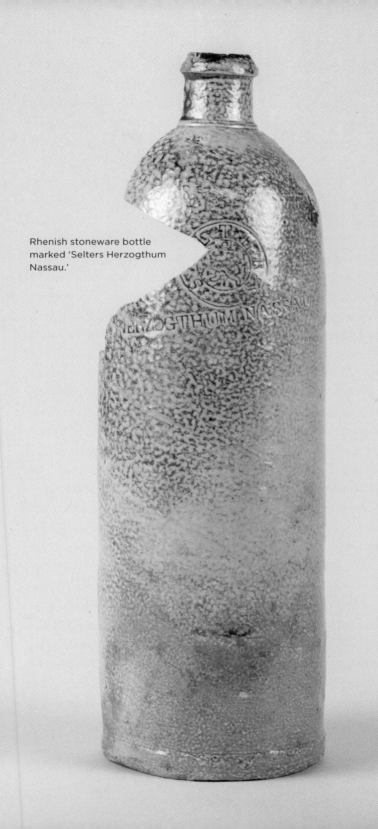

Rhenish stoneware bottle
marked 'Selters Herzogthum
Nassau.'

the time they finally cracked the recipe, the English glass wine bottle was emerging as a viable alternative to the Bartmann. As the eighteenth century approached, the Rhenish Bartmann bottle had competition in England from two new domestic products, so imports declined.

That was not the end of Rhenish stoneware exports to England, however. The Bartmann was out, but English consumers had a growing appetite for another Rhenish product: the stoneware beer mug. This mug was durable and could take a beating in a tavern. It came in various sizes and could be fitted with a pewter lid. Its base colour was grey, but blue and purple were added onto designs of flowers, hearts, checkers, and whimsical geometric motifs. English royal medallions were commonly applied, proof of the value of the English market to the Rhenish stoneware industry. The mugs, elegant as well as purposeful, were a hit and an indispensable commodity for much of the eighteenth century.

Eventually, English fervour for the beer mugs waned and these, too, slowly disappeared from taverns and homes – and, consequently, the archaeological record. Rhenish stoneware was replaced again by domestic alternatives, in stoneware, earthenware, and glass. But even though the English had all but dropped Rhenish stoneware, the industry in the Rhine Valley continued to steadfastly manufacture products for the domestic market and continental European neighbours.[2]

Furthermore, a new opportunity presented itself to the *Kannenbäckerland*, or 'Country of Pot Bakers,' as the region was known. Mineral springs of naturally carbonated water, renowned for its crisp, sharp flavour and curative qualities, were located in nearby Selters. Selters mineral water was chiefly marketed as a remedy for various ailments. Though Selters water had been exploited for centuries, interest in carbonated water grew after artificially carbonated water became available in the late eighteenth century.[3] The competition bolstered international sales of Selters' naturally carbonated water, and it was reliably bottled and shipped in Rhenish stoneware. The word *Selters* was eventually pronounced 'seltzer' in English and became synonymous with all carbonated water.

For centuries, Rhenish stoneware had been a desirable commodity in and of itself. By the nineteenth century, however, international

NICOLE BRANDON

interest had shifted to its contents. Consumers bought Rhenish stoneware bottles in 1650 because they wanted a bottle; by 1850 the consumer bought mineral water, which happened to be bottled in Rhenish stoneware. The archaeological record reflects the shift with increasing and then decreasing quantities of Rhenish stoneware artifacts in English colonial contexts over three hundred years.

From the Bartmann bottle of the seventeeth century, to the beer mug of the eighteenth century, to the mineral-water bottle of the nineteenth century, Rhenish stoneware exports have left their mark in Canada. Shards of Rhenish Bartmann bottles abound on the shores of Newfoundland, where the English established their earliest Canadian settlements. At the seventeenth-century site of Ferryland, for example, Rhenish Bartmann bottles are among the many material goods excavated from the artifact-rich soils. Moving west to Nova Scotia, where the Fortress of Louisbourg dominated the colonial landscape in the first half of the eighteenth century, archaeologists have found Rhenish stoneware beer mugs with blue highlighting the English heraldic medallion 'GR,' for King George II. Though French, Louisbourg was for some years occupied by the English, and the material culture left behind reflects both cultures' tastes.

England's love affair with Rhenish stoneware had largely played itself out by the time English settlers pushed into Ontario in the late eighteenth century. Britain's entrepreneurs supplied her subjects with most needed commodities, including ceramic and glass drinking vessels. This is not to say the English were not importing foreign goods, but the nature of imported goods had shifted from practical items to exotic ones. Despite the availability of domestically produced, artificially carbonated water in nineteenth-century England, the naturally carbonated mineral water from Selters, Germany, was still a desirable product.[4] The Rhenish stoneware bottles that contained this prized water occasionally show up on nineteenth-century-Ontario archaeological sites – including ours in The Ward.

Sheridan Building, 86–90 Chestnut Street.
The image is from the Fashion Hat & Cap
Company's stationary.

WORK LIFE

# A TOOL FROM ANOTHER TIME:
# THE PROJECTILE POINT

## RONALD F. WILLIAMSON

A N ASTONISHING AND mysterious object appeared amidst the house remains and refuse thrown out by the immigrants who lived in The Ward. One hot day in the summer of 2015 , archaeologists excavating the privy behind the former residence at 76 Chestnut Street recovered a 2,000-year-old spearhead from near the bottom of the pit. Made from a chert – a flintlike rock that outcrops along the north shore of Lake Erie between Fort Erie and the Grand River – this Indigenous tool is about fifty millimetres long and twenty-eight millimetres wide. The archaeologists had no idea what it was doing in the privy.

While it is possible the projectile had been found elsewhere and brought into The Ward, it is far more likely that the piece had been discovered on the very lot on which the privy was situated. While now a sewer, the small stream known as Taddle Creek originally wound its way from its headwaters on the glacial Lake Iroquois shoreline near Wychwood Park southeastward through The Ward, to its mouth at Lake Ontario near the Distillery District. Its course across The Ward can be seen on the 1842 James Cane map of the city (page 29). But by the 1850s, it had been buried less than one hundred metres from the former location of the creek.

The proximity of the Armoury Street parking lot to the creek is important: almost all of the more than 18,000 Indigenous archaeological sites in Ontario are within a few hundred metres of water. While this is due mainly to the enduring necessity of potable drinking water for small camps and more extended communities, larger streams

also facilitated travel by canoe and most water sources represented opportunities for fishing. If we therefore assume the spearhead had been lost on that parcel of land originally, there are actually several mysteries here. How had the point been misplaced thousands of years ago? How had it been encountered in the nineteenth century? And why and when was it deposited in the privy?

2,000-year-old projectile point or spearhead made from Onondaga chert, from a source along Lake Erie.

One possible scenario to explain its original loss would be similar to the hypothesis developed for hundreds of other isolated projectile points found previously in Ontario – a hunting loss. Imagine, about 2,000 years ago, Indigenous hunters winding their way along the creek when, having spotted a large deer, they threw several spears at the animal. Fatally wounded, the deer ran along the stream, where one of the spear shafts and its stone point came loose and fell. When the hunters finally caught up with the animal, they removed their spears, only to find one missing. Having travelled a considerable distance, there was no chance to quickly find it. Besides, the party had more important work: butchering the animal and returning to their camp with the prized pieces of meat and hide.

This scenario may have occurred in the fall, when meat and pelts were in prime condition for taking by families harvesting wild plants and animals at locations where they occurred in greatest abundance. These would be spots like wild rice beds, fish spawning runs in the spring or fall, and places in forest openings where deer and acorns were abundant in the fall. Such seasonal activities likely occurred within well-defined territories, probably along river drainages. Individual bands or extended families, each with a population of a few hundred people, may have returned repeatedly over years to certain preferred sites. The hunting technology was similar to that of previous times with the use of both spears and the 'atlatl' – a throwing board used to hurl stone projectile-tipped darts. Some archaeologists believe the bow and arrow was in use by this time as well.

The Ward point, however, is too large and heavy to have tipped an arrow or a dart, and thus likely tipped a spear shaft. This style of projectile point is also only rarely found in south-central Ontario (i.e., north of Lake Ontario). In fact, including the Ward point, there have been only two of its age and kind found in Toronto. The other one, similarly shaped but a bit longer, was located in a park near the intersection of Eglinton Avenue East and Leslie Street, about twenty metres east of Wilket Creek, which drains westward into the main branch of the West Don River.

These larger projectile points are more common in southwestern Ontario. For example, a unique and very large site was located about five hundred metres north of the Lake Erie shoreline on a creek west of the mouth of the Grand River, some sixty kilometres south of Hamilton. It consisted of four dense, overlapping concentrations of stone-artifact debris spread across an area of approximately 3,000 square metres. All but two of the nearly three hundred projectile points have shapes similar

RONALD F. WILLIAMSON

to the Ward spearhead. These forms, common in Michigan and northern Ohio, are considered part of a widespread cultural complex centred in Ohio that dated to between 2,500 and 2,000 years ago. That projectile points were made at this camp is suggested by the recovery of almost 3,000 pieces of chert flakes discarded during their manufacture.

This period is also known across the Great Lakes region for heightened interaction – exchanging of customs and material – among distant groups. This is especially in evidence for shared burial ceremonies. It was common during this period for people to sprinkle powdered iron hematite (an iron oxide) around and on the remains of their deceased, as well as on their grave offerings. This substance, sometimes known as ochre, was bright red in colour and likely symbolized blood, restoration, and rebirth.

Points identical to the Ward artifact have been found in graves. This suggests there might be a different answer to the question of how the point was lost. It may, in fact, have been intentionally placed in a grave along the banks of Taddle Creek that was then disturbed in the nineteenth century. The chert from which the Ward point and others like it were made was itself considered sacred material. Both Iroquoian- and Algonquian-speaking societies of the Great Lakes region link the origin of chert or flint to creation stories and the actual spilled blood and to broken bodies of key figures in those stories. Perhaps hunters occasionally returned to the earth artifacts made of the stone so central to their lives – a giving back of an important cosmological figure's blood or body.

Regardless of how the point originally came to be on the banks of Taddle Creek more than 2,000 years ago, it is also curious that it ended up more than a metre deep in a wood-lined, nineteenth-century privy amid an assemblage of mid-nineteenth-century artifacts. The person who found the artifact likely lived at 76 Chestnut Street and used the backyard privy. The residence there was built between the first lease of the land in 1840 and 1842, as it appears on the 1842 map. The point may therefore have been discovered during the construction and soil disturbance that took place on the lot in the 1840s. The documentary record links this period with William Percy, who was possibly Black, like many other residents of the street. It may also have been found by

Richard Cross, an Irish immigrant who occupied the residence from 1856 to the 1860s.

It is also possible the artifact was discovered when Taddle Creek was channelized and buried, probably in the late 1840s. This would have entailed considerable excavation of the banks of the stream and therefore disturbance of anything that had been placed in the ground or lost along its banks over the millennia. The workers would have had to dam the stream while they prepared the channel, excavating and then lining the new channel with wood and perhaps even stone to prevent the channel from migrating. While the displaced dirt and banks would have been restored once each section of the creek was buried, substantial rains would reveal artifacts near the surface of the dirt.

Archaeologists find artifacts regularly on the surfaces of plowed fields; in fact, surface searches are a prescribed method for surveying properties in advance of land development. They also find artifacts in the spoils of groundhog holes and tree throws or any other disturbed ground surface. Any person walking along that area could have found the piece and recognized it as a curiously shaped stone from the past.

As for its loss or discard in the privy, this action likely occurred around the same time as its discovery, given the mix of nineteenth-century artifacts in which it was found. One imagines it may have fallen from a pocket or the folds of a person's clothing. Or might it have been regarded as unimportant and thrown away with the trash? Some mysteries are never solved.

What is to become of this ancient Indigenous object? Currently, it is a provincial licensing obligation for archaeologists to store such objects for the people of Ontario. In the context of the recommendations of the Truth and Reconciliation Commission of Canada (TRC), however, there is an urgent need to respect and promote the inherent rights of Indigenous peoples including those related to their cultural heritage. In response to the TRC calls for action, the provincial government is beginning to make changes in how they are managing aspects of Indigenous heritage in Ontario. Perhaps then, the third life of this projectile point will be determined by the Indigenous people on whose traditional lands it was rediscovered.

RONALD F. WILLIAMSON

# ADDING SPARKLE TO EVERYDAY LIFE

SARAH B. HOOD

A MONG THE MOST plentiful artifacts recovered from the Armoury Street excavation are the scores of branded bottles from local soda-water factories. The two most common – Clark Bros. and James Walsh – are represented by dozens of bottles each. Clearly, between the 1860s and the 1930s, residents of The Ward consumed a lot of soda water. Also, even though The Ward had a reputation as an impoverished neighbourhood, the story of its soda producers shows that it was possible to build a business there quickly, to the point of profitably supporting a comfortable family life for the business owners.

Starting a seltzer business required an investment in equipment and bottles. The water had to be filtered and carbonated, then bottled and distributed to a roster of regular customers. The bottles had perceived value, and empties were exchanged for freshly filled containers, exactly like today's water-cooler bottles.

Today, these bottles inspire delight in collectors. Solid, generally well designed and usually embossed with striking typography, they also tended to be reissued with myriad variations over the decades. James Walsh (1868–83) emblazoned the company's address – 124 Berkeley – on its bottles, as well as a crown (and, occasionally, a beaver). Clark Bros. (1879–1900), operating at 229 Queen West and 30 William,[1] used a wheel logo because the company originally made carriages.

Throughout the life of the business, these companies might have used bottles of clear, pale blue, or teal glass, or sometimes stoneware. Clark Bros. and S. (for Stephen) Charlton, of 28 Richmond Street (1862–74), were among those firms that sometimes used 'torpedo' bottles, whose bottoms ended in a rounded point; they were meant to stand in a metal holder.

Clark Bros. bottles, in turn, often closed with a 'Hutchinson stopper,' made of a rubber plug attached to a springy wire loop. This was the most commonly found bottle stopper in The Ward, but some bottles also used corks or crown caps (like today's non-twist-off bottle caps). A few relied on the 'Codd's ball stopper,' which utilized the pressure of the carbonation to hold a glass ball in place. By the twentieth century, many soda bottles were also topped with a siphon instead of a removable sealer.

Soda water, or seltzer, was hardly new in the nineteenth century. British scientist Joseph Priestley had invented a technique for carbonating water in 1772, and the Schweppes Company was founded in Switzerland in 1783. By the 1820s, notes Robert Barratt in *The Canadian Encyclopedia*, 'small carbonated bottling operations were established in Canada, producing carbonated drinks in refillable bottles which were merchandised as medicinal elixirs or tonics.'[2]

In crowded urban areas like The Ward, bottled water was important because safe drinking water was scarce. As immigration historian Ellen Scheinberg points out, even by 1911, fewer than 10 per cent of homes in The Ward had indoor plumbing.[3] Excavations in similar locations, like Manhattan's Five Points neighbourhood, also turned up numerous soda bottles.[4] However, other factors contributed to their proliferation.

Waves of immigrants, particularly The Ward's plentiful Irish population, had brought with them an almost spiritual belief in the healing powers of spring waters. When few could afford a high standard of medical care, patent potions abounded, and pharmacies purveyed tonics and pick-me-ups of all kinds, often as a soda drink (hence the evolution of the drug-store soda fountain, which could be found by 1900 in downtown Toronto). The growing temperance movement in the latter decades of the nineteenth century further encouraged the consumption of non-alcoholic beverages.

Throughout Europe in the nineteenth century, people flocked to baths and spas to drink mineral waters (or to bathe in them), hoping to cure everything from general lassitude to serious diseases. Germans in particular embraced seltzer consumption (as they still do),[5] but Eastern

SARAH B. HOOD

Clark Bros. soda water bottle.

Europeans likewise fondly remembered seltzer from their homelands. Indeed, the possession of a sparkling siphon bottle also appealed to those with aspirations to middle-class luxury.[6]

From the mid-nineteenth century, soda- or mineral-water bottling companies sprang up in increasing numbers in Toronto. By 1895, there were more than a dozen, mainly started by British immigrants.[7] Besides the aforementioned Clark Bros., Walsh, and Charlton, the Armoury Street Dig unearthed bottles from John Verner (1881–97), T. Smith Steam Soda (1867–81), Boyle & Libby (1892–c. 1914), John O'Connor (c. 1891–94), Burns & Armstrong (1888–90), James Bushby (1891–93), Charles Wilson (1876–1900), and J. Eves Soda Water.

The last mark belonged to James Eves, a manufacturer of soda water, ginger beer, and mineral water who 'heralded from Brighton, England. If his own advertising can be believed, he originally established his soda water business in 1845.'[8] By the late 1850s, he was selling his beverages in Belleville and Kingston, and also shipping crates of ten dozen bottles by steamboat and railway to other markets.[9] He relocated to Toronto in 1861, and ran the business for twenty years. His bottles carried the motto 'This bottle never sold,' meaning they remained the property of the company. Oddly, Eves also dabbled in 'old coins, Indian and other curiosities,' according to the 1869 Province of Ontario Gazetteer and Directory.

Around the turn of the century, Eastern European Jews moved into the seltzer market. From this later period come bottles from Fauman Bros. (c. 1907–29); Halpern Brothers (1902–11); Paris Soda Water Manufacturing Company (1906–08); Union Soda Water Mfg. Co. (c. 1909–31); Toronto Soda Water Manufacturing Company (c. 1914–c. 1931), and Ontario Soda Water Manufacturing Company (c. 1914–23).

Whereas the nineteenth-century soda manufacturers of UK ancestry had tended to use their own names as brands, the Jewish soda manufacturers mostly used generic company names. There are different theories about the naming practice: they might have been intended to disguise the ethnicity of the manufacturers (although the bottles of the Paris Soda Water Manufacturing Company were proudly embossed with a prominent Star of David – presumably to achieve the opposite effect). But

some research done for the Armoury Block excavation suggests that many firms had multiple partners, making the use of people's names in the brand impractical. Alternatively, it might simply have been an indication that commercial marketing was becoming more sophisticated.

Union Soda Water Mfg. Co., 28 St. Patrick, December 9, 1918.

The Toronto Soda Water Manufacturing Company, mentioned by Ellen Scheinberg in *The Ward*,[10] was likely typical of the seltzer businesses run by Jewish immigrants. Founded around the end of World War I by Chaim (Hyman) Teichman, Sruel (Sami) Shumaker, and Moishe (Morris) Silverberg, it continued to operate until the 1940s. The company was originally located in The Ward, at 183 Elizabeth Street,[11] but moved in 1924 to 61 Oxford in Kensington Market.[12] The shift was characteristic of the European Jewish arrivals, who established themselves in The Ward before moving their families and businesses to nicer digs in Kensington.

A family memoir[13] tells us that Teichman bought an existing company and brought in partners from his home village of Ivansk, Poland.

His son, Ben Teichman, recalls that '[w]ithout any experienced employees the partners learned to run the machinery and blend ingredients to produce seltzer, ginger ale and other flavors of soda pop. They worked inside the plant, say two days a week, and then with horse and wagon went on the road delivering to customers inherited from the previous owners. All work ceased on Shabbos. It did not take long before things really took off and they were doing quite well.'

Another, the Paris Soda Water Manufacturing Company, was in operation from 1906 to 1908 at 134 (then 77 and 79) Agnes (later Dundas). The business, with branches in London, Ontario, and Montreal,[14] was run by Chaim Saliter, David Schwartz, and Max Shea. A descendant of Saliter recalls his somewhat checkered career: he left Iasi, Romania, to enter the business, 'which apparently was the first [Jewish-run] one in Toronto.' However, he soon decamped, deserting a wife and two daughters, and moved 'to Detroit where he had another wife and two sons.' According to family lore, 'after Detroit, Chaim went to Quebec City and had yet another family. From there, Chaim went to Palestine to die and be buried on the Mount of Olives.'[15]

Some of these companies survived a long time. The Ontario Soda Water Manufacturing Company, whose distinctive bottles featured an embossed elephant, was founded by Harry Weintraub, Sami Silver, Isadore Budner, and Reuben Rosenberg around 1914. Toronto resident Allan Rosenberg recalls[16] visiting his grandfather's seltzer company at 229 Manning Street in the mid-twentieth century, by which time it had been renamed the Nu Jersey Creme Company. The seltzer was delivered to regular clients in elegantly etched siphon-topped bottles, six to a wooden crate, stacked in an open truck.

As of 2018, this industry has not quite been extinguished: Frank Samel of Magda Soda Water still carries on his family's business – probably the last of its kind in this country – using 'the same glass bottles his father once washed, filled and delivered when he arrived in Canada from Hungary more than 50 years ago.'[17]

# WHEN EATON'S PITCHED ITS TENT

WAYNE REEVES

FROM THE 1910S through to the 1920s, the production of tents and awnings, two rather prosaic canvas goods, brought together two disparate sorts of entrepreneurship in The Ward. On one side was Henry Greisman, a Jewish businessman of local renown. On the other was Canada's retail magnate, Sir John Craig Eaton, who occupied a spot much higher up the socio-economic ladder. Their lives intersected in a factory building at 86–90 Chestnut Street – a property that offers a glimpse into the driving personalities and commercial dynamics behind redevelopment in The Ward in the first decades of the twentieth century.

Starting in 1915, the Canadian government began ordering large quantities of military gear such as 'bags, buckets, haversacks, holdalls, mess tin covers, tents, valises, canvas covers, kit bags, line gear bags, nose bags, [and] ration bags.' The T. Eaton Company

Officers of the Royal Flying Corps Canada with their tents and canvas gear at the University of Toronto, 1918.

won substantial tenders to supply these canvas goods to the Canadian Expeditionary Force in Europe. Similar contracts were awarded to a local competitor, tellingly named the American Tent and Awning Co. of Toronto. According to historian Patricia Phenix, Eaton's donated all profits from its government contracts to the war cause.

Besides its war-related production, Eaton's had long made canvas goods for the domestic market. From 1896 on, tents and awnings were featured in Eaton's spring and summer catalogues; in-house manufacturing began by 1899. By 1916, Eaton's was selling wall and wedge tents in various sizes, though potential buyers were no longer urged to submit custom orders. Local sales likely increased after Ward's Island became a summer 'tent city' in the early 1910s. 'The workmanship we guarantee,' stated an Eaton's pamphlet from the 1920s, 'as they are all made in our own workrooms.'

The T. Eaton Company traced its roots to a modest shop on Yonge Street, near Queen, founded in 1869 by Timothy Eaton, a Methodist merchant. By the end of the century, Timothy was running Canada's leading department store. He had instituted manufacturing in Toronto in 1889, and was soon making clothing, jewellery, furniture, upholstered goods, window shades, harnesses, horse collars, suitcases, and leather trunks.

His youngest son, John Craig, was born in Toronto in 1876. He became company president upon his father's death in 1907, and embarked on a major expansion of Eaton's factories, in Toronto and other Canadian cities. His corporate success was reflected in Ardwold, the fifty-room mansion he built atop the Davenport Ridge in 1911.

Picture postcards and other promotional items from the early twentieth century depict a swath of commercial and industrial buildings owned by Eaton's, spanning some twenty-two acres along The Ward's eastern edge. Two of John Craig's factories reached twelve storeys, looming above the nearby working-class neighbourhoods.

Early in the war, Eaton's decided to lease additional factory space further inside The Ward, likely due to those large canvas-goods contracts for the Canadian military. It was a move that saw the fortunes of the patrician retailing mogul intersect with the ambitions of a Jewish immigrant who was busy building his own commercial empire.

Henry Greisman was born in 1867 in what is now Radomyśl Wielki, Poland, then part of the Austrian province of Galicia. He came to Toronto in 1888, joining a large family of peddlers living and street-trading in The Ward. By 1919, Greisman was affluent enough to move his home from University Avenue, on the edge of The Ward, to Admiral Road in the Annex.

Greisman's upward mobility was marked by his changing occupations. He earned enough as a peddler/jobber to buy his own house on Chestnut Street in 1897. He became a partner in the Empire Suspender Co. in 1904, then sole owner of the King Suspender Co. in 1909, enabling him to acquire additional lots along Chestnut and Armoury. Greisman constructed a row of brick houses there in 1908–09, which, notes historian Stephen Speisman, 'were built as

The Eaton's tent and awning factory (below centre) sports twelve windows on its rear side. Flanking it are the British Methodist Episcopal Church and another loft built by Henry Greisman. The Toronto Armouries is over, left (July 1930).

investment, not philanthropy, but he did rent them at a reasonable rate.'

When it came to real estate, Greisman's business model was to erect, own, and lease out his buildings. In the 1910s, his construction focus turned from residential to manufacturing. Perhaps prompted by rising land values, Greisman demolished six frame houses on Chestnut Street, erecting in their place two brick loft buildings in 1913–14. The structure was just what Eaton's needed. By September 1916, Greisman's sole tenant in the four-storey structure at 86–90 Chestnut was Eaton's new tent and awning factory/warehouse.

Greisman's manufacturing firm, the King Suspender Co., also bene-fitted from World War I, receiving additional contracts from the federal government, including one for 30,000 pairs of braces for Canadian soldiers.

That John Craig Eaton's landlord was Jewish is a delicious irony, given the bitter 1912 factory strike at Eaton's that involved many Jewish garment workers. At the time, Eaton's was the largest single employer of Jews living in The Ward. The strike, crushed by John Craig, allegedly kept Jewish staff off Eaton's retail floors for decades. The protest also prompted Toronto's Jews to form small garment-related industries, many of whom sold their goods to Eaton's. Greisman – already well-established in the menswear accessories business – possibly had Eaton's as a client for his suspenders, braces, and neckwear.

John Craig Eaton died from influenza in 1922, at just forty-six. His successor, cousin Robert Young Eaton, had different plans for the Eaton's factory on Chestnut Street. With reduced demand for canvas goods after the war, coupled with excess capacity in the company's

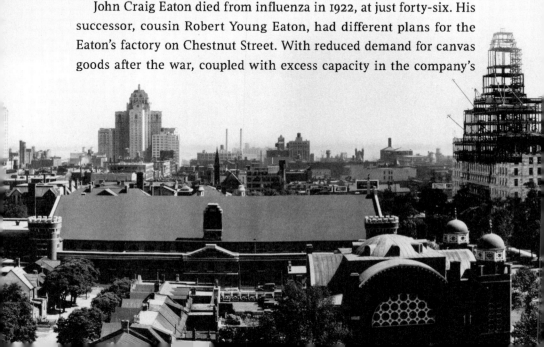

manufacturing system, Eaton's terminated its lease with Greisman in September 1924. The department store continued to carry canvas tents and awnings, but their manufacturing location is unknown.

After his ventures on Chestnut Street, Greisman did not pursue further property development inside The Ward, though he continued to build and lease out industrial space in downtown Toronto. Besides his King Suspender headquarters at 240 Richmond Street West (1916), Greisman's loft projects from 1919 to 1926 included 116 and 129 Spadina Avenue and 30–34 Duncan Street. All are currently standing, unlike John Craig's Toronto buildings, which were swept away in the 1970s to make way for the Eaton Centre. Greisman died in 1938, leaving an estate worth over $2 million in today's dollars – modest compared to John Craig's fortune, but accompanied by a sterling reputation in the city's Jewish community.

As for 86–90 Chestnut, the building continued to serve as a factory and warehouse for numerous small-scale enterprises after Eaton's departure. It was demolished in 1969–70 to make way for a parking lot.

But the factory at 86–90 Chestnut was not entirely gone. During the 2015 archaeological assessment for the new Toronto courthouse, two below-grade walls were exposed, and trenching revealed part of the building's basement, including the boiler room. 'The building has little archaeological value and its basement was sufficiently deep to negate the potential for recovery of deposits relating to the previous 19th century occupations of the lot,' concluded the archaeologist's report. No objects from Henry Greisman's factory building – or John Craig Eaton's tent and awning operation – were recovered.

# CAP AND TRADE

ELLEN SCHEINBERG

D URING THE EARLY twentieth century, hats were worn by both men and
women on a daily basis. They came in a wide array of fabrics and
styles and were a sign of respectability and sophistication. The popular
choices for businessmen during the 1940s and 1950s included the fedora,
homburg, and bowler hats. Wool caps, such as the Ivy or newsboy, offered
a more casual and comfortable alternative. Men of all classes typically had
several hats in their wardrobe, to suit different occasions. The popularity
of this accessory led to a flourishing hat-manufacturing trade in Toronto.

Two of the artifacts unearthed during the archaeological excavation
were hat moulds used by the Fashion Hat and Cap Company. The firm
operated out of the factory warehouse at 86–90 Chestnut Street from the
early 1940s until 1970. The rubber moulds, each approximately thirty to
thirty-five centimetres wide, were likely used to manufacture men's felt
brimmed hats. The manufacturing process in the factory started off with
the tailors sewing the hats and caps according to a pattern. The item was
then rounded out, using a metal tool that resembled a pestle. The next
step was to place the hat on the mould and steam the item into the
desired shape. And finally, the company label was either sewn or stamped
inside the hat to identify each item as a Fashion Hat and Cap product.

The firm started off as the Fashion Cap Company. Located at 126
Elizabeth Street, just south of Dundas, it was established by Harry Zweig
and his son Morris during the late 1920s. The Zweig family were Polish
Jews who came to Toronto just before the First World War. Harry was a
skilled tailor who had worked for other cap companies before setting up
his own factory.

The company moved to 130 Dundas Street West around 1930. As the business grew, the Zweigs realized that while they were both adept at handling the manufacturing side of the enterprise, they also required someone who could tackle sales. In 1935, they brought in a third partner, Ben Banks, to fulfill this role. Banks was an Eastern European Jew who had tremendous talent and tenacity as a salesman, according to his descendants.

By the early 1940s, the company changed its name to Fashion Hat and Cap, and the owners purchased the four-storey building at 86–90 Chestnut Street, with the land title registered in the names of their wives – Doris Zweig, Elizabeth Zweig, and Agnes Banks. The first floor was used as office space while the upper floors housed the manufacturing divisions. Initially, they rented out the basement and upper floors to other companies, including Sheridan Hosiery, after which the building was named. But by the late 1950s, they had grown significantly and took over the entire building.

The owners' children and grandchildren recall visiting the factory as children, viewing rows of operators behind sewing machines, as well as hat moulds on the second and third floors of the building. Morris's daughter, Monica Zweig Zigerstein, vividly remembered taking the old elevator up to the second floor and helping out a little before heading out to the nearby cinema for a matinee.

At its pinnacle, during the 1950s and 1960s, the company employed forty to fifty people. Despite his status as the founder of the firm, Harry

Rubber Hat Mould. One of two rubber moulds used by the Fashion Hat and Cap Company in their factory warehouse at 86–90 Chestnut Street. Recovered from demolition debris.

felt most at home behind a sewing machine (he continued working until his death in 1972, at age ninety-four). He had ceded control of the business to Morris and Ben. Ben's grandson, Stephen Banks, described them as 'the inside and outside men': Morris minded the manufacturing side of the business, and Ben was responsible for promotion and sales.

While the early products manufactured by the company included fur, felt, and wool caps and hats for men and youth, their offerings expanded dramatically during the postwar years. They worked with Sheridan Hosiery to produce knit headwear, such as toques and balaclavas. And during the 1950s, they rolled out Davy Crockett coonskin caps, all the rage among young boys eager to emulate their TV hero. In many respects, it was the Fidget Spinner of its day, topping the *New York Times*'s must-have toys of that decade. Ben's involvement in the scouting movement also enabled him to secure the rights to produce hats and caps for Scouts Canada. And he capitalized on his sports contacts to acquire the licensing rights for an Arnold Palmer golf line, as well as Maple Leaf baseball caps.

Fashion Hat and Cap's products were sold in cities across Canada in many of the major department stores, including Eaton's, Simpson's, and Sears, along with men's clothing chains like Jack Fraser. To reach smaller markets, Ben traversed the province – to destinations as far north as Kapuskasing and Cobalt River – by train, pitching FHC's products to prospective clients. The company also relied on ads in newspapers to promote their hats. By the 1950s, Fashion Hat and Cap had opened a handful of factories in other parts of Canada, including Hamilton and Winnipeg.

In the mid-1960s, the City of Toronto began pressuring the three partners to sell their factory property on Chestnut. While Stephen Banks says the firm had around 3,300 active accounts at this time, the partners nonetheless capitulated to the city. They sold their felt-hat division to Biltmore Hats in Guelph, and some of their other lines to the Stetson Hat Company. The building was torn down around 1970 and replaced with a parking lot. (The Chinese United Church, located next door at 92–96 Chestnut Street, remained standing until the late 1980s.) The three partners, however, continued to work in the hat industry, toiling for other manufacturers for the remainder of their lives.

ELLEN SCHEINBERG

# THE MULTIPLE LIVES OF ORDINARY BUILDINGS
JOHN LORINC

I F YOU LIVED in Toronto between the 1940s and the late 1970s, and found yourself scanning the classified ads for cheap furniture, it's possible you might have ended up paying a visit to 29 Centre Avenue, just north of Armoury, home to the Pearl Furniture Company. The bargain basement retailer didn't advertise per se, but over many years, its address appeared in hundreds of two- or three-line notices in the city's newspapers, suggesting the owners may have sold furniture taken on consignment.

Compared to the giant Eaton's and Simpson's department stores located just a few blocks south, Pearl's wasn't much to look at: a squat, two-storey brick building with a pair of display windows on either side of the main entrance and a flat roof.

At the time, Centre wouldn't have been a shopping destination. In the 1940s, that block was home to a hodgepodge of commercial/industrial businesses, including firms that made handbags, sanitary wipes,

Pearl Furniture c. 1970, formerly Standard Foundry and then Shaarei Tzedec.

and bottled beverages. Property maps and aerial photos taken during the 1950s and 1960s – a period when municipal officials had began expropriating all the land that later became Nathan Phillips Square/City Hall – show the block was increasingly given over to parking lots. By the early 1970s, the only buildings still standing were Pearl's and the church immediately behind it (initially the British Methodist Episcopal and then, after the mid-1950s, the Chinese United Church).

The abundance of parking would certainly have been convenient for Pearl's customers, who likely had to bring some kind of vehicle to haul away their purchases, or, if Pearl's was a consignment store, bring in furnishings. There's no way to determine who Pearl's customers were. But furniture stores typically locate near their markets. When Pearl's opened, in the early 1940s, the surrounding downtown neigh-bourhoods, both to the north and also west of University Avenue, were home to predominantly immigrant and working-class residents – in other words, people who would be interested in purchasing inexpensive and possibly used furniture rather than the more high-end products sold by department stores.

Because much of the building had been rendered visible by the gradual demolition of its immediate neighbours, customers approach-ing Pearl's along Centre may have noticed a few subtle architectural details about its construction: that the brick on the facade was newer and cleaner than the bricks used for most of the rest of the structure, and that the eight arched sash windows on the ground-floor sidewalls didn't match the square-topped second floor and facade ones.

It's certainly possible a few customers, especially in Pearl's first years of operation, would have remembered this place *before* it became a furniture store, and a time when it played a very different role in this corner of The Ward.


SOME BUILDINGS CAN only ever perform the task they've been designed to carry out. Office towers and cathedrals aren't meant to yield to new uses. But many others will have multiple lives over a prolonged period, their evolving roles determined by shifts in ownership, their urban sur-roundings, and the imaginations of architects, tenants, or contractors.

In current heritage parlance, we talk about 'adaptive reuse,' but the practice itself is long-standing, and certainly predates the label: residential homes on main streets that acquire additions suitable for retail space, abandoned factories that fill up with clandestine artists lofts and eventually turn into trendy warehouse-based offices, or deconsecrated churches sold to developers who convert them into post-liturgical condos.

Toronto figured out how to save and repurpose dozens of brick-and-beam warehouses, thanks to land-use planning reforms introduced in the mid-1990s. But there are other recent imaginative examples, including the reuse of the old Don Jail as the administrative offices for Bridgepoint Health and Maple Leaf Gardens, which Ryerson University transformed into a multi-use space – retail, institutional, recreational facilities – that also contains a smaller hockey arena. Even the city's first municipal abattoir, infamous for its stench and the shrieks of animals headed for slaughter, is being converted into a residential development.

In the post–World War II era, much of The Ward was bulldozed, thus closing off any possibility of adaptive reuse of the built form. But the area's earlier history showed ample evidence of this kind of recycling: a Black Baptist church at Bay and Dundas transformed into a Yiddish-language theatre; numerous residential dwellings that became cafés and restaurants and, in one location on Centre Avenue, a shvitz bath; and a notorious welfare shelter (the former House of Labour at Elizabeth and Elm) that became a seniors home (Laughlen Lodge).

So it was with Pearl's.

According to insurance maps and property records, the land where Pearl's stood was once occupied by wood frame cottages likely built in the mid-to-late decades of the nineteenth century. The municipal address in that period was 49 and 51 Centre, although it later changed to 29 Centre. Directories show that the occupants included a shipbuilder, druggist, labourer, plasterer, and even a farmer.

Around 1890, those lots were purchased and combined by the Standard Foundry Company, which erected a two-storey brick factory there. Foundries tended to be long, low-slung structures designed for manufacturing metal goods or large pieces of industrial equipment. Fitted out with furnaces for forging iron and steel, foundries would have fallen into the category of heavy industry – places that emitted plenty of noise and smoke, and employed labourers such as moulders.

Occasionally, these buildings experienced violent explosions, as happened at the Gurney Foundry in West Toronto in June 1915. But it's also worth noting that some of nineteenth-century Toronto's most majestic factories and foundries survived all the way into our era, repurposed as condos, offices, and theatrical spaces.

As of 1890, the Standard's neighours to the south were residential houses; at least one Centre Avenue resident worked at Standard. Immediately to its north sat the Trinity Sunday School, a mission meant to serve poor immigrant children in the area. (By the turn of the century, this two-hundred-seat chapel became a 'Jewish mission' dedicated to converting 'distressed Jews of Russia,' as the *Globe* noted in 1905.)

Around 1909, a seven-year-old congregation of Russian Jews purchased the foundry and began the process of converting it into a synagogue. (The Standard Foundry Company relocated to a larger, and better situated, factory at Jarvis and the Esplanade.) In 1912, a local architect, Isadore Feldman, drew up elaborate plans for the new Shaarei Tzedec. Feldman worked for Hynes, Feldman & Watson, an architectural firm that designed, among many other projects, Allen's Danforth theatre (1919), now known as the Danforth Music Hall. Feldman's blueprints, which are in the City of Toronto Archive, show the facade with a roofline evoking the tablets given to Moses. The details include leaded glass windows, a Star of David, and an oak door. It was to become one of several synagogues in the immediate vicinity.

There's no record of what would have been required to transform this foundry into a place of worship, or who did the work. But one can imagine a messy, labour-intensive process that would have required an almost complete gutting, with the heavy equipment and contaminated industrial residues hauled away before any kind of architectural refurbishment could begin. As happens, the finished building didn't turn out exactly as the architect had imagined on his plans.

While the Shaarei Tzedec congregation was in the midst of making this significant investment in a new synagogue, city officials were mulling over a sweeping urban redevelopment plan proposed by the

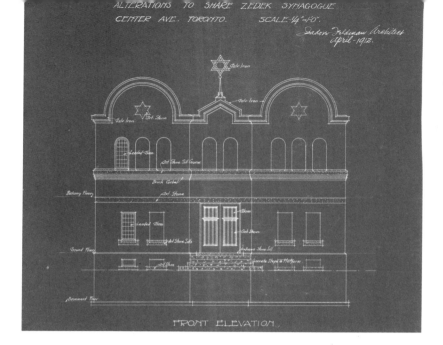

Blueprint, Shaarei Tzedec Synagogue, April 1912. Architect Isadore Feldman.

1911 Civic Improvement Committee[1] that would have eliminated this entire portion of Centre Avenue, transforming the block into a parade ground adjacent to a proposed garden and new civic buildings. (That plan didn't come to fruition but led to a series of reimaginings of The Ward, which eventually produced Nathan Phillips Square.)

The synagogue, as Simon Rogers discusses in 'The Synangogue on Centre Avenue' (pages 173–177), operated at 29 Centre Avenue for almost two decades, until 1937, at which point the congregation decamped to 397 Markham Street. As with the foundry, that move also involved repurposing an existing building, but the conversion was likely more straightforward: its new shul had previously functioned as a semi-detached Victorian home.

Pearl Furniture opened in that same building about three years later, its facade once again reworked to include large display windows, and with the various religious detailing – Stars of David, and the twin tablet-shaped arches on the roofline – removed. The store occupied 29 Centre Avenue longer than either of its predecessors (almost forty years), and was demolished sometime in the late 1970s.

# THE COMMERCIAL TENANTS OF CHESTNUT STREET'S FACTORIES

IN THE LATE-1910S, several small cottages south of the British Methodist Episcopal Church were demolished to make way for two brick-and-beam factory structures. One would house Eaton's Tent and Awning Factory and, later in the 1920s, a radio manufacturer that became part of Edward Rogers's broadcast empire.

| | 80–84 CHESTNUT | 86–90 CHESTNUT |
|---|---|---|
| 1917 | Canadian Ice Machine Co.; Lempert and Leranbaum (tailor); Coulter J. Co. (jewellery cases); Louis Frelfeld (furrier); Cleveland Pneumatic Tool Co. | T. Eaton Co. |
| 1921 | United Electric Co.; Lempert and Peranson (tailor); J. Coulter Co. (jewellery cases); Louis Frelfeld (furrier); Cleveland Pneumatic Tool Co. | T. Eaton Co. |
| 1925 | Peranson & Wilder (clothier); Confectioners Trading Co.; J. Coulter Co. (jewellery cases); Eastern Fur Co.; Cleveland Pneumatic Tool Co. | Canadian Radio Corp. (radio manufacturer); Canadian Independent Telephone Co.; Canadian Machine Telephone Co. |
| 1930 | Peranson & Wilder (contractor); Confectioners Trading Co. (confectioners' supplies); All Weld Co. Ltd. (machinist); Cleveland Pneumatic Tool Co. of Canada Ltd.; Fit Right Pant Co. | Vacant |

| | 80–84 CHESTNUT | 86–90 CHESTNUT |
|---|---|---|
| 1940 | Durable Shoe Co.; Confectioners Trading Co.; All Weld Co. Ltd. (machinist); Jobbers Supply Co. (auto accessories); J. D. Carrier Shoe Co. (shoe manufacturer); Leader Printing Co.; Toronto Printing Co.; Michael Burkhardt (jewellery manufacturer); William Pugh Co. (jewellery manufacturer); Albert E. Smith (jewellery engraver); Essential Supplies Co. (notions); Service Hat Lining Co.; Cleveland Pneumatic Tool Co. of Canada Ltd.; Imperial Pant Co. | P. F. Ross Co. (steel can manufacturer); Good-Wear Shoe Co.; Superior Upholstering Co.; Baker & Sporn Shoe Co. Ltd.; G. P. Hurlbut Shoe Co. |
| 1950 | Canadian Silversmiths Ltd.; York Plastic Industries (plastic fabrication) | Fashion Hat & Cap Co.; Sheridan Hosiery Ltd.; Colour Mark (Canada) Co. (paint finisher) |
| 1960 | Canadian Silversmiths Ltd.; Vac Products | Fashion Hat & Cap Co. |
| 1965 | Jack Kirshner & Co. (commercial photographer); Jackir Studios Ltd. (commercial photographer); Canadian Silversmiths Ltd.; Victor Vermeiren Interiors Ltd.; S & S. Vending Machine Co. | Fashion Hat & Cap Co. Ltd. |
| 1970 | Parking Lot | Fashion Hat & Cap Co. Ltd. |
| 1971 | Parking Lot | Parking Lot |

Examples of glass and ceramic tableware.
Left: Glass cruet for liquids like oil and
vinegar. Right: Blue Willow transfer-printed
serving dish.

# SOCIAL LIFE

# THE HISTORY OF A BLACK CANADIAN CHURCH

ROSEMARY SADLIER

ON APRIL 20, 1895, the *Globe* ran a series of impressive photographs of the new British Methodist Episcopal (BME) Church (right). 'The building is a handsome red brick structure, situated at 94 Chestnut Street, finished inside with oak and capable of seating a congregation of 600,' the accompanying article explained, noting that construction on the $8,000 building had begun the previous September. Half the funds came from the sale of the Colored Wesleyan Church on Richmond Street.

The unveiling of this grand building, which rose above the surrounding working-class neighbourhood, occurred almost fifty years after a small group of Black residents established a modest wood-frame Methodist chapel on the property. Among the founders was Ellen Toyer Abbott, the wife of Wilson Ruffin Abbott, a highly successful Black merchant and property owner who had come to Toronto from Alabama in 1835.

The congregation grew as Toronto's Black population increased in the years preceding the American Civil War, and the Chestnut Street church was rebuilt in 1871. But over the next two decades, the broader BME, which included churches across southern Ontario as well as Atlantic Canada and the Caribbean, nearly collapsed during a lengthy conflict with the American denomination from which it had originated many years earlier and due to the high costs of overseas missionary work. In the late 1880s, however, BME elders began a rebuilding process in Canada, culminating with the new Chestnut Street church and the continuance of the BME in the lives of Black Canadians.

The British Methodist Episcopal Church of Canada is one of the oldest continuously operating African Canadian religious institution founded and maintained by Black people. It was established in Chatham, Ontario, in September 29, 1856, by formerly enslaved Africans and some free Black people, with the first Toronto congregation situated on Sayer Street (later Chestnut).

Thanks to the British parliament's decision to ban slavery throughout the empire as of August 1, 1834, the inclusion of 'British' in the denomination's name was, for the time, a symbol of freedom to the thousands of enslaved Africans making their way to Upper Canada, where their right to be free was protected under the law. In fact, the BME church in Chatham was named Victoria Chapel after Queen Victoria, who reigned over the British Empire at that time.

Interior, newly expanded British Methodist Episcopal Church, 1895.

British Methodism began in 1729 as an offshoot of the Church of England. It supported systematic study, personal responsibility for spiritual development, and a zeal for creating missions, including in North America. With support for abolition growing in eighteenth-century Britain, Methodist founder John Wesley spoke out against slavery as 'an execrable villainy.' For Black people, Methodist Episcopalianism was seen as a means to regain both freedom and human dignity.

In 1787, Richard Allen, a Methodist preacher born to enslaved parents, established a church in Philadelphia. Dubbed the Bethel African Methodist Episcopal in 1816, it became the first Black congregation in the U.S.

Upper Canada soon became a rich mission field for the AME. By 1831, AME ministers were organizing missions in every Black settlement in what's now southern Ontario. In 1838, the AME leadership had created a Canada Conference, a group of churches with a common administration.

With the passage of the second Fugitive Slave Act in the U.S. in 1850 and the significant rise in the numbers of Blacks fleeing to Canada, AME leaders had to consider how to protect their their congregants and clergy from bounty hunters coming to Canada searching for fugitives. They also wanted to ensure that their clergy attending conferences in the United States would be able to return to Canada without risk of enslavement.

During the AME's Canadian Annual Conference in Cincinnati, in May 1856, the leadership sought permission to split from the U.S. parent. A few months later, ministers and delegates met in Chatham and formally established the BME, which effectively replaced all AME churches in Canada and assumed ownership of their properties, including the one on Chestnut Street. Rev. Willis Nazrey, an AME bishop living in Canada, was elected unanimously to lead the new church.

Born in the U.S. in 1808, Reverend Nazrey was ordained as an AME bishop on May 13, 1852, in New York City. He migrated with his wife and family to Chatham to further serve the AME Church and emerged as the obvious choice to lead the new BME. Under his leadership, the BME strengthened the churches already in Toronto, Chatham, St. Catharines, Owen Sound, Windsor, Sandwich, Brantford, Hamilton, and Queen's Bush, among others, as well as establishing new ones in Nova Scotia, Bermuda, and British Guiana.

By the time of Nazrey's death in 1875, the BME had built an extensive administrative foundation to support missions in the Caribbean and South America. Yet because of the BME's independence from the well-financed AME, the BME's leaders realized they required more from the broader local community to help support this mission work.

To ensure the training of new ministers and older ones who had not had that opportunity, the BME also established a 'Literary Association' for continuing education and as a place to house those who had retired. To keep congregants informed about the issues of the day, the BME began publishing the *Missionary Messenger* – the official voice of the church. The BME helped to fund itself through the sales of this newsletter.

ROSEMARY SADLIER

Sherd of coloured and textured glass
from a window in the British Methodist
Episcopal/Chinese United Church.

The BME's second bishop was Rev. Richard Randolph Disney, who travelled to Britain to raise funds for the church soon after his appointment. Disney also organized a talented singing group called the Jubilee Singers, who became very popular in Ontario. They travelled with Disney to England, Scotland, and Ireland to help him raise funds for other church projects.

Reverend Disney wasn't the only BME official who journeyed to Britain. Josiah Henson, also known as the figure who inspired Harriet Beecher Stowe's 'Uncle Tom,' was an ordained BME minister who made two trips to Britain to raise funds for the Dawn Settlement, a self-help project of his for Black people in the Dresden, Ontario, area.

In the late 1870s, with the gradual decline in Canadian congregations following the end of the U.S. Civil War, BME and AME leaders began discussing ways to co-operate with the funding of missionary work in the West Indies and South America. Initially, these 'reunion' talks went well, but it soon became evident to the Canadian ministers that the AME felt the BME in Canada should become just another district, not an equal partner. On September 5, 1880, at the BME's Toronto General Conference, the Canadian delegates rejected the plan.

Despite that decision, Reverend Disney a few years later accepted an appointment to become an AME bishop and proclaimed the union of the two branches. The BME was stripped of its seal and many younger BME ministers in Canada left for the AME Church in the U.S. with Disney. The 1884 crisis left the BME wounded but not dead. In fact, the Chestnut Street church maintained its BME designation following the merger.

Not long after, Rev. Walter Hawkins, a Massachusetts-born minister who had served under both Nazrey and Disney at the BME on Chestnut Street, came out of retirement to rebuild the Canadian Church. The BME had been reduced to twenty-five churches in eight districts in Ontario, as well as Nova Scotia, New Brunswick, the Bermudas, and British Guiana. But in 1891, an energetic network of BME Church women raised $10,000 for mission work while the Chestnut Street BME was designated the 'banner church.'

Over the next six decades, the BME Church continued to evolve and grow. In 1898, for example, the first woman delegate was admitted to a

ROSEMARY SADLIER

BME General Conference. Soon, the BME Church recognized women as missionaries or evangelists in their own right.

To mark the BME's seventieth anniversary, in 1926, Church leaders produced a commemorative tablet, which was installed at Queen's Park. (It can still be found on the second floor, close to the main entrance of the Legislative Assembly.)

Black community organizations increasingly looked to the BME for support. For example, Donald Moore and Harry Gairey, both members of the Negro Citizenship Committee, joined with BME leaders to protest the use of force against striking labourers in the British West Indies.

In 1949, Rev. Thomas H. Jackson was appointed as the general superintendent of the BME Church. Since 1902, Jackson had served as a local preacher, a travelling licentiate, a deacon, and an elder. His work with the Chestnut Street BME had begun in 1944, so he was familiar with the issues facing this church, such as the ordination of women. It was on his initiative that, in 1951, the first woman, Rev. Addie Aylestock, was received into the BME Connection as a deacon and the elder. She was the first Black woman minister in Canada.

With the congregation dwindling, Jackson began working diligently with another church, the Afro Community Church, at 460 Shaw Street, which was also struggling with declining membership and consequent financial pressures. After lengthy negotiations and property sales, the BME Church on Chestnut amalgamated with the Afro Community Church and moved to Shaw; the combined congregations opted to use the BME name. (The United Church of Canada bought the Chestnut Street property in 1953.) Sadly, Reverend Jackson died three years before the union was completed.

The history of the BME Church continues to this day, at a church at the corner of Dufferin and Eglinton. This latest chapter continues to help frame the BME as a local, regional, national, and international body – ongoing, proud, resilient, and dedicated.

# FREEDOM ABOUNDS

NATASHA HENRY

A UGUST 1, 1852
At sunrise, a large crowd gathered for an early church service at the Sayer Street Chapel (later the British Methodist Episcopal Church). Church services were an integral part of Emancipation Day observances – marking the day, eighteen years earlier, when slavery was legally abolished in what we now call Canada. The annual commemoration began with the congregation giving God thanks for delivering them, their relatives, and their ancestors from bondage. As the *Globe* reported, celebrants then gathered at Richmond and York Streets at 11:00 a.m. to march through the streets, led by the City Brass Band. They made their way to Holy Trinity Anglican Church (now surrounded by the Toronto Eaton Centre), where Rev. Henry Grasett delivered a sermon. The procession carried on to City Hall, then to St. Lawrence Market, where the parade's grand marshal, Black resident William Harris, delivered a welcome.

The crowd partook in an elaborate lunch at a location east of Yonge Street, hosted by freedom-seeker and master saw maker Thomas Smallwood. Black abolitionist Samuel Ringgold Ward, Presbyterian minister Robert Easton Burns, and Congregationalist minister Adam Lillie all spoke. The paraders regrouped in front of St. Lawrence Hall and marched back to Richmond and York. After cheers for Queen Victoria, the City of Toronto, the day's speakers, and the City Brass Band, the crowd dispersed. In the evening, however, there was a soiree at St. Lawrence Hall organized by local Black women. The well-attended program consisted of music, singing, toasts, and speakers.[1]

THE 1793 ACT to Limit Slavery, passed in Upper Canada, did not abolish the slave trade in Canada, as some mistakenly believe. Although slavery was gradually being phased out, it still existed in Canada when Britain passed the Slavery Abolition Act, affecting most of its colonies, on August 26, 1833. This act became law on August 1, 1834, a day of celebration for those who were freed immediately. Those forced into apprenticeships after that date would have to wait until August 1, 1838, to be completely freed.

Emancipation Day was commemorated in Canada from the day the Slavery Abolition Act took effect.[2] Marking the end of enslavement had significance in early Toronto, where Blacks were enslaved at the turn of the eighteenth century. Town of York censuses from between 1797 and 1808 counted thirteen enslaved Black men, women, and children owned by provincial administrator Peter Russell, provincial secretary and registrar William Jarvis, and Solicitor General Robert Gray.[3]

By the early 1800s, there were more freed and free Blacks in Toronto. Some had been held in bondage in Ontario and received their freedom as the province phased out slavery. Black Loyalists were escaped slaves who had won their freedom by fighting in defence of Britain during the American Revolution, and were then evacuated to the northern British colonies (i.e., Upper Canada). Finally, a trickle of African American freedom-seekers had fled to Canada after the 1793 Act to Limit Slavery stated that Blacks entering Ontario would be considered free.[4] Consequently, the Slavery Abolition Act, forty years later, freed enslaved Blacks while simultaneously making Canada a free land for African Americans who remained enslaved. Thus the ideal of Canada as a safe haven for African American freedom-seekers was born. Thousands of freedom-seekers and free Blacks arrived between 1834 and the 1850s and celebrated their newfound liberty.

In the mid-nineteenth century, Toronto had become a centre of abolition activity in the fight to end American slavery. Mary Ann Shadd Cary published the *Provincial Freeman*, a weekly newspaper headquartered and printed for a short time on King Street just west of Jarvis, to dispel stereotypes of Blacks, promote anti-slavery ideals, denounce American slavery, and discuss the problems facing freedom-seekers in the province. The *Toronto Globe*, a mainstream newspaper edited by George Brown, supported anti-slavery and the Black community, and helped found the Anti-Slavery Society of Canada. Many anti-slavery meetings were held at St. Lawrence Hall, including speaking engagements with guests such as renowned African American abolitionist Frederick Douglass. During the 1851 North American Convention of Coloured People, delegates passed a resolution declaring Canada West 'by far the most desirable place of resort for coloured people, to be found on the American continent.'[5]

This background informed the social climate around Emancipation Day celebrations. Blacks were dealing with the after-effects of 206 years of racial slavery in Canada and ushering in an uncharted era of liberty. Celebrations in Toronto began in the 1830s and continued to grow over the next two decades as an annual event. A diverse Black population commemorated Emancipation Day: former locally enslaved Blacks and their descendants; Black Loyalists and their descendants; free Blacks, freedom-seekers, Canadian-born Blacks, and West Indian immigrants. Some white community members also joined in. Men and women of different racial, social, and economic backgrounds came out in the hundreds from around the province and the United States. Emancipation Day became a public arena where the evolving social interactions between races, genders, and religious denominations played out.

According to various accounts, commemorations through the years shared a number of key traditions: church services, invited speakers, parades, feasts, and other social and leisure activities, such as dinners, balls, musical concerts, baseball games, carnivals, and picnics. Celebrants worshipped, sang, and broke bread together. Several Toronto churches hosted Emancipation Day festivities, including the Chestnut Street BME. Both mainstream and Black newspapers published detailed accounts that captured the spirited atmosphere of these events.

## AUGUST 1, 1854

The twentieth anniversary of the passage of the Slavery Abolition Act was a grand affair in Toronto's Black community, approximately half of whom – or about five hundred – lived in St. John's Ward. Committee members, both male and female, from Black churches in and around The Ward (the Sayer Street Chapel, the First Baptist Church, and the Second Wesleyan Chapel), made elaborate plans. The Sayer Street group began with a prayer service at 5:00 a.m. Several hours later, celebrants gathered at the Government Grounds on Front Street, between John and Simcoe. A parade marshalled by William Thompson and Charles Peyton Lucas, and led by Scott's Brass Band, marched to Brown's Wharf, at the foot of Yonge Street, to welcome celebrants arriving from Hamilton on the steamer *Arabian*.

Thomas Smallwood Sr., a freedom-seeker and one of the organizers, addressed the visitors:

> **A Grand Display of Fire Works!**
> THOMAS SMALLWOOD,
>                    *President of the Day.*
> CHARLES FREEMAN,
>                    *Secretary.*
> Toronto, July-29, 1854.              19

Fellow subjects of this noble province, and citizens of Hamilton, It is my pleasing duty, in behalf of a portion of my fellow citizens of Toronto, to welcome you, who have honoured us this day with your presence, to partake of a festival in commemoration of one among the greatest events in British history, when that magnanimous nation swept the bonds from 800,000 bondsmen, and made them free...[6]

The parade continued on to St. James Cathedral, where Reverend Grasett, a regular Emancipation Day speaker, delivered a sermon. Afterwards, celebrants marched back to the Government Grounds for a lavish lunch, followed by speeches and entertainment. Smallwood, the event's president, invited George Dupont Wells, a local white lawyer, to read a speech written by the organizing committee and dedicated to Queen Victoria, expressing gratitude – on behalf of Toronto's Black community – to Britain for abolishing slavery:

May It Please Your Majesty:
    We, the Coloured Inhabitants of Canada, most respectfully, most gratefully and most loyally approach you Gracious Majesty, on this, the

anniversary of our death to Slavery, and our birth to Freedom. With what feelings, or what words can we adequately express our gratitude to England for such a boon?...

What a happy, what a proud reflection it must be to your Majesty, to know that the moment the poor crushed slave sets foot upon any part of your mighty dominions, his chains fall from him – he feels himself a man, and can look up...[7]

To close the lunch program, the group made several cheers, resolutions, and toasts to the Queen, colonial officials, and 'our wives and sweethearts.' In fact, such toasts and resolutions were a common feature of Emancipation Day celebrations. They often expressed the Black community's loyalty to, and appreciation of, the British Crown. But these declarations also highlighted the various forms of racism that Black Canadians were still working collectively to address.

Finally, on that day, celebrants regrouped to march together to see a new Black lodge and then returned to the Government Grounds for a soiree. The activity-filled day was capped with a spectacular display of fireworks accompanied by a band, with tea served.

Also in the 1850s, Dr. Anderson Ruffin Abbott became the first Canadian-born Black doctor after graduating from the Toronto School of Medicine. His parents, Wilson Ruffin Abbott and Ellen Toyer Abbott, were free Blacks of means, and active in providing assistance to freedom-seekers and participating in local Black church organizations. For Anderson Abbott, one of the most memorable sights that day was a tall Black man marching with the 92nd West India Regiment – 'a drummer,' as he later recalled, 'known as Black Charlie.'[8]

AUGUST 1, 1858

The *Globe* reported that the 1858 Emancipation Day celebrations began with an early-morning service at the BME Church, conducted by Bishop Walter Hawkins. The parade, led by a band, started just after 10:00 a.m. Waving flags and carrying banners, the marchers went to St. James Cathedral to attend a full service by Reverend Grasett and the Reverend Canon Edmund Baldwin, St. James's assistant minister.

Baldwin preached a stirring sermon, expressing hope that slavery in the U.S. would soon end.

When the service concluded, the celebrants marched through the main streets to the university grounds for a splendid lunch. Following the meal, Rev. William M. Mitchell, a Black abolitionist minister at the Coloured Regular Baptist Church at Terauley (Bay Street) and Edward, addressed those assembled. To bursts of applause, he spoke about the great boon of 1834 that saw 800,000 enslaved Blacks freed from bondage. He also condemned the U.S. for not ending the heinous institution.

The *Globe* described the rest of the day: '[A]bout five o'clock the procession again got into marching order, and proceeded along Queen and down Church streets to the wharf where they all went on board the *Fire Fly*, Captain [Robert] Moodie having invited the party to a free excursion to the Island. Nearly sixty persons partook of tea on the Island, and spent a few hours in a very happy manner.'[9]

During the evening, there was a party in St. Lawrence Hall, with tea, a lineup of speakers, and live music. The funds raised through ticket sales were directed toward the construction of a new church. Some attendees then went to Louis Kurth's Tavern and Concert Hall, on Adelaide Street, across from the York County Court House, for dinner, cocktails, song, and lively conversation.[10]

OVER ALMOST TWO centuries, Emancipation Day celebrations have continued to evolve, but they remain a cultural fixture in Toronto's Black community. There is a contemporary connection to Emancipation Day celebrations in the Caribana Festival introduced to the city by West Indian immigrants in 1967. They drew on familiar traditions from their countries of origin, but also continued the long history of Black Canadians who celebrated freedom in the streets of the city they all called home.

Emancipation Day paraders in Toronto, July 29, 1961, led by the Toronto Negro Band. The procession is arriving at Victoria Memorial Park at Niagara and Portland.

# RESISTING STEREOTYPES: AFRICAN TORONTONIANS PROTEST MINSTRELSY

KAROLYN SMARDZ FROST

*'[Blackface performers are] the filthy scum of white society, who have stolen from us a complexion denied them by nature, in which to make money, and pander to the corrupt taste of their white fellow citizens.'*

*– Frederick Douglass*

ONE OF THE most fascinating artifacts recovered at the Armoury Street Dig is a porcelain figurine about nine centimetres high. The piece is much worn but depicts a white actor in blackface makeup, playing a banjo. It is also broken, so there is no maker's mark evident, but was probably of German manufacture and intended for North American, British, Australian, and New Zealand markets. The object is evocative of the minstrel shows that were so popular in the English-speaking world starting in the early nineteenth century. Its discovery in the soils of Lot 10, at 35 Centre Street, highlights how pervasive the intensely racist minstrel tradition was in Canadian entertainment.

Minstrel shows were born out of racial prejudice. In the 1820s, European-American actors began putting lampblack or burnt cork on their faces and presenting themselves as 'blackface' performers at circuses and other venues. Thomas Dartmouth ('Daddy') Rice, considered 'the father of American minstrelsy,' is believed to have been inspired by an African American with a disability whom he observed in Louisville, Kentucky, in the early 1830s. The man was sweeping out a stable while singing and dancing with a halting, shuffling step. From this, Rice developed his signature 'Jump Jim Crow' song-and-dance routine.[1]

The invention of blackface minstrelsy initiated two profoundly discriminatory aspects of American popular culture: the minstrel tradition that turned racist perceptions of Black Americans into figures of fun for the amusement of white audiences; and the identification of the term *Jim Crow* with African America. So pervasive was the latter that *Jim Crow* became the common term for racial segregation, culminating in the draconian Jim Crow laws enacted in the last decades of the nineteenth century. These laws, and their attendant customs, demanded a separation of African Americans from European-Americans in nearly every walk of life.[2]

The minstrel tradition combined sentimentality and comedy, ridiculing African Americans and romanticizing plantation slavery. It caricatured both enslaved and free Black people in a series of stock characters that grew more exaggerated over time. Early on, minstrel productions also developed a formulaic structure incorporating song, dance, musical recital, often slapstick comedy, and parodies of well-known theatrical and literary works. Instruments included the bones (a pair of animal bones or wood sticks), banjos, fiddle, and tambourine.

Painted ceramic figurine depicting a minstrel playing a banjo.

By 1843, the Christy Minstrels of Buffalo, New York, had devised a standard three-act format consisting of the prologue; the second act, a hodgepodge of comic routines and skits known as the 'olio'; and the afterword, which usually comprised a one-act musical. This formula influenced minstrel shows for decades. The group's signature song was 'Old Folks at Home,' by Stephen Foster, who also authored such classic works of the era as 'My Old Kentucky Home,' 'Oh! Susanna,' and 'Camptown Races.' The Virginia Minstrels, established soon after in New York's Bowery, were the first such act recorded as caricaturing life on the plantation, turning the cruelty and oppression of agricultural slavery into a comedic medium that undervalued African American suffering and contradicted abolitionist campaigns to raise awareness about the horrors of the slave condition.[3]

Nor was the appeal of the blackface performance limited to the U.S. Soon after the invention of blackface, travelling players brought the minstrel tradition to Canada, Great Britain, and Europe, as well as Australia, New Zealand, and South Africa, where it proved an enduring form of public amusement. Songs written for minstrel performance, both professional and amateur, were widely published, some of them in Toronto.

Not surprisingly, Toronto's respectable, hard-working, and politic-ally aware African Canadian population, largely comprised of African American expatriates, protested such performances. The majority lived in the future St. John's Ward (known as The Ward by the 1890s). As early as 1840, concerned African Torontonians petitioned city council to stop licencing travelling minstrel shows and circuses – including blackface burlesques – to mount shows within the city limits. In a series of impas-sioned appeals to city council, the community representatives complained that the stock characters, and the itinerant groups of actors who played them, were endeavouring 'to make the Coloured man appear ridiculous and contemptible in the eyes of their audience' and 'contaminating the wholesome air of Our City with Yanky [sic] amuse-ment of comic songs known by the name of Jim Crow and Aunt Dinah.'

The first such petition was signed by dozens of the city's Black male residents. It was presented on July 20, 1840, by Wilson Ruffin Abbott, a tobacconist and real estate investor destined to become the wealthiest African Canadian resident of the nineteenth-century city:

> The subscribers of this humble petition represents to his Worship the Mayor and the Corporation, that they have remarked with sorrow that the American Actors who from time to time visit this City, invariably select for performance plays and characters which by turning into ridicule and holding up to contempt the coloured population cause them much heart-burning and lead occasionally to violence ... They therefore respectfully entreat His Worship and all those to whom the right pertains to forbid in future the performance of plays likely to produce a breach of the public peace.

The 1840 petition fell on deaf ears, so there were annual presentations to Toronto city council over the next three years. However, it was only after a letter, dated April 21, 1843, pointed out that the City of Kingston had already ceased to licence these 'demeaning' and 'insulting' performances that Toronto's municipal officials followed suit. Apparently preserving the public peace was a factor, since, as Abbott's fourth petition stated, 'certain acts and songs such as Jim Crow and what they call other Negro characters performed by them has heretofore been productive of many broils and suits between the white and coloured inhabitants of this City.'[4]

Toronto's prohibition against minstrel shows was short-lived. Even venerable literary works, such as Harriet Beecher Stowe's iconic anti-slavery novel *Uncle Tom's Cabin,* first performed as a play in Toronto in 1853, were recreated as burlesque satires in the minstrel tradition.[5] Minstrelsy turned Stowe's paternalistic abolitionism on its head and, in the words of Ryerson University visual studies scholar Dr. Cheryl Thompson, 'served to reaffirm widely held beliefs about the inferiority of Blacks and the docility of slaves on the Southern plantation.'[6]

A final Toronto petition, dated August 15, 1856, and 'praying the Council to prohibit the exhibition of a circus in the city during the current year was presented to Councillor Cameron and read ... passed,' noted on page 568 of the Minutes of City Council for that date.

McCormick Playground Minstrels, January 29, 1920.

In succeeding decades, newspapers advertised minstrel performances at St. Lawrence Hall, the Amphitheatre, the Royal Lyceum Theatre, and other more formal venues, often playing to standing-room-only audiences. Less professional performances were staged in the upper rooms of the city's hotels, taverns, and saloons, at the fairgrounds, racetracks, or in the open air by travelling players. Toronto even produced its own very famous blackface actor, theatre director, and composer, Colin 'Cool' Burgess, who gained an international reputation and whose songs have entered the North American folk repertoire.[7]

Amateur productions employing blackface makeup, minstrel-style clothing, musical performance, and song were popular well into the mid-twentieth century. There were even handbooks published for groups wishing to present their own minstrel shows, as fundraisers by service and professional organizations, school presentations, or variety show entertainments. A photo of the McCormick Playground Minstrels

KAROLYN SMARDZ FROST

(1920, left) survives in the collections of the City of Toronto Archives. The Toronto Reference Library has programs for minstrel shows mounted by the Cantanks of the 1st Canadian Army Tank Brigade, which they performed while stationed in England in 1918, as well as the Toronto Canoe Club Minstrels (1919).

On at least one occasion, a minstrel show was written specifically to denigrate successful and well-regarded members of Toronto's own Black community. In 1909, the Toronto Press Club put on *Uncle Tom's Taxi-Cabin*. Produced in blackface with the enthusiastic support of *Telegram* newspaper publisher John Ross Robertson, ordinarily a strong advocate of the city's African Canadian community, the show poked fun both at *Uncle Tom's Cabin* and Thornton and Lucie Blackburn, a well-known, formerly enslaved Toronto couple whom Robertson had personally interviewed in 1888.[8]

Arriving in the city from Kentucky in 1834, the Blackburns had started the city's first, highly successful, taxi business. With the profits, they supported abolitionism and built a series of homes in St. John's Ward to provide inexpensive housing for incoming refugees from American slavery. Thornton Blackburn had attained a position of sufficient wealth and respect to be listed as a 'Gentleman' in the city's tax records, and the couple were among the largest African Canadian landowners in The Ward at the time of their deaths in the 1890s. Many members of the Toronto community, white and Black, would have remembered the Blackburns. Yet this cruel spoof performed at the Royal Alexandra Theatre on June 18 and 19, 1909, attracted large audiences.[9]

The original owner of the porcelain minstrel figure brought to light on Lot 10 in the Armoury Street Dig will never be identified. But this single artifact reveals the racial stereotyping and discrimination that Toronto's early African American immigrants suffered, even after they had reached their new homes on Centre Street. And today, however much Canada's oft-touted multiculturalism policies seek to legislate away prejudice and inequality, descendants of the freedom-seekers continue their long struggle against the ever-present, insidious fact of racism.[10]

# REMEMBERING UNCLE TOM'S CABIN

CHERYL THOMPSON

HARRIET BEECHER STOWE'S *Uncle Tom's Cabin* (1852) was a best-selling novel, but it also gave rise to a series of best-selling commodities and popular minstrel shows. Its sentimental narratives appealed to white, middle-class women, but its anti-slavery themes appealed to abolitionists who condemned slavery. The book was an instant national bestseller and international hit that was quickly translated into thirty-seven languages.[1]

Stowe's novel tells two stories – one of escape, one of martyrdom. The former is told through the story of a fugitive slave named Eliza Harris, who flees with her young son over ice floes on the Ohio River and then, with the help of northerners, comes to Canada to reunite with her husband, George. The latter focuses on Uncle Tom, who was born a slave on a Kentucky plantation but is eventually sold to a plantation owner in New Orleans. While there, Tom endures the worst violence of his life. And while others, like Eliza, escape, Tom does not run. Eventually, as the novel's martyr, he is whipped to his death by his white master. By personalizing for readers the lived experiences of the enslaved, Stowe's words profoundly influenced public attitudes about slaveholding, especially abolition.

However, as U.S. cultural historian Robin Bernstein observes, most scholars have characterized *Uncle Tom's Cabin* as either a novel, an archival fixture, or a cultural phenomenon, rather than as a combination of all three.[2] Stowe was American, but the novel was amplified by hundreds of derivatives, and its success was in no way confined to the United States. All over Europe, *Uncle Tom's Cabin* was avidly read, translated, and discussed.[3] In Britain, the term *Tom mania* spread through dozens of minstrel troupes and even dedicated minstrel halls.[4]

Drawing on the novel's immense and sustained popularity, travelling blackface minstrel shows known as 'Tom Shows' made their way to Toronto in the 1850s, and continued to appear on stages through the 1920s. While these productions mostly originated in New York State, local actors were also cast in leading roles. In 1857, for example, Colin 'Cool' Burgess (1840-1905) put on blackface to sing at the Royal Lyceum in the chorus of *Uncle Tom's Cabin*, in which Denman Thompson, an American who spent the better part of two decades in Toronto, played Uncle Tom and local thespian Charlotte Nickinson (1832-1910) performed Eliza.[5]

In that period, the downtown theatre houses where these and other shows played were the exclusive domain of Toronto's business and governing elites, all of whom were white, English-speaking, and Protestant.[6] The Royal Lyceum – Toronto's first professional theatre – burned down and was replaced in 1874 by the Grand Opera House, which stood at 11 Adelaide Street West, on the south side just west of Yonge Street. The Princess Theatre – which also burned down, and was rebuilt in 1895, and would burn down and be rebuilt again in 1915 – sat a few blocks away, on the south side of King Street West, halfway between Simcoe and York Streets (not far from the present-day Royal Alex).[7]

At the turn of the twentieth century, audiences still longed for *Uncle Tom*. On December 20, 1898, the *Evening Star* declared, 'The best "Uncle Tom's Cabin" ever presented in Toronto is now giving a week's engagement at the popular theater, the Toronto Opera House.'[8] Three years later, the *Toronto Globe* proclaimed, 'A large audience attended the Princess last night to see the Valentine Company's improved version of "Uncle Tom's Cabin."'[9] There were likely dozens of *Uncle Tom's Cabin* minstrel troupes that performed on stages in Toronto, such as Stetson's Uncle Tom's Cabin Company, one of the largest and longest-lived of the travelling Tom Shows, operating from 1886 to 1931.[10]

The derivative representations of *Uncle Tom's Cabin* were not just onstage; the novel's illustrations were equally as popular. While illustrations were not usually found in antebellum fiction – especially that of a first-time novelist[11] – in the U.S., Stowe's publisher, John P. Jewett of Boston, hired Hammatt Billings, a local illustrator and architect, who drafted six full-page engravings. In Britain, John Cassell published the best-selling version, which included twenty-seven illustrations by George Cruikshank, who was known for illustrating the work of Charles Dickens.

There were important differences in the British and American *Uncle Tom's Cabin* illustrations. When Americans saw Billings's drawing of Eliza, she was a diminutive, nearly white figure shielded by a wisp of shawl as she swaddled her child and stripped barefoot in flight. British readers saw something slightly different. In choosing the same scenes that Billings had singled out from the story, Cruikshank took his lead from the American but also modified Billings's drawings to fit his own interpretation of the story.[12] For example, in Cruikshank's version, Eliza is similarly a nearly white figure shielded by a shawl and carrying her child barefoot in flight, but the viewer's attention is also drawn back to a plantation owner and two enslaved Black men left behind.

The passive, loyal Black male slave as a literary and visual trope begins with Uncle Tom as text, but also as image and theatrical character. Where, as art historian Jo-Ann Morgan notes, 'Stowe used the qualities of loyalty and devotion to a master, which were presumed of slave uncles, to advocate an allegiance,'[13] illustrators reinforced this trope as well. This explains why, even today, Uncle Tom is remembered as both a character and racial stereotype.

Copyright protection did not extend from the printed page to the stage until 1865.[14] As had happened in the theatre, without copyright protection for creators, publishers too were free to amend, abridge, and bowdlerize Stowe's text.[15] The plate depicting Eliza's escape, which was recovered from the Armoury Street Dig, could therefore be read in multiple ways.

Ceramic historian Jill Weitzman Fenichell notes that this scene would have reminded nineteenth-century viewers that slave owners separated family members from one another for commercial reasons, as bounty hunters were sent across state lines to find escaped slaves and return them, as chattel, to their owners.[16] This imagery likely resonated

CHERYL THOMPSON

UNCLE TOM'S CABIN.

ELIZA CROSSES THE OHIO

Mid-nineteenth-century moulded earthenware
plate with a transfer-printed scene from Harriet
Beecher Stowe's novel *Uncle Tom's Cabin*.

more with British abolitionists, who were at a literal distance from the brutalities of slavery.

Given their immense popularity in Britain and France, ceramic objects could not have been made in the U.S. because no American ceramic factory could create the quantities of inexpensive objects to meet the demand generated by the popularity of the novel.[17] Thus, the Armoury Street ceramic plate was likely manufactured in Britain with Cruikshank's engraving of Eliza.

The plate depicts a light-skinned Eliza with long, flowing hair. In the background stands the Southern plantation – a white slave owner and two enslaved Black men, one of whom can be read as Uncle Tom. Visual culture scholar Marcus Wood notes that 'mid-nineteenth-century com-mercial wood-engraving leaves little room for subtle distinctions in the representation of degrees of skin tone,' and characters like Eliza con-sequently appeared in illustrated editions, prints, and ceramics as white.[18] That Eliza is light-skinned also puts her in the tradition of anti-slavery appeals, which used female images with whom northern women would be most likely to empathize.[19]

In the theatrical conventions of minstrelsy, 'fugitive slaves' were also thought to have white ancestry, and it was this ancestry that was seen as 'escaping slavery.'[20] However, University of Toronto theatre professor Stephen Johnson opines that while 'no minstrel character could ever "pass" for white,' and 'no minstrel character could ever enter a "middle class" culture...in performance...the minstrel tradition invaded and undermined the abolitionist intent' because the only slaves depicted as escaping into freedom were played as 'white.'[21]

Ultimately, by recognizing blackface minstrelsy conventions such as the wearing of burnt-cork makeup – a confection of scorched, crushed champagne corks and water or petroleum jelly – and the trad-ition of white actors speaking and singing in mock 'Black' dialects that combined popular music, dance, and comedy ostensibly found on Southern plantations, we gain a better understanding of the overlap between the theatre and the home. University of Cambridge scholar Sarah Meer observes that when we read a variety of *Uncle Tom's* in rela-tion to Tom mania, it directs us to the extent of blackface's influence,

CHERYL THOMPSON

'spilling out of the minstrel halls and into the parlors even of those who never went to minstrel shows.'[22]

In the 1920s, after the Tom Shows had finally faded away, Toronto's demographics were changing significantly, with large populations of non-Anglo immigrants settling in The Ward and elsewhere. It's not that public attitudes toward the city's Black community had completely changed. Rather, consumer demand for Uncle Tom as a theatrical production had waned while other popular media, such as film, increasingly captured the public's imagination throughout that decade.

Toronto's Black community had also evolved. While the privileging of white immigrants at the Canadian border remained common practice until the 1960s, a growing number of West Indians, including many from Jamaica, came to Toronto in the 1920s to work as domestics and railway porters, and to provide the labour needed to support economic growth.

The city had three Black churches – Grant AME (originally on Elm and then at 23 Soho Street after 1929), the University Avenue Baptist Church (at Edward), and the BME Church at 94 Chestnut – as well as the *Canadian Observer*, the first Black newspaper to reach a national audience.[23] While these churches were not officially segregated, some members of the Black community tried to worship in white churches and found they were not always welcome.[24] The Grant AME was primarily led by African American ministers, while many West Indians attended the BME, and the Baptist church was split.

As Toronto's Black population established businesses and church congregations grew, its community members began to attract media attention. The appearance of an editorial in the Women's Daily Interest section of the *Toronto Daily Star* on July 29, 1926, announcing the wedding of Rachel Adina Stephenson to Mr. J. M. Williams, both originally from Jamaica, at the BME Church on Chestnut Street, speaks to a connection between BME congregations and the newspaper's mostly Anglo-Saxon readership. 'To the strains of Mendelssohn's wedding march the bridal party entered the church and took their place under the floral arch, the Union Jack and the Jamaican flag, intertwined with the roses,' the report noted.[25]

The photograph (pages 168–169) also speaks to the important role women played in community-building. As the Cornell University scholar Noliwe Rooks writes of African American women, fictional and cultural narratives 'posited marriage as the primary means of achieving a desired relationship to domesticity and of uplifting an entire race.'[26] The description of Williams, the bridegroom, as a 'well-known merchant, dealing in West Indian products,' tells us that a link existed between entrepreneurship and the public image of the Black community during the decade. In addition to business, marriage and children were means for Black people to integrate into Toronto's majority white society. Such imagery also speaks to the legacy of Uncle Tom and the widely celebrated image of Black men as non-violent, passive, and loyal. Historical images of Black subjects, like this one, must therefore be placed *in time* and not interpreted based on modern notions of race and representation that did not exist in the early twentieth century.

After centuries of enslavement, the 1920s marked a moment of great promise, as free Black people (the first generations not born into slavery) sought to provide services to, and uplift the moral character of, Black women, men, and their children, who were seen as the emblems of a new identity – one might say a 'new Negro' for a new century. At the same time, Stowe's novel still had a profound effect on popular culture, creating an enduring image of Black passivity that shaped representations of Black characters in Hollywood, most notably the Shirley Temple and Bill 'Bojangles' Robinson films in the 1930s that repackaged Stowe's (and the illustrator's) Uncle Tom and his child-patron Little Eva for movie audiences.

CHERYL THOMPSON

# A BLACK LITERARY SOCIETY

## HEATHER MURRAY

THIS BRIEF ENTRY from *Caverhill's Toronto City Directory for 1859-60* is the first and most detailed evidence of the Moral and Mental Improvement Society (African), one of the many social and educational groups that sprang into being in the 1850s to serve the burgeoning Black population of Canada West.[1] *Caverhill's* does not list the group under the heading of 'Literary, Scientific, and Associate' organizations, placing it instead under 'Religious and Benevolent Institutions,' along with the Anti-Slavery Society, the Ladies Colored Fugitive Association, and the Elgin Association (a settlement group). These groups intended to provide both political

MORAL AND MENTAL IMPROVEMENT SOCIETY, (AFRICAN).

This Society has for its object, the improvement of its members by means of essays and debates; it meets every Monday evening in the upper part of No. 120 Elgin buildings in Yonge st., at 8 o'clock during the summer months, and 7½ during winter. R. P. Thomas, president ; F. G. Simpson, 1st vice-president; E. J. Baily, 2nd vice-president ; W. H. Taylor, treasurer ; G. W. Cary, secretary ; G. W. Squirrel, chairman ; W. H. Taylor, E. J. Bailey, H. Jones, S. Stout, council.

support and assistance to escaping slaves as well as endangered freemen and women fleeing to Toronto either directly from the United States or from points of arrival elsewhere in the province.

With the aim of reading and discussing original essays and staging debates, the Moral and Mental Improvement Society (African) would have had much in common with the literary and debating groups established by European-descent settler men of Toronto at the same time (e.g., the Ontario Literary Society, the Toronto Literary Association, or the Osgoode Debating Club), as well as the racially inclusive Toronto Mechanics' Institute (a precursor of Toronto's first library). Even more significantly, the name of the new organization places it in the lineage of societies with similar names and aims that had operated for decades among the free Black population of the northern U.S. states.

For example, the Philadelphia Association for Moral and Mental Improvement of the People of Color began as early as 1835, and other societies restricted to young men soon emerged in its wake, like the Washington, D.C.-based Young Men's Mental Improvement Society for the Discussion of Moral and Philosophical Questions of all Kinds.[2] The 'moral' element of these groups' mandates was both direct and indirect. Characteristically, their leaders exhorted young men to abstain from alcohol and tobacco, and to lead an otherwise upright life. The groups also were intended to provide a convivial but safe alternative to the street corner or the tavern. Yet, as the eclectic title of the Washington group suggests, participants may have taken this mandate as a prompt for the discussion and debate of moral questions.

Black literary societies (i.e., reading groups) and educating societies, for both men and women, already operated in Cannonsburg, Chatham, Toronto, and Windsor. In 1855, the *Provincial Freeman* reported the existence of a predecessor organization in Toronto known as the Young Men's Excelsior Literary Association.[3] The founding of such organizations was a priority for the local Black community: in addition to raising the level of literacy and rhetorical skills among their own members, these groups staged educational entertainments and 'mental feasts' for wider audiences, and often undertook forms of civic work such as providing school supplies for young students. In the absence of much information about the Moral and Mental Improvement Society itself, these contexts are important to understanding what its members may have set out to achieve.

The directory entry, however, does provide several clues that connect the society to St. John's Ward in the mid-nineteenth century, when it was a teeming, vibrant, and swiftly expanding home for Toronto's new immigrant populations. The listing includes the society's leading members: R. P. Thomas as president, F. G. Simpson as first vice-president, E. J. Bailey as second vice-president, W. H. Taylor as treasurer, G. W. Cary as secretary, and G. W. Squirrel as chair. H. Jones and S. Stout joined Bailey and Taylor as members of the society's council.

While identification can be tricky – given some common family names, the use of initials only, and the slipshod transcription in city directories – it is possible to specify these members by cross-referencing

HEATHER MURRAY

city directories, while some have emerged in the historical record by virtue of their other achievements.[4]

Francis Griffin Simpson, a shoemaker by trade, was a key figure in Toronto's Black community at mid-century, active in many initiatives to assist the newcomers. Simpson then was located at 45 Park Lane, just north of Queen Street, although soon he would move to Elizabeth Street. George W. Cary was one of the four Cary brothers, free-born Virginians who had achieved economic stability not long after arriving in Toronto in the early 1850s. Like his brother Thomas F. Cary, George was an active abolitionist. His hairdressing (i.e., barber) shop was in an enviable location at 154 Yonge Street in the newly developing business district; he lived outside of The Ward on Church Street.

The Cary name brought to the fledgling society some important cultural connections, for in 1856 brother Thomas had married Mary Ann Shadd, publisher of the newspaper the *Provincial Freeman* and a founder of the Provincial Union Association.

George W. Squirrel (elsewhere spelled Squirell) was a labourer who, in 1861, is shown living at 26 Christopher Street, a short street of small cottages at the northern-most edge of The Ward. S. Stout is presumably Samuel Stout (elsewhere Stoute), who was also a hairdresser, as was the association's president, R. P. (Robert) Thomas, and both had shops near the market.

A shared métier, as well as a common street of residence, suggest that Bailey, Jones, and Taylor were the Edmund Bailey, Henry Jones, and (possibly William) Taylor living at 202, 16, and 22 Centre Street respectively, all working as waiters. (Jones worked at the North American Coffee House and, later, the prestigious new Rossin Hotel.) While these club members may have had different religious or congregational adherences, they were linked through ties of neighbourhood, work location, vocation, and, feasibly, political belief.

In all probability, this group got underway sometime in 1858, in time to make the 1859 directory. While Robert Thomas was the eventual president, surely Francis Simpson was a prime mover, and he may well have been responding to a heated political incident that occurred in August 1858. As John Lorinc has described it, at a nomination meeting held in the tavern of 'Captain Bob' Moodie on Terauley Street, where Black voters were being canvassed for their support along with other local residents, arguments and fights broke out. Simpson was there to win Black voters to the Liberal Party cause (many members of the Black community worried that the Grits were on the slippery slope to republicanism and annexation with the United States, and that they were better protected by Canada's imperial connections).[5] Witnessing the melee, Simpson may well have felt that the men of his community deserved a better venue for the discussion of differing points of view, and that they should be provided with training in rational thought and persuasive speaking to make them more effective political actors.

Whatever the reason, the location for the Monday-evening meetings of the society put it in the Liberal orbit. Convening in the upper rooms at 120 Yonge Street, in the Elgin Building, the members met above the offices of the *Echo*, a newspaper representing the evangelical wing of the Church of England in Canada. Publisher Thomas Sellar, an immigrant Scot who had worked as a sub-editor of the *Globe,* had remained a close friend of *Globe* editor and Liberal Party stalwart George Brown, and presumably shared Brown's anti-slavery views. It may or may not be a coincidence that the society seems to have wound down after Sellar relocated the *Echo* to Montreal.

While the 1861 and 1862 directories included a listing for the Moral and Mental Improvement Society (African), the 1866 directory contains no such entry, which suggests the society had ceased to exist by 1865 or perhaps even earlier. This is not unusual: cultural and voluntary organizations of the mid-century, no matter their demographic composition, were often short-lived, and this was especially the case for the freedom-seekers, given the uncertainties of their lives, the need for frequent relocation, and a constantly shifting political climate.

But perhaps the winding-down of the society offers evidence of its success, and a sign that it had, at least partially, fulfilled the goals its members shared with so many others in their community: to acquire, or to improve, their literacy skills; to become cultured, or 'literary' in understanding; and to develop the rhetorical strengths necessary for participation in Toronto's broader civic life.

HEATHER MURRAY

# 'FASHIONABLE JAMAICAN WEDDING'

KATHY GRANT

THE FRONT PAGE of the July 29, 1926, edition of the *Globe and Mail* contained three images: a photo of young artist Francis J. Haxby; the portrait he painted of the late Sir Adam Beck, founder of the Hydro-Electric Power Commission of Ontario; and a portrait of members of a wedding party, entitled 'Bridal Party at Fashionable Jamaican Wedding.'

A story about this same wedding also appeared in the *Toronto Star* on the same day, back on page twenty-five, in a section entitled 'Women's Daily Interests.'

'One of the most brilliant weddings ever solemnized between members of the Jamaican colony in Toronto took place at 7:30 last evening in the British Methodist Episcopal Church at 94 Chestnut Street,' the *Star* article began. 'To the strains of Mendelssohn's wedding march the bridal party entered the church and took their place under a floral arch, the Union Jack and the Jamaican flag, intertwined with the roses.'

Below the article was an ad for Martins Holiday Specials Cooked and Jellied Meats. 'Let Martin's help you fill the outing hamper and family picnic basket – from their two score and more ready to serve cooked and jellied meats,' read the ad, noting that meats sold for fifty-five cents per pound. These were the prices of food in 1926.

I first saw the image of the seven members of that 1926 wedding party in the spring of 2015. The photograph was part of a JB's Warehouse and Curio Emporium blog post about a play called *The Wild Party*, about life and jazz in the Roaring Twenties. I saved the picture.

The blog's author, Jamie Bradburn, wrote:

Among the weddings detailed on the social and women's pages of Toronto's major newspapers on July 29, 1926, regular readers might have noticed something unusual about one of them. As the *Toronto Star*'s headline put it, 'Toronto Jamaica Folk Attend Smart Wedding.' The *Star*, along with the *Globe* and the *Telegram*, covered the union of merchant Michael Joshua Williams and Rachel Adina Stephenson.

Perhaps the most remarkable thing about the original coverage is that, apart from references to the couple's West Indian origins, it could have passed for any other society wedding. For example, Stephenson was 'charmingly gowned in white satin, with the cap of her embroidered net veil banded with orange blossoms, [and] carried a shower bouquet of Ophelia roses and baby's breath. Miss Gladys Bramwell, the maid of honour, and the five bridesmaids, all wore gowns of pink georgette, with drooping pink hats and carried bouquets of delicate pink rambler roses.'

The newspaper accounts also recorded what the guests and child ring bearers wore, as well as the newlyweds' honeymoon destination (Niagara Falls). Had it not been for the photograph of the wedding party, one might have been unaware that the participants were Black.

The following month, as part of a Black-veteran oral history project, I interviewed the Hon. George Carter, Canada's first Canadian-born Black judge, who had served in World War II. He graduated from the University of Toronto in 1945. Judge Carter articled with the only Black lawyer practising in Ontario (B. J. Spencer Pitt), and then opened his own Bay Street practice covering real estate, family, and criminal law. Carter was named to the bench in 1979. He was the first of fourteen children of Barbadian parents, John and Louise Carter. They immigrated to Canada in the late 1910s. As a little boy, George recalls walking with his mother as she pushed a giant wicker-basket carriage carrying three of his siblings – the baby lying on her back and two toddlers propped up in the corners. His father, in turn, worked in an iron foundry. During George's early teens, his family lived in The Ward and attended the BME Church on Chestnut Street. 'I think back to the wonderful good fortune I had in having two great parents,' he told me. 'They were just ordinary folks... At home, that's where the real lessons were learned.'

During our interview, George showed me his parents' 1920 wedding photo. The groom bore an uncanny resemblance to the best man in the 1926 photo of the elegant Jamaican wedding. Two years later, when a student researcher and I searched for information about that 1926 wedding through online newspaper clippings and Ancestry.ca, we discovered that Michael Joshua Williams's best man's name was John Carter – George's father!

I called George a few days later and shared the names of the members of the 1926 wedding party. Remarkably, he confirmed that he knew the families and the children in the photograph, and how they were connected. George's dad, the groom, and those attending the ceremony were all members of the Universal Negro Improvement Association (UNIA), a Black nationalist fraternal organization founded by Marcus Mosiah Garvey. Garvey's philosophy was 'Up, up, you mighty race! You can accomplish what you will.'

Many of the families attending the ceremony, including the groom, arrived in Canada from 1911 to 1915, George recalled. Michael Williams had become a porter after he settled in Toronto, as this was one of the few jobs available to Black men in those days. He worked for seven years on the railroad before returning to Jamaica.

In 1921, Michael came back to Canada with a $1,400 in his pockets, according to immigration records, and started his own import business selling Jamaican coffee and West Indian produce. He was known to all as 'Coffee Williams.' Like many West Indians who came to Canada, Michael was Anglican and joined the BME Church because Blacks were not made to feel welcome at Anglican churches. His wife was Presbyterian.

Michael eventually joined UNIA and became its president. One week after the wedding story was published, he appeared in the *Toronto Star* again. Most of the wedding party was part of a three-hundred-member delegation to the St. Catharines/Niagara Falls area for the annual August 1 Emancipation Day picnic. By coincidence, George's birthday, in 1921, also fell on Emancipation Day.

The paper's headline read, 'Colored Folks Picnic on Emancipation – 500 Strong Make Merry at Port Dalhousie.' It was an extended celebration, as three hundred members of the Toronto churches made their way to the town to continue the merriment. The *Star* article did not hesitate to mention, more than once, that 'there were large quantities of fried chicken.'

'The picnic was sponsored by the Universal Negro Improvement Association, of which Mr J. M. Williams is president,' the article explained. 'The following churches [are] represented in Force: First Baptist Church, corner of Edward Street and University Avenue, of which Rev. McEwan Williams is pastor, the British Methodist Church at 94 Chestnut Street, Rev J. Stewart pastor, and the African Methodist Episcopal Church situated at the corner of Elm and University whose pastor is Rev. W. C. Carpenter.'

The reporter also noted that 'the colored people celebrated Emancipation Day in an appropriate manner with fifteen hours of emancipation from the duties and restrictions of their daily tasks.'

A couple weeks after we'd done this research, I obtained a copy of that elegant wedding photo taken ninety years earlier and presented it to Judge Carter as a Father's Day gift. His family and friends were on hand for the viewing.

The people in the photo, from left to right, include John Carter, best man; Michael Joshua Williams, groom; Miss Rachel Adina Stephenson, bride; Agnes Brown, bridesmaid; Doris Bailey, flower girl; Francie Gibbons, train bearer; Thomas Foster, ring bearer.

Foster became a photographer and died in 2011. He was in his nineties. Doris Bailey's sister Ruth would go on to become one of the first Negro nurses permitted to practise in Ontario.

# THE SYNAGOGUE ON CENTRE AVENUE

SIMON PATRICK ROGERS

S HAAREI TZEDEC[1] CONGREGATION was founded by new Russian
immigrants around 1902, and the earliest surviving ledgers indicate a thriving membership by 1905. The congregation would have
first met in a *shtibl*, or small synagogue in a converted house or store,
likely on Edward Street. In 1907, they found a new home in the former Standard Foundry Company, at 29 Centre Avenue, which backed
onto the British Methodist Episcopal Church on Chestnut Street.
They renovated the building into a synagogue, or shul, including giving it a new facade. To undertake these refurbishments, they hired a
contractor named Philip Rosenbes, a Russian Jewish immigrant who
had arrived in Toronto in 1895, and local architect Isadore Feldman.
The Centre Avenue shul was a two-storey brick building with a capacity of between three and four hundred people, constructed with a
traditional central bimah – a raised altar from which the Torah is
read – and a separate second-storey women's gallery. Full occupancy
probably commenced in 1910, a year often erroneously given as the
shul's founding date.

Centre Avenue was already decidedly Jewish in character by 1912,
with four established synagogues on the two-block strip between
Armoury and Edward Streets. Within a few blocks, members could
visit Riman's Russian Baths, which maintained a mikveh for ritual
purification, dine at kosher restaurants, read Yiddish newspapers at
Dworkin's news agency on Elizabeth Street, or attend Yiddish shows at
the Lyric Theatre. The creation of new shuls coincided with the steady
arrival of Eastern European Jews, who naturally gravitated to the area

for its proximity to work in the textile factories, the cheap rents, and the familiar atmosphere that approximated the shtetls, or segregated communities, they had fled in Eastern Europe following the pogroms of the late nineteenth century. Here the devoutly Orthodox community maintained important cultural, business, and regional affiliations that helped sustain them through the difficulties of emigration and the precariousness of their living and working conditions in Toronto.

The early records of Shaarei Tzedec indicate a membership base in flux. Even over a relatively short span, the shul's ledgers record frequent changes of address for most of the affiliated families, the majority of whom lived within walking distance of the shul. Many of the members worked as general labourers and tradesmen, with the whole family often contributing piecework from the home for nearby garment factories. Representative examples of employment held by members listed in the 1911 census and 1922 city directory include grocer, labourer, laundryman, furrier, and factory operator.

Much of the initial membership would have been drawn from earlier established synagogues such as the Goel Tzedec on University Avenue and Chevra Tehillim on McCaul Street. In fact, dual membership would have been common, with many congregants choosing their synagogue according to convenience of location, as well as customs of worship and their regional affiliation with kinsmen of the same origin and language. Between 1880 and 1920, dozens of new congregations were founded by Romanian, Galician, Polish, and Lithuanian Jews newly arrived in Toronto. Many of these congregations were short-lived and left behind little in the way of historical record of their existence as important social centres for the Jewish immigrant communities that flocked to The Ward.

Shaarei Tzedec's early documentation shows that Nathan Gold was the first president of the shul. The treasurer was paid the nominal sum of one dollar per annum, according to the 1902 constitution. The fee for a wedding was ten dollars for non-members, but for members, use of the shul was free. Membership dues were waived for members of ten years' standing who were too old, too poor, or too sick to pay, codes that indicate the social principles of the faithful.

SIMON PATRICK ROGERS

Raising the necessary funds to purchase the original building on Centre Avenue would have constituted the primary fundraising effort of the congregation's founders. In addition, mutual benefit societies formed an important part of the Jewish social network, and one of the first orders of business for a new shul was always the establishment of the *chevra kadisha*, or burial society. This volunteer group within the shul purchased a cemetery allotment in Roselawn Cemetery, where 678 Shaarei Tzedec burials are registered.

Translation: 'Congregation Shaarei Tzedek, prayer services are held daily, morning and evening, everyone is welcome!' Sign from Centre Ave. synagogue.

It was a dispute over burial rights that led a number of families to form the First Russian Congregation of Rodfei Sholem Anshei Kiev, commonly called 'the Kiever,' in 1912, under the leadership of father and son Louis and Max Bossin, who had been among the earliest members of Shaarei Tzedec. Strong similarities of faith and tradition have remained, however, between the various downtown Orthodox synagogues in spite of such ideological differences. The members of different congregations frequently attended services at more than one shul, suggesting the consistency of practices in the downtown Orthodox community.

Rabbi Solomon Langer (d. 1973) was affiliated with Shaarei Tzedec as well as the First Narayever Congregation. Though he did not typically lead services, he acted as a spiritual leader and teacher. His involvement with several different congregations in the Annex and Kensington Market areas is telling of the humble beginnings of many of the Jewish community's earliest institutions, which often could not afford to retain the services of a full-time rabbi. In the early twentieth century, the shul ran a choir under the direction of Cantor Meyer Zimmerman (1884–1954), a highly regarded choral director and rabbi. Joseph Woolf, another early member of the congregation, was the executive director of the Jewish Philanthropies of Toronto in the 1920s. The shul continues to be associated with social work in the Jewish community, and the city more broadly.

When Shaarei Tzedec moved from The Ward to the Annex in 1937, it occupied the family home of Louis Gurofsky (1871–1934), an influential Jewish business leader who ran the North Atlantic Trading Company. Renovations were undertaken to convert the residence on 397 Markham Street into a synagogue according to the design of the prominent Jewish architect Benjamin Swartz. Rabbi Saul Wolfe Gringorten (1876–1959), an executive officer of the Toronto chapter of the Zionist Organization of Canada, lived next door at 395 Markham Street and, until the late 1930s, operated a cheder there, where the congregation's children received their basic and religious education. Toronto's first rabbinical seminary, Yeshivah Torath Chaim, was founded in 1937 by Rabbi Avraham Aharon Price (1900–94) across the street from the Markham Street shul. It was the site of the education of many spiritual leaders in the Orthodox tradition.

The shul's move to Markham Street would have represented the ascendancy of the community from its working-class status of the early twentieth century to a more mercantile-class norm of the 1920s and 1930s. The original plan of the congregation's executive, in purchasing

SIMON PATRICK ROGERS

the Markham Street buildings, was to demolish the houses in order to build a new synagogue on the site as a replacement for the larger building on Centre Avenue, which had become too costly to maintain during the Depression. However, the funds for the new building could not be raised and, as a cost-saving measure, the congregation renovated the Markham Street properties instead. The hand-to-mouth survival of the congregation throughout the 1950s, 1960s, and 1970s ironically led to the continued use and preservation of the Markham Street synagogue, which was declared a Category C Ontario Heritage building in 2001 (the designation means the building is part of a historical streetscape).

Today the Markham Street shul is a living historical monument to the thriving Jewish culture and community that once attracted such prominent figures as Rabbi Price to the Annex. As the Jewish community increasingly moved to the northern and outlying suburbs of Toronto, this trend began to take its toll on the membership of Shaarei Tzedec into the 1960s. The congregation declared bankruptcy in 1968. However, a concerted fundraising effort by Jewish community leaders in the area re-established the congregation in 1970, under the spiritual and administrative leadership of the shul's president, Dr. Joseph Greenberg, who died at the age of ninety-four in 2017.

The pews, Torah crown, Torah ark, and plaques listing the original founders were brought over from the Centre Avenue building and are still in use today. The congregation has also kept a number of its original light fixtures and the original founding stone of the Centre Avenue building that names Philip Rosenbes as the contractor. When Agudath Israel Anshei Sfard Congregation closed its Palmerston shul in 1978, the pews and other fixtures from that building were distributed by Sholom Langer and Frank Zomerfogel to Shaarei Tzedec and other shuls in the downtown core for their ongoing use.

Today, Shaarei Tzedec is home to a diverse assortment of resident and visiting members, who come to the shul to experience services in the Orthodox tradition. The intimate heritage building in the multicultural Annex neighbourhood preserves and recalls its historical roots in the vibrant Ward community.

# ANIMAL BONES, BROKEN DISHES, AND A CUP FOR ELIJAH

HOLLY MARTELLE

A RCHAEOLOGY IS A combination of science and storytelling. While the scientific method is paramount in the recognition, collection, and analysis of raw archaeological data (artifacts, features, structural remains, and so on), it is the interpretive narrative that weaves the data together in a holistic and culturally meaningful way. Explanatory models and frames of reference are, for archaeologists, the storylines that breathe life into stagnant material remains.

Apart from its intellectual foundation, archaeology is also an intuitive and sensory exercise. Smells, colours, shapes,

An archaeologically derived table setting. Among the items shown: a decanter for wine, a glass cellar containing apple seeds, a spoon fragment, gilded plates, a lamb shank and walnuts, and wine goblet.

textures, and patterns all affect archaeological experience during excavation and in the laboratory; they mould our 'feelings' about the data and, although never catalogued and inventoried, can be as powerful as the data themselves in stirring intuition and directing archaeological lines of inquiry.

During the excavation of the Armoury site, one particular privy deposit stood out. Among its wealth were beautiful dishes rimmed with gold and elaborately cut and pressed glassware that sparkled brightly in the fall sunlight when we cleaned off a century of encrusted muck. Immediately intrigued, I spent some time poking around in the piles, finding other archaeological treasures (whole eggs, mass quantities of butchered animal bones, utensils, serving vessels, nuts of various kinds), and thinking about what might have made this privy so different. The gilded ceramics were an extravagance that seemingly had no place in The Ward. They were virtually absent in the other privy deposits I had seen, where inexpensive and plainer wares were plentiful, as would be entirely appropriate for folk of limited means. Not only that, the same pattern of gilding and printing was repeated on several dishes, indicating they were from a set. Matching wares were almost non-existent in other privies.

Eager to know more about the social, economic, or cultural behaviours that left their mark in this exceptional privy, I started by putting it into context. The feature was identified in the rear of Lot 12 on Centre Street, behind a large brick building at 29 Centre Avenue that was built around 1895, as the Standard Foundry. In 1906, it was converted to the Shaarei Tzedec synagogue. The privy pit sat just inside the outline of a two-storey warehouse and car garage built around 1940, and had been cut through and heavily impacted by deep, cinder-block foundations.

The privy's wood lining and a central partition had been knocked down by those foundations, collapsing into the privy chamber. On the surface, the privy was much longer than most others and its excavation profile revealed that it was, in fact, three chambers spaced closely together – although not all were likely in use at the same time. The artifacts we recovered from that privy dated from the 1860s through the 1930s. However, based on their decorative style, the gilded ceramics are characteristic of the 1910s through 1930s, the period during which 29 Centre Street functioned as a synagogue. Tax-assessment records indicate that the rear of the property, where the privy was located, had been occupied by the synagogue's two caretakers, Solomon Yellman and then, after 1916, Israel Lerman. The 1909 (revised to 1917) fire insurance plan depicts their one-storey wood-clad dwelling (opposite), as does a 1937 photograph taken when the building had fallen into disrepair after Lerman moved out, and just before the property was purchased and converted for use by the Pearl Furniture Company.

City directories and tax records indicate that Israel Lerman was the synagogue's *shammas*, or caretaker. Although the word *caretaker* denotes a person responsible for looking after a building, the shammas was all of that and more. He ensured that day-to-day activities went smoothly, prepared the building for prayer and services, and offered support to the rabbi and members. As an individual integral to the successful functioning of the synagogue, Lerman likely took his beliefs very seriously.

HOLLY MARTELLE

Placed in the context of a shammas's privy, the concentration of fine china and formal glassware finds meaning. These are not just broken sherds of glass and ceramic,

Privy behind Shaarei Tzedec synagogue at 29 Centre, February 16, 1937. The rear wall of the BME Church is at right.

but potentially also the remains of formal table settings used during Jewish holidays, particularly the Seder, a ritual feast served on the first nights of Passover that commemorates the Jews' exodus from slavery in Egypt. Passover is a time of great celebration and for giving thanks. In the nineteenth and early twentieth centuries, the Seder was associated with elaborate table settings that reflected the joyous occasion. And it still is today. The finest tablecloths, china, utensils, and glassware are used to both colourfully and symbolically decorate the Seder table. In some cases, families had two sets of dishes specifically for Seder, one for meat and the other for dairy.

Each Seder-table place setting includes a plate, flatware, waterglass, wineglass, and Haggadah, a book containing the story of Passover. Among the table settings are bottles or decanters of wine, small vessels for salt water, and candles, which are lit at the beginning of the Seder meal. Each table is also adorned with a plate containing three matzos –

loaves or sheets of unleavened or crackerlike bread – and a Seder plate, tray, or platter containing five individual food items: *zeroa* – a roasted shank bone of lamb; *beitzah* – a roasted hard-boiled egg; *moror* – bitter herbs such as horseradish; *haroset* – a sweet mixture of fruits and nuts, often apple and walnut; and *karpas* – a green leafy vegetable, often parsley or lettuce. Finally, a separate wineglass is placed near the centre of the table for the prophet Elijah, who is invoked as part of the Seder ritual and symbolizes hope for redemption. Elijah's cup is filled, but its wine is not drunk.

As with all Jewish meals, the foods on the Seder table are highly symbolic:

› Matzos – Unleavened or 'poor man's' bread is a reminder of Jewish life under slavery and reflects the fact that the Jews left Egypt so hurriedly that they did not have time to wait for their bread dough to rise. During the week-long Passover holiday, consumption of leavened bread is prohibited.
› Zeroa – The roasted bone represents the paschal lamb that was sacrificed on the altar of the great Temple in Jerusalem on Passover.
› Beitzah – The roasted egg symbolizes the second offering that was traditionally offered in the Temple of Jerusalem on every pilgrimage festival.
› Moror – These bitter herbs symbolize the bitterness of slavery.
› Haroset – This mixture of finely chopped fruit, nuts, spices, and wine of a red-brown colour represents the clay and mortar used by Jewish slaves to make the bricks that built the towns and pyramids in Egypt; its sweet taste is a reminder of the sweetness of God's redemption from slavery.
› Karpas – Leafy vegetables or herbs, or 'fruit of the earth,' signify the arrival of spring and the gathering of spring harvest; the karpas are dipped into the dish of salt water before being eaten, as the water symbolizes the tears and sweat the ancestors shed while suffering from slavery. These vegetables are often some of the first to appear in the spring; the rebirth of plant life reflects the rebirth of Jewish people when they escaped bondage in Egypt.

›	Yayin – Wine is a gift from God consumed to make the heart glad and merry; four cups are meant to be consumed at specific points during the meal.

Understandably, and given preservation and disposal biases, we didn't find all of the elements of a Seder table in this privy. But we found at least enough to prompt some observations about the deeper cultural meaning of food remains recovered from the site, as well as the opportunities the data offer for identifying cultural practices around food acquisition, preparation, consumption, and disposal, and considering those within a context of immigration and acculturation.

Derived from the Torah's Books of Leviticus and Deuteronomy, the basic laws of Kashrut define what foods can be eaten by Jews, and how they must be prepared and consumed. These laws ensure that eating is both a ritual and a sustaining act that reifies, on a daily basis, what it means to be Jewish. While traditionally the Kashrut laws have been proscriptive, history has shown that Jewish cuisine is both regionally variable and highly adaptable, incorporating local ingredients into traditional dishes. This makes our archaeological studies of late-nineneenth- and early-twentieth-century Jewish households important for understanding how Eastern European Jewish immigrants, most of them Orthodox, adapted to life in Canada.

Koşher laws around what animals could be eaten and how they must be slaughtered should also be visible archaeologically and offer interesting lines of inquiry. Further, other kosher rules regarding the cooking and eating of certain foods together ensured that Jewish households had separate sets of cooking vessels, dishes, and utensils for meat and for dairy. Kosher rules around all forms of cooking utensils, then, could also leave archaeological signatures.

Eggshells. Fish scales. A glass goblet. Gilded pieces of porcelain. A glass bottle stopper. Walnut shells. A lamb leg bone. Apple seeds. A knife. Fragments of an ornate candlestick holder. A transfer-printed serving platter. Peach pits. By no means mere food scraps and broken dishes, these archaeological remnants open a window to the ways immigrant Jewish families lived and what they believed.

# THE ROLE OF THE SHAMMAS

ELLEN SCHEINBERG

M ANY OF THE smaller synagogues in Toronto, like Shaarei Tzedec, did not have the resources to hire permanent clergy. Typically, they shared a rabbi with other synagogues and/or temporarily secured a rabbi or cantor for special events, like the High Holidays. According to its constitution, the shul's board members fulfilled a number of important functions, in areas like management, administration, and finance. While Shaarei Tzedec was situated on Centre Avenue, the congregation turned to the *shammas*, or caretaker, to maintain the shul. A rear dwelling behind the synagogue served as residence for the shammas and his family.

The Hebrew word *shammas* means servant. Indeed, the ninth candle of the Chanukah menorah is referred to as the shammas (or shammash), since it is set apart and used to light the other eight ceremonial candles. The synagogue shammas not only illuminated the building and supported the ceremonial functions of the shul, but kept everything running efficiently. Traditionally, the shammas was the building manager, responsible for both the interior and exterior of the facility. However, it was not uncommon for this individual to also oversee security.

Israel Lerman held this position for Shaarei Tzedec from 1916 until the 1930s. Born in Kiev, Russia, he immigrated to Toronto around 1907. Lerman's wife and son – Sara and Sam – arrived a few years later, in 1911. Both Israel and Sam – ages fifty-eight and nineteen when they started – worked in tandem to maintain the shul. They earned salaries of $600 and $700 respectively, according to the 1921 census. Their remuneration

פ״נ

איש צדיק וישר

ישראל בר גרשון

לערמאן

נפטר כב אלול תרצו

ת נ צ ב ה

ISRAEL LERMAN
DIED SEPT. 19, 1936
AGED 82 YEARS

LERMAN

would have also included free housing and potentially other benefits, like a family membership to the synagogue and burial plots.

Their responsibilities for the shul likely included safeguarding the congregation's members from the perceived aggressive and egregious proselytizing of Rev. Henry Singer. His 'Jewish mission' was located next door and sought to convert Jews to Christianity.

Sam eventually married, had a family, and moved to Detroit during the 1920s. As for Israel, he retired in the mid-1930s and died in 1936, at the age of seventy-eight. He was laid to rest with the other members of the congregation in the Shaarei Tzedec section of Roselawn Cemetery, near Bathurst north of Eglinton. The family memorialized him with a lovely monument; unfortunately, the age inscribed on the stone is incorrect according to his death certificate.

# WORSHIP SERVICES IN TRANSLATION

GREER ANNE WENH-IN NG 伍吳詠嫣

*In the early 1950s, the British Methodist Episcopal Church on Chestnut Street was sold to the United Church of Canada, which had selected the facility to become the city's first purpose-built place of worship for a Chinese-Canadian congregation. Chinese-Christian organizations had operated in the city as far back as 1911, when the first association was founded on Church Street. By 1933, the United Church of Canada had expanded that Chinese mission and moved it to 58 Elm Street. Its location, a block from the Elizabeth Street playground, attracted local children to the mission to play basketball. The congregation was renamed the Bay Street Chinese Church in 1939, with a celebration held the next year to mark its twenty-second anniversary.*

*In the 1940s, the Chinese Canadian Institute opened in an old mansion at the northwest corner of Dundas and University. It provided space for Chinese language classes and other extracurricular activities, as well as a home for ill and elderly members of the Chinese community.*

*After the Chestnut Street church was sold and demolished in 1988, the congregation relocated to 3300 Kennedy Road, in Scarborough, and has operated there ever since.*

CAME WITH THE Rev. Kam-Yan Ng 伍錦仁 and our two children from New York to minister at the Toronto Chinese United Church in 1970. What we discovered when we got here was that the main part of the congregation was Cantonese-speaking, consisting of the first generation of old overseas Chinese who had come from China. But these members already had second-generation children who by that time

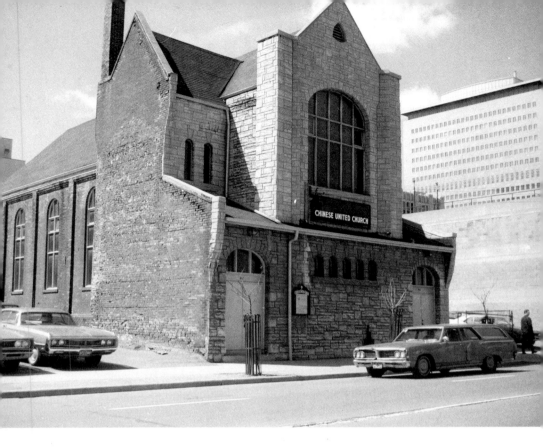

were adults. Of this second generation, I still remember several of the most active women leaders who had grown up here, among them Lily Howe, Laura Wong, Lily Yee, and Mary Ko-Bong. They mostly functioned in English: they could not read much Chinese. They were on the governing board and represented the church at presbytery as lay representatives. They also acted as liaisons between the congregation and the larger, wider denomination. This was one group of people who really needed English.

Chinese United Church, 92–96 Chestnut, 1977.

What we had to do, then, was conduct Sunday school in both English and Chinese, and any church publication – a newsletter, an annual report, anniversary notices, the weekly Sunday bulletin – would always have to be in both languages. There were several Chinese dialects, too. For example, most of the older folk came from a cluster of four villages in the southern part of Guangdong Province. They spoke a distinct sub-dialect, *Toishan*, which the second-generation adults also spoke. The third-generation children were in Sunday school and the youth groups: their functioning language was English, especially in written form. More recent immigrants from Hong Kong would speak Cantonese and most of them were bilingual.

In order to be able to do ministry effectively with this particular congregation, we really needed things to be bilingual, not just in publications, but in day-to-day communication and of course in the worship service every Sunday. What were the alternatives? There was always the possibility that you could set up a separate English-speaking group. But the congregation at that point was not large. So we set out to see if there was a way, without dividing into two separate linguistic entities and while ministering to the original Chinese-speaking members in Chinese, to involve the English-speaking members more so they could feel they were part of the congregation. That was the motivation: there was this second-generation group who were already very active church leaders, and then there was the third generation. It was important that everyone could take an active part.

On top of that, we soon actually had a non-Chinese couple who became members: they were Caucasians – Douglas and Allegra Smith. Why were they interested in becoming part of this congregation? Doug was a missionary child who grew up in Szechuan/Sichuan and had gone to the Canadian School in West China. He became quite active, and of course he was English–speaking – he hadn't learned much Chinese.

We thought, how do we accommodate everybody? We started seeking ways of doing that. The church already had a huge bazaar every year: the children and young people were very active in it. Also, a lot of community people came, including United Church colleagues and members of other churches. After a while, my husband suggested, 'We could translate some of the new hymns.' A new English hymn book had just been published in 1971, and we translated some of the new hymns to Chinese so the congregation could sing them in that language as well. But this wasn't enough – it didn't address the need to be able to communicate bilingually within one worshipping congregation.

It was thanks to Bill Cheung that we found a solution. Bill had come to Canada in his late teens, so he was himself bilingual, as were congre-

GREER ANNE WENH-IN NG 伍吳詠嫻

gants Joseph and Loretta Leung from Hong Kong. Bill, who had attended the Presbyterian church on Beverley Street, said, 'I think they have a way of doing this. Let me

Worshippers, Chinese United Church.

go and check.' He went over to attend services there and reported back: 'They have this simultaneous translation system – you don't have to stop every so often to translate what the minister speaks. Why don't we try it?' We already knew how the United Nations functions with many languages using a simultaneous translation system: we thought we could try it with just one other language.

The balcony of the church was already enclosed for a nursery for young children. Bill, who was an electrician, suggested, 'Maybe I can use a corner of this space to turn it into a little broadcasting place.' He involved Joseph Leung, as well as some other young people, to help. He installed headphones in the last few rows of the pews in the sanctuary downstairs, and we started by interpreting the sermon into English, since the sermon was central to United Church worship. This would make it possible for someone like Doug Smith, who spoke almost no Chinese, and the second-generation adults, who could catch phrases but couldn't grasp the whole sermon, to follow along. Soon Doug was saying, 'I can get the sermon now, even though I can't hear the minister speaking.'

As we were getting this new system in place, we thought, 'What about the younger people, the third generation, who are studying Chinese in Chinese school at the church on Saturdays but don't read enough Chinese? How about, since the bulletin is in both languages anyway, we involve the younger people in doing announcements, and also reading the day's scripture lessons, as readers from the broadcasting booth?'

This took a while to set up. I was one of the first to take on the responsibility of interpreting the sermon. Then I formed a team and there were three or four of us. We discovered that it really was effective in involving the participation of the younger people. They weren't just sitting there, feeling bored – they felt they could participate actively, as they did at the bazaars. That was how that system facilitated the congregation bringing its younger generations, up to the third one, together into one big family. At the same time, it allowed for the participation of English-speaking visitors, rendering the service accessible to them.

Up to that point, there hadn't been much involvement on the minister's part in the wider Church. Reverend Ng believed that we should not only be part of the Chinese community in the neighbourhood, but also be active in the greater United Church. So, with his encouragement, the congregation hosted presbytery several times, and Doug Smith invited the alumni of his West China Canadian School to meet there for reunions. Outreach such as this helped the church involve not only its own people but also be part of the wider United Church.

Such involvement was important because developers, even in those early days, were always after the United Church of Canada (who owned the property) via the presbytery, saying, 'We want you to sell us the property.' So the minister went to the presbytery for support. He asked presbytery to put a moratorium of ten years on any attempt to sell the building site at 92–96 Chestnut Street, and presbytery agreed. This gave the congregation some stability for over a decade. In its current location, on Kennedy Road since 1988, the congregation is celebrating its 100th anniversary in 2018.

GREER ANNE WENH-IN NG 伍吳詠嫣

# MEMORIES OF THE CHINESE UNITED CHURCH

GORDON CHONG

I N THE LATE forties, I lived on Phoebe Street, just outside The Ward, in a second-storey apartment across from Osgoode Hall, where the opera house is now. I was always in the neighbourhood. My father had married a white Brit, whose family disowned her. After she started to fall apart, most of my time was spent in Chinatown with my father – many of my Chinese relatives were in that area. If you simply looked at me, you wouldn't know I was only half-Chinese. But there were several mixed-race families in the neighbourhood.

I went to the Chinese United Church, on Chestnut Street, for Sunday services with the other Canadian-born Chinese children. The inside of the church was plain, with wooden pews. When it was first built, it had been very modern-looking. But over time, it got old. Yet it was comfortable.

We would cut through the parking lot of the Lichee Garden restaurant to get to the church to play table tennis on the second floor. I was also very familiar with the back alleys in the Centre, Chestnut, Armoury, and Louisa Streets vicinity. As you went further south, there were abandoned parking lots and alleyways where we'd play marbles.

On Sundays, I was part of a choir at the Chinese United Church – we often met for rehearsals during the week. We used to sing some of the hymns and Christmas songs in Cantonese and in English. Our group would also go through the whole Christmas ceremony at the Christmas service. I have stayed in touch with several people I met there over the years.

During the week, I was sent to the Chinese school on University Avenue at Dundas. School started at 5:00 p.m., but we'd get there at five-thirty, after public school sports programs ended, and the teachers would be very annoyed with us. Then at six o'clock, it was recess, which was supposed to last fifteen minutes. We'd take off and didn't come back on time. They had to go out and round us up!

The original Canary Grill was on Dundas just west of University. During the breaks, we used to go there to get something to eat. Or we'd go running around the block because we wanted to stay in shape. And at 7:00 p.m., school was over. In two hours, you should learn a lot, but we really didn't.

In those days, if you were going to Chinese school, chances are you were Canadian-born and your parents wanted you to learn Chinese. But the interest in language classes petered out over the years, as it does in every ethnic group. Looking back, one of my biggest regrets is that I didn't pay attention. But the way Chinese was taught at the time wouldn't have motivated many students.

I did speak some Chinese, though – not like a native, but enough. A lot of my friends were Canadian-born Chinese, but they left the central part of the city and lived in the suburbs, which denied them daily inter-action with Chinese-speakers.

My father's family association, the Lung Kong Brotherhood Associa-tion, is comprised of four clans – the Chongs, the Kwans, the Chus, and the Los. I used to go to the banquet-hall restaurants all the time and I grew up frequently eating banquet-calibre Chinese food.

Our clan association had moved up from Queen Street to a new home directly facing Lichee Garden across the street. There were houses on Chestnut and Centre Streets where some of the smaller associations had their official homes, but generally in buildings they owned. On Sunday, they would operate the credit unions and have mah-jong games. It was like a community centre, but one with mul-tiple addresses where each building played a separate role.

As we got a bit older, Kwong Chow, at Dundas and Elizabeth Streets, became one of the three restaurants that people would go to regularly. The Chinese went there as well – it wasn't just non-Chinese. Sai Woo was another popular eatery, and then Lichee Garden. But Lichee

Garden's main clientele was non-Chinese. Across from Lichee, there was another restaurant called Lotus Garden.

Weekends, but Sundays especially, was a gathering time. I would go to the Kwong Chow because I worked there on weekends. We would load up the takeout containers and then we'd go on picnics. At 3:00 p.m., when we were finished our shifts, Jean Lumb, who co-owned Kwong Chow for twenty-three years, would take the family, and I went along, down to Kew Gardens and the beach. We would spend the rest of the afternoon lying around in the sun, just playing.

Jean was very extroverted and friendly, as well as being a foil to her husband, Doyle. She was Canadian-born but grew up in an environment more Chinese than where I was brought up, and became a spokesperson for the city's Chinese community – but not because she was looking for glory. She was a natural-born leader who spoke better English than many of the male leaders, who were shrewd enough to concede that territory to Jean. She became even more involved around World War II, when the Chinese were clamouring for citizenship. She recognized an opening when she saw one!

When the first Canadian Citizenship Act was introduced in 1947 and proclaimed in 1948, she was active with the Liberals and then later with Conservative PM John Diefenbaker – she was always a community activist.

I'm sure some of the men of the era resented that Jean's English was significantly better than theirs. There was no way they could outmanoeuvre her. But Jean was genuine. She wasn't manoeuvring to run for public office. Both the Liberals and the Conservatives asked several times, but that was never one of her ambitions. Jean was the first Chinese-Canadian director of Women's College Hospital and later a citizenship court judge. She was also the first Chinese-Canadian woman to be named to the Order of Canada, in 1976. Her daughter, Arlene Chan, has written extensively about the history of Canada's Chinese communities.

INDIVIDUAL LIVES

# WRITING HOME

### EDITED BY TATUM TAYLOR

IN 1872, WILLIAM STILL, the son of formerly enslaved parents who had fought for their own freedom, published a carefully documented account of his experience as an abolitionist. He titled it *The Underground Railroad: A Record of Facts, Authentic Narrative, Letters, Etc., Narrating the Hardships, Hair-breadth Escapes and Death Struggles of the Slaves in Their Efforts of Freedom, as Related by Themselves and Others, or Witnessed by the Author.*

Based in Philadelphia, Still had been a 'conductor' on the Underground Railroad, the secret network of abolitionists who had established safe routes for enslaved African Americans to escape to free states and to Canada. Prior to the Civil War, Still had helped hundreds of refugees reach freedom, and many of them kept in touch with him from their new homes, including those who reached Toronto and settled in St. John's Ward. At considerable personal risk, he collected and then published much of this correspondence in his book, which he hoped would 'testify for thousands and tens of thousands, as no other work can do.' Several of these letters are reproduced here, mostly unchanged from their original transcriptions.[1]

*Hidden in a dark, stifling space near the boiler on a steamship, thirty-two-year-old James Mercer and several other refugees had made the journey from slavery in Richmond, Virginia, to freedom in Toronto in*

*March 1854. Though he had left his wife and mother behind, he wrote to Still of his good spirits, three weeks after his arrival.*

TORONTO, MARCH 17th, 1854.

My dear friend Still: – I take this method of informing you that I am well, and when this comes to hand it may find you and your family enjoying good health. Sir, my particular for writing is that I wish to hear from you, and to hear all the news from down South. I wish to know if all things are working Right for the Rest of my Brotheran whom in bondage. I will also Say that I am very much please with Toronto, So also the friends that came over with. It is true that we have not been Employed as yet; but we are in hopes of be'en so in a few days. We happen here in good time jest about time the people in this country are going work. I am in good health and good Spirits, and feeles Rejoiced in the Lord for my liberty. I Received cople of paper from you to-day. I wish you see James Morris whom or Abram George the first and second on the Ship Penn., give my respects to them, and ask James if he will call at Henry W. Quarles on May street oppisit the Jews synagogue and call for Marena Mercer, give my love to her ask her of all the times about Richmond, tell her to Send me all the news. Tell Mr. Morris that there will be no danger in going to that place. You will also tell M. to make himself known to her as she may know who sent him. And I wish to get a letter from you.

JAMES M. MERCER.

*Isaac Forman, twenty-three years old, had also escaped from Richmond via steamship. He wrote to Still of his gratitude, but also of his despair at having left his enslaved wife; he had not been able to tell her of his intention to flee.*

TORONTO, MAY 7, 1854.

MR. W. STILL: – Dear Sir – I take this opportunity of writing you these few lines and hope when they reach you they will find you well. I would have written you before, but I was waiting to hear from my friend, Mr. Brown. I judge his business has been of importance as the occasion why he has not written before. Dear sir, nothing would have prevented me from writing, in a case of this kind, except death.

My soul is vexed, my troubles are inexpressible. I often feel as if I were willing to die. I must see my wife in short, if not, I will die. What would I not give no tongue can utter. Just to gaze on her sweet lips one moment I would be willing to die the next. I am determined to see her some time or other. The thought of being a slave again is miserable. I hope heaven will smile upon me again, before I am one again. I will leave Canada again shortly, but I don't name the place that I go, it may be in the bottom of the ocean. If I had known as much before I left, as I do now, I would never have left until I could have found means to have brought her with me. You have never suffered from being absent from a wife, as I have. I consider that to be nearly superior to death, and hope you will do all you can for me, and inquire from your friends if nothing can be done for me. Please write to me immediately on receipt of this, and say something that will cheer up my drooping spirits. You will oblige me by seeing Mr.

Black porcelain doll of likely German manufacture, similar to those produced by the Hertwig Company. It depicts a person with features representing African ancestry. Many other nineteenth-century manufacturers of Black dolls used moulds of Caucasian porcelain dolls and painted them black.

Brown and ask him if he would oblige me by going to Richmond and see my wife, and see what arrangements he could make with her, and I would be willing to pay all his expenses there and back. Please to see both Mr. Bagnel and Mr. Minkins, and ask them if they have seen my wife. I am determined to see her, if I die the next moment. I can say I was once happy, but never will be again, until I see her; because what is freedom to me, when I know that my wife is in slavery? Those persons that you shipped a few weeks ago, remained at St. Catherine, instead of coming over to Toronto. I sent you two letters last week and I hope you will please attend to them. The post-office is shut, so I enclose the money to pay the post, and please write me in haste.

I remain evermore your obedient servant,

I. FORMAN.

*Over the course of five years, Still received over a dozen letters from John Henry Hill, who had escaped from a slave auction in Richmond at the age of twenty-five. The following is Hill's third letter, written a month after his arrival in Toronto.*

TORONTO, November 1853.

So I ask you to send the fugitives to Canada. I don't know much of this Province but I beleaves that there is Rome enough for the colored and whites of the United States. We wants farmers mechanic men of all qualification &c., if they are not made we will make them, if we cannot make the old, we will make our children.

Now concerning the city toronto this city is Beautiful and Prosperous Levele city. Great many wooden codages more than what should be but I am in hopes there will be more of the Brick and Stonn. But I am not done about your Republicanism. Our masters have told us that there was no living in Canada for a Negro but if it may Please your gentlemanship to publish these facts that we are here able to earn our bread and money enough to make us comftable. But I say give me freedom, and the United States may have all her money and her Luxtures, yeas give Liberty or Death. I'm in America, but not under Such a Government that I cannot express myself, speak, think or write So as I am able, and if my master had allowed me to have an education I would make them American Slave-holders feel me, Yeas I would make them tremble when I spoke, and when I take my Pen in hand their knees smote together. My Dear Sir suppose I was an educated man. I could write you something worth reading, but you know we poor fugitives whom has just come over from the South are not able to write much on no subject whatever, but I hope by the aid of my God I will try to use my midnight lamp, untel I can have some influence upon the American Slavery. If some one would say to me, that they would give my wife bread untel I could be Educated I would stoop my trade this day and take up my books.

But a crisis is approaching when assential requisite to the American Slaveholders when blood Death or Liberty will be required at their hands. I think our people have depened too long and too much on false legislator let us now look for ourselves. It is true that England however the Englishman is our best friend but we as men ought not to depened upon her Remonstrace with the Americans because she loves her commercial trade as any Nations do. But I must say, while we look up and acknowledge the Power greatness and honor of old England, and believe that while we sit beneath the Silken folds of her flag of Perfect Liberty, we are secure, beyond the reach of the aggressions of the Blood hounds and free from the despotism that would wrap around our limbs by the damable Slaveholder. Yet we would not like spoiled childeren depend upon her, but upon ourselves and as one means of strengthening ourselves, we should agitate the emigration to Canada. I here send you a paragraph which I clipted from the weekly Glob. I hope you will publish so that Mr. Williamson may know that men are not chattel here but reather they are men and if he wants his chattle let him come here after it or his thing. I wants you to let the whole United States know we are satisfied here because I have seen more Pleasure since I came here then I saw in the U.S. the 24 years that I served my master. Come Poor distress men women and come to Canada where colored men are free. Oh how sweet the word do sound to me yeas when I contemplate of these things, my very flesh creaps my heart thrub when I think of my beloved friends whom I left in that cursid hole. Oh my God what can I do for them or shall I do for them. Lord help them. Suffer them to be no longer depressed beneath the Bruat Creation but may they be looked upon as men made of the Bone and Blood as the Anglo-Americans. May God in his mercy Give Liberty to all this world. I must close as it am late hour at night. I Remain your friend in the cause of Liberty and humanity,

JOHN H. HILL, a fugitive.

If you know any one who would give me an education write and let me know for I am in want of it very much.

Your with Respect,

J.H.H.

*Still also received letters from fellow abolitionists working with the Underground Railroad, such as this note from Agnes Willis, wife of a 'distinguished reverend' and 'Treasurer to the Ladies' Society to aid colored refugees.'*

TORONTO, 15th June, Monday morning, 1857.

TO MR. STILL, DEAR SIR: – I write you this letter for a respectable young man (his name is James Morris), he passed through your hands July of last year (1856), and has just had a letter from his wife, whom he left behind in Virginia, that she and her child are likely to be sold. He is very anxious about this and wishful that she could get away by some vessel or otherwise. His wife's name is Lucy Morris; the child's name is Lot Morris; the lady's name she lives with is a Mrs. Hine (I hope I spell her name right, Hine), at the corner of Duke street and Washington street, in Norfolk city, Virginia. She is hired out to this rich old widow lady. James Morris wishes me to write you – he has saved forty dollars, and will send it to you whenever it is required, to bring her on to Toronto, Canada West. It is in the bank ready upon call. Will you please, sir, direct your letter in reply to this, to a Mrs. Ringgold, Centre street, two doors from Elam street, Toronto, Canada West, as I will be out of town. I write this instead of Mr. Thomas Henning, who is just about leaving for England. Hoping you will reply soon, I remain, sir,

Respectfully yours,

AGNES WILLIS.

# CORRESPONDENT: CECELIA HOLMES

KAROLYN SMARDZ FROST

A SMALL INKWELL BEARS mute testimony to the importance of literacy in St. John's Ward. The conical, salt-glazed stoneware artifact, dating to the mid-nineteenth century, was retrieved from a pit dug in the backyard of the brick-fronted frame home on the northwest corner of Lot 7, on the east side of Centre Street just north of Osgoode Hall.

While many of the area's residents of this period, both Black and white, were unable to read and write, African Torontonians made education a major priority – witness the Sunday school that operated out of the British Methodist Episcopal Church on Sayer (Chestnut) Street in the same block. Both adults and children attended, as those who had escaped the South availed themselves of the chance to obtain the education they'd been denied while enslaved.

One of those residents who gained literacy upon achieving freedom was a young woman named Cecelia Jane Reynolds. She had fled her Louisville, Kentucky, owners when they visited Niagara Falls in 1846. During her stay, a waiter named Benjamin Pollard Holmes rescued Cecelia, brought her home to Toronto, and married her. There, she learned to write in order to ask the price of her beloved mother's freedom. Thus began a correspondence with her childhood playmate and erstwhile owner, Fanny Thruston Ballard, that would endure for more than twenty years and have no parallel in the annals of the Underground Railroad.

Lot 7 was a double-width property originally purchased in 1844 by Holmes and his first wife, Ann Eliza. He was most likely responsible for having the first house built on the site, probably by the noted local construction-company owner John M. Tinsley. Tinsley was a free Black carpenter born near Richmond, Virginia, where he had owned a successful building firm. He built many houses in St. John's Ward. Tinsley and his extended family had come to Toronto by way of Cincinnati in 1842, and lived in a pair of semi-detached houses on Agnes Street, near what is now the southwest corner of Dundas at Bay.[1]

Like Tinsley, Holmes was also a Virginian, the son of a county clerk by his enslaved housekeeper, Katie Hoomes, or Holmes. Benjamin had been brought up and educated in his father's home at King and Queen Court House, a town near Richmond, Virginia. When his father's health failed, Benjamin was sent to live at Melrose, a nearby plantation owned by his white half-sister Elizabeth and her husband, Alexander

Stoneware inkwell.

Fleet. A teenager when Nat Turner's slave revolt[2] broke out in August 1831, Benjamin was then sent off to Richmond, Virginia, likely to protect him from the violent retribution meted out in its wake, since young, literate African Americans were considered particularly suspect. He was hired out to tobacco merchant James A. Fisher Jr., in whose household Benjamin worked as a domestic servant pending his own father's death, at which point he had been promised his freedom.

While living in the Fisher home in Richmond, Benjamin became a Methodist Church convert and married Ann Eliza, an enslaved woman who was nursemaid to the Fisher children.[3] The couple had a little boy, Ben Alexander Holmes. But Benjamin burned with the desire to liberate himself and his family. Approaching a missionary from the African Colonization Society, he managed to convince the Fleets and the Fishers to issue freedom papers for his little family, on the condition that they join the free African American colonists in Liberia, on the African coast.

On August 4, 1840, the Holmeses set sail from Norfolk Harbor aboard the *Saluda,* bound for Liberia. But once out at sea, the ship sprang a leak and put into the Philadelphia harbour for repairs. There, abolitionists boarded the boat and convinced the family to escape to Canada instead. Abandoning their voyage to Liberia would mean their freedom papers were worthless, yet Benjamin and Ann Eliza, along with their toddler son, took the opportunity to travel northward in secret. Upon reaching Toronto, they were welcomed by missionary Hiram Wilson, a U.S.-born white minister educated at Oberlin College, Ohio, who had been sent to Canada to assist freedom-seekers. On August 28, 1840, Reverend Wilson wrote a long letter to a U.S. antislavery newspaper, the *Emancipator,* describing the Holmes family's perilous flight to freedom.[4]

Benjamin and Ann Eliza initially lived in rented rooms on Richmond Street, and Benjamin used his experience in household service to gain employment as a steamboat waiter. He sailed aboard the *Transit,* the *Chief Justice Robinson,* and the *City of Toronto.* Carrying both passengers and cargo, such vessels were luxuriously appointed and made regular circuits of Lake Ontario. In the winter, Benjamin worked in restaurants and hotel dining rooms, saving his tips so he and Ann Eliza could buy a home.

KAROLYN SMARDZ FROST

Waiting tables on the steamers was both lucrative and an excellent opportunity to assist other freedom-seekers on their way to Canada. Benjamin worked for Toronto-based Capt. Thomas Dick, later owner of the Queen's Hotel, where the Royal York would one day be built, and also Capt. Hugh Richardson, who would be appointed the city's first harbour master. Both captains were notably sympathetic to the cause of the fugitive slave. With their clandestine support, Benjamin became a conductor on the Underground Railroad networks operating between the U.S. and the Canadian Great Lakes ports.[5]

In 1841, Ann Eliza gave birth to another son, James Thomas Holmes. Three years later, she and Benjamin purchased Lot 7, on the east side of Centre Street, and set about building a two-and-a-half-storey frame house with a brick front. Their home was just north of Osgoode Hall, in an area where many of the city's most recently arrived African American immigrant families, both formerly enslaved and free, had settled. This was a vibrant neighbourhood with shops and businesses, many of them African Canadian-owned, as well as a school at the corner of Albert and Terauley (Bay) Streets, a few blocks to the east.

The British Wesleyan Methodist Church, where Benjamin would have been welcomed as a talented 'exhorter,' or lay reader, was also within easy walking distance. It was just south of Queen Street near the corner of Richmond and York Streets (the location is currently part of the parking-entrance area of the Sheraton Hotel). There, the Holmeses rubbed shoulders with leaders of the city's African Canadian community, including the up-and-coming real estate magnate Wilson Ruffin Abbott, born free in Richmond, Virginia, and his wife, Ellen Toyer, a native of Baltimore.[6]

Sadly, Ann Eliza contracted tuberculosis and died on April 16, 1845, at age twenty-eight, leaving behind Benjamin and their sons, who were just five and three. About a year after her death, Benjamin helped engineer the rescue of Cecelia Jane Reynolds. Purchased as a baby by the wealthy Louisville-based Thruston family, Cecelia had grown up in their household. Committed to reaching free soil, she arranged with Underground Railroad operators to escape during an upcoming trip to Niagara Falls. The Thrustons planned to holiday at the famed Cataract

House hotel, on the American side of the Falls. Holmes stayed there in the weeks before Cecelia's arrival, arranging with the hotel's all-Black wait staff to spirit Cecelia across the river to Canada. She was just fifteen when Benjamin brought her to Toronto in the summer of 1846. By November of that same year, they married at St. James Cathedral.

Cecelia had learned to read as a lady's maid for the Thrustons' daughter, Fanny. But as soon as she settled down in her new home on Centre Street, she also learned to write. Cecelia sent a letter to Fanny Thruston Ballard, in Louisville, to ask the price of her mother's and brother's freedom. She and Fanny would correspond for another two decades, their surviving letters bearing witness to an affectionate but unequal relationship built on the stark, cold cruelty of slavery.

Benjamin and Cecelia had many adventures trying to raise the $600 price set on Mary Reynolds's head. Benjamin even travelled across the world to the Australian gold fields, but all their efforts failed. In 1856, he and Cecelia built a second house on their land, at 31 Centre. The new dwelling was intended as a rental property and a legacy for Benjamin's two sons. However, Benjamin died just three years later, and Cecelia promptly rented out her home and moved to Rochester, New York. Back in the U.S., Cecelia lived an eventful life, first as an associate of African American abolitionist Frederick Douglass in Rochester, and later, following her second husband, William Henry Larrison, to the battlefields of the Civil War. In her later years, Cecelia finally returned to Louisville to rejoin her mother, now liberated as a result of the Thirteenth Amendment to the American Constitution that freed nearly four million enslaved African Americans. Impoverished in her later life, Cecelia in 1889 sold her Toronto property to the man who had previously served as her rental agent, Francis Griffin Simpson.[7]

Twice widowed, Cecelia died in Louisville in June 1909. As an instrument of correspondence, the inkwell discovered in the privy of her old Toronto home in the fall of 2015 can be seen to symbolize the intense desire expressed by so many residents of St. John's Ward to both gain an education and reunite the beloved families they had been forced to abandon in their own desperate quests for freedom.

Drone imagery (2015) of the foundations of the house occupied by Benjamin and Cecelia Holmes, built in the early 1840s. Modern upgrades to the basement included a cement floor and coal bin.

# MORE THAN A SHOEMAKER: FRANCIS GRIFFIN SIMPSON

KAROLYN SMARDZ FROST

O NE INTRIGUING ARCHAEOLOGICAL discovery at the Armoury Street Dig was a cache of scrap and damaged leather, evidently the product of shoe repair. This had been buried in the backyard of 33 Centre Street, on the northwest corner of Lot 7 on the east side. Painstaking research has dated these extraordinarily well-preserved leather artifacts to the 1890s, when both Lot 7 houses (by then renumbered as 7 and 11 Centre) were the property of African Canadian shoemaker Francis Griffin Simpson and his wife, the former Elizabeth Burke.

Both a skilled artisan and a well-known African Canadian community spokesperson, Simpson had been born free at Manorton, in upstate New York, about eighty kilometres from Albany, and arrived in Toronto in 1854, where he trained as a shoemaker. He was an articulate, well-educated man. Over the course of a long life, Simpson served as an implacable opponent of slavery and racial discrimination, and an impassioned advocate of both political and economic self-determination on behalf of African Torontonians.

The Simpsons' first recorded home in Toronto was on Park Lane, which ran parallel to the east side of the modern University Avenue, extending north from the Osgoode Hall grounds. In 1859, Francis and Elizabeth had a son they named Francis (Frank) Simpson Jr. By 1861, the family was living at 26 Elizabeth Street, just below Albert, and Simpson was listed in the Canadian census for that year as a 'Boot & Shoemaker.'[1]

Simpson was devoted to community service, assisting formerly enslaved African Americans in finding employment in the city. He worked closely with John M. Tinsley, Toronto's most successful African Canadian construction company owner, to provide incoming freedom-seekers with their first Canadian jobs. Literate and politically engaged, Simpson also was involved in a number of organizations serving Black Toronto. For instance, on October 10, 1854, he served as an agent for the purchase of tickets to the upcoming Grand United Order of Odd Fellows Soiree, and was later listed as the first vice-president of the Moral and Mental Improvement Society (African) in *Caverhill's Toronto City Directory for 1859.*[2]

Frank Simpson, son of Francis G. Simpson, with wife Laura and their children.

Through his activism in causes important to Black Torontonians, Simpson was likely already acquainted with many of his St. John's Ward neighbours, including Benjamin Pollard Holmes and his wife, Cecelia (see 'Correspondent: Cecelia Holmes,' pages 202–207). The couple owned all of Lot 7 on the east side of Centre Street, and resided at number 33.

Francis Griffin Simpson's name appeared alongside those of other prominent and politically engaged African Canadians of the time. Indeed, through marriage, Simpson was connected to one of the most noted such families in the province. In 1862, his older brother, Rev. Henry Livingston Simpson, had married Emeline Shadd. She was an award-winning graduate of the Toronto Normal School (teachers college) and sister of Mary Ann Shadd Cary, the outspoken abolitionist lecturer and publisher of the *Provincial Freeman* newspaper.[3]

On September 5, 1863, Simpson had the opportunity to narrate his own life story, including his personal observations regarding Canadian race relations, in a wide-ranging interview conducted by Samuel Gridley Howe of the American Freedmen's Inquiry Commission.[4] President Abraham Lincoln had recruited Howe and two other representatives to investigate the condition of the refugees from U.S. slavery resident in what is now Ontario. Lincoln wanted to learn how formerly enslaved African Americans were faring in Canada, with a view to planning how best to assist the South's millions of enslaved men, women, and children in the aftermath of anticipated Union victory. (For an edited version of the interview, see pages 213–218.)

Simpson was well positioned to offer insights. In the years leading up to the American Civil War, he had organized meetings of Black voters and was instrumental in persuading much of the community to support the election of *Globe* publisher George Brown, a staunch abolitionist and future Father of Confederation. In his later life, Simpson became involved in union activities. Most unusually, given the depth of racial prejudice in late-nineteenth-century Toronto, he served in 1878 as an officer on the committee of the almost entirely white-dominated Liberal Working Men.[5]

In addition to his participation in such activities, Simpson was also energetic in resisting discrimination and racial prejudice. He served as recording secretary for at least one important meeting protesting the mistreatment of Toronto's first African Canadian postman, Albert Jackson, who for a time in 1882 was prevented from delivering the mail.[6]

For all his activism, connections, and political commitment, Simpson still had to earn a living. The leather artifacts discovered in

Below: Iron shoe lasts, forms for moulding and repairing shoes. These would have been turned upside-down and mounted on a long shaft that extended from a cobbler's work bench. Opposite: Shoe-making and repair debris.

the pit behind 33 Centre demonstrate his skill as a craftsperson. Indeed, it was his business acumen as a shoemaker that provided him with the wherewithal needed to acquire several pieces of Toronto real estate.

In the 1870s, Simpson began accumulating property in St. John's Ward. Benjamin Pollard Holmes had died in 1859 and the widowed Cecelia moved to Rochester, where she remarried. Cecelia never returned to live in Toronto, but depended on the rental income from her home at 33 Centre for many years. Her stepsons, who had inherited 31 Centre, next door, also used their Toronto house as an income property.

Simpson first leased 31 Centre from Cecelia's stepsons, and eventually purchased the property outright. According to the *Globe* of December 4, 1876, he immediately ordered a new home constructed there. It was a 'neat brick-fronted cottage; side and rear walls roughcast,' erected by carpenter and builder Daniel Lewis.[7] Simpson also acted as Cecelia's rental agent for the house next door (number 31), paying her property taxes and maintaining the house until 1889, when he was able to buy the rest of Lot 7, the neighbouring house included, from the aging woman.

Frank A. Simpson, the son of Francis G. and Elizabeth Simpson, waited tables in both Niagara Falls and Toronto. He and his wife, Laura, resided briefly in the home once occupied by Cecelia and Benjamin Holmes. Indeed, it may have been during his time at the

house that his father buried a cache of scrap leather and worn and damaged shoe parts in the backyard.[8] After his son Frank moved to new accommodations, Simpson continued renting out Cecelia's old home to a series of tenants.

One of Simpson's last recorded acts was to support Cecelia in acquiring access to her second husband's Union Army pension. He signed an affidavit on October 21, 1896, attesting to his friendship with Cecelia and her first husband, Benjamin, and that he died before she remarried.[9] On October 11, 1899, Cecelia finally began receiving the monthly twelve-dollar stipend due her as the widow of her second husband, William, who was a Union Army veteran injured in service to his country.

Simpson died the following March. His obituary, which appeared in the *Globe* on March 19, 1900, read, in part,

> An Old Resident Dead: Mr. Francis Griffin Simpson, aged 68 years, died at the residence of his son, 155 Richmond Street West, on Saturday morning. Mr. Simpson was taken suddenly ill about a week ago with a severe cold, which developed into pneumonia. He was originally from Schenectady, N.Y. but had been a resident of this city for over 45 years. He was a member of the York Pioneers and took a prominent part in the anti-slavery movement. In politics, Mr. Simpson was a lifelong Liberal. He is survived by a wife and one son, Mr. Frank Simpson of the Rossin House [hotel]. The funeral will take place this afternoon at 2:30 o'clock to Mount Pleasant Cemetery.

The cache of shoemaking and shoe-repair debris discovered in the backyard of No. 33 Centre Street during the 2015 excavation offers clues about the life of a remarkable man, an African American immigrant who had made Toronto his home in 1854, and lived to see, in part at least, the outcome of his twin struggles: battling slavery and promoting African Canadian political engagement. In 1894, a few years before Simpson's death, voters elected William Peyton Hubbard (1842–1935), the son of a Virginia-born couple, to serve on Toronto council, paving the way for his appointment as Toronto's first – and also our city's last – acting mayor of African descent.[10]

KAROLYN SMARDZ FROST

# FRANCIS SIMPSON ON BEING BLACK IN 1860S TORONTO

EDITED BY JOHN LORINC

*On September 5, 1863, a Boston physician and social activist named Samuel Gridley Howe arrived in Toronto with an ambitious series of interviews on his agenda for the day. A gaunt man with a thick beard and deep-set eyes, Howe was travelling through Canada West (Ontario) on a fact-finding mission, investigating the way free Black Canadians lived, worked, learned, and worshipped.*

Samuel Gridley Howe.

*A year earlier, Edwin Stanton, President Abraham Lincoln's secretary of war, had appointed Howe to the American Freedmen's Inquiry Commission (AFIC), which had a mandate to scope out what freedom would look like for millions of African Americans. By the time Howe arrived in Toronto, Lincoln had signed the Emancipation Proclamation (on January 1, 1863), and it seemed likely that the Unionist forces would prevail in the bloody Civil War.*

*On his journey, Howe had talked to both whites and Blacks. In Toronto, he sought out George Brown, the* Globe's *publisher and an outspoken abolitionist. Later in the day, Howe found himself conversing with Francis G. Simpson, a thirty-three-year-old shoemaker originally from New York State living in a little cottage on Elizabeth Street, a few steps from where the Nathan Phillips Square snack bar now stands.*

*It's not clear how Howe found Simpson; according to Toronto lawyer Matthew Furrow, who did his graduate research on the AFIC, Howe typically stopped in at local Black churches, like the British Methodist Episcopal on Chestnut Street, to identify community leaders. But five years earlier, Simpson, who had worked to settle fugitive slaves, met Brown while the newspaper publisher was rallying support among Toronto Blacks during his bid to win a seat in the provincial legislature. It's possible the introduction came from Brown.*

*In any event, Simpson offered Howe a detailed account of life in Toronto: the bracing weather, the economic difficulties, the successes of some Black businessmen, and the Black community's self-help societies. The churches and courts were tolerant, he said, yet the people could still be bigoted. 'This country is not so good a country to make money and get along in as the States,' Simpson observed. But, he added, '[o]ur children suffer not the slightest inconvenience in regard to their color.'*

*When the AFIC's members – there were two others besides Howe, who travelled to Haiti and through the non-slave states of the West – compiled their findings into a report, they submitted it to Stanton and the U.S. Senate; Lincoln drew on the conclusions to fashion a postwar policy on the transition from slavery. Several quotes from Simpson are in the final document.*

*What follows is an edited version of Simpson's interview with Howe.*

TESTIMONY OF F. G. SIMPSON (SHOEMAKER), SEPT. 5, 1863.[1]
I have been here about eight years. I was born in New York State. I can't say that I have found this a better country than New York State. It answered my purpose when I came here, but of course I should prefer the United States.

This country is not so good a country to make money and get along in as the States. It is a newer country, and the people are not so go-ahead as the Yankees are. They go ahead and spend their money for the improvement of the country, whereas the Canadians keep their money for the benefit of themselves. That makes the difference. I learned my trade in this city. Though the colored people may manage to eke out a scanty living, they don't do much more, many of them. Some few are doing pretty well. I think all those who came here from the free States, or from the Slave States, who were free, came because of the prejudices under which they labored. I know persons living here who came from Philadelphia, Richmond, Charleston, and Cincinnati, who were free; and they came for the purpose of bettering their social condition...

I must say, that leaving the law out of the question, I find that prejudice here is equally strong as on the other side. The law is the only thing that sustains us in this country. There is not the slightest prejudice here to keep us out of the churches. We are treated with the utmost respect in the best churches here. The highest seat in the synagogue is not too good for us. The people here don't want the colored people to have the separate churches. In fact, they would be far better off if they had no [Black] churches. I am certain they would. It would help to allay and break down the prejudice against color...

Our children suffer not the slightest inconvenience in regard to their color. There are very few here so poor that they cannot find books for their children. I belong to a society for furnishing poor children with books for the common schools, and we have had but one or two applications. The schools are pretty well attended by colored children. We undertake to clothe children here and send them to school, but there are very few that require it...

The climate is rather hard upon the people, generally. The kind of labor they get is far different from what they get in the States, and hence they are exposed a great deal, and the climate may work more strongly upon their constitutions. Perhaps they may not be so warmly clothed as they should be to face the inclemency of the season... But I notice that many of them die of decline or consumption here. I don't think there are any diseases peculiar to colored children...

Since the war, a great many colored people have come here. The churches take care of what poor belong to them. But in jail, there are no poor of any consequence. I don't see them going about begging, & I don't think you will find one in the poor house...

[T]he poor house... is called a 'house of industry,' and those who are not able to work much are sent there. There are very few beggars here, white or colored. I never was in a place of its size where there were so few. Our people, as a general thing, are self-supporting. There are quite a number that have acquired property, but I think the greater number of these brought some little nucleus with them when they came here... A good many go to the other side to wait and cook & then come back to spend the money they have earned. I tell them they might as well stay there, if they are obliged to go there to earn their money. If I went over there as they do, I would not come back.

I have seen the colored people from Hamilton to Kingston, and I find them all just about alike, though I must say, that I found more people in Kingston who were in rather poor circumstances than in any other places. After you leave Kingston, you find very few East. You find quite a number in Port Hope, Coburg and Bellville [sic].

There are perhaps twenty or thirty families in each of those places, and they are all very prosperous – as a general thing, more so than they are in these large cities, because where they are so few, the competition is not so great in the kinds of work they get to do, and the people give them a better chance...

We have shoemakers, carpenters, blacksmiths and tobacco manufacturers. There are three benevolent societies among the colored people – one male society, and two female societies. Then there is one literary and social society. There are men here who have been here between thirty and forty years... I am almost inclined to doubt whether even those who have lived here a great many years have feelings of loyalty to the government. Many of them might not desire to leave their property, but that there is anything like a firm satisfaction on the part of those who were born on the other side, I very much question.

I think the early local attachment would carry them back. Some year & a half or two years ago, there was an excitement raised about emigration to [Haiti]; and some of our oldest inhabitants...went to [Haiti]. It was an unfortunate experiment, and I was very much opposed to it... [M]y little influence was unable to prevail, but I persuaded some of my friends to wait awhile, and they are very glad now that they did. Some of the emigrants have come back, utterly broken down, and they will never recover as long as they live. My opinion is, that if the people felt they would be as secure in the United States as here, the major part would move over to the States; many of those who have property here would not, perhaps.

I was talking to a gentleman some months ago about countries, and he intimated to me that we had no disturbances here under the Queen. I said that they would soon be over their difficulties at home.

He said, 'Home! Where is your home? I thought this was your home.'

'Oh, no,' I said, 'this is not my home.'

'Why,' said he, 'I thought you were a British subject.'

'So I am a British subject,' said I. 'I had to become a British subject so as to be able to enjoy all the rights and privileges the country afforded; but of course,' said I, 'the Queen would not give much for her adopted subjects...because they could not make good subjects, if they had no love for home. We are exiles, not from justice, but oppression, and of course, we are like the Hungarians, and all the other exiles; when home becomes tranquil & secure, of course we must return to our homes.'

That is my feeling; and I suppose, if I had not been young & foolish, and not willing to submit to the many little inconveniences and disagreeable things that I met with in [New] York State, I should have [stayed] there. And if I had had the knowledge I have now, I should not have moved here. The fact is, I could not stand it. The older I grew, the harder it became to bear.

When I came here, I swallowed all those little things, because I had redress. I don't think the removal of the major part of the colored people of Canada to the United States would be at all injurious to the United States, because I feel certain there is not a more industrious class than the black, in Canada. And they have to be so, because this country calls for great exertions.

The climate is invigorating, and we are in the midst of an industrious people, and all these things make a difference. I can assure you that the difficulties in the way of laying up money here are very great. There is no mistake about it; because, in the first place, you make very little, and the long winters take every thing you can make to feed, warm & clothe yourself.

[T]here are thirty-one families that I can count over in my mind, that have purchased houses for themselves since I came here... I do not count Mr. Tinsley or Mr. Abbott, who had something when they came here. I happen to be familiar with these parties, because I have been here quite a long time, and I was connected with the Anti-Slavery Society...and it brought me into contact...with the fugitives who came over during the great influx in 1854.

I have kept pretty good watch of [sic] them. A gentleman came to me a little while ago and said,

'How do you do, Mr. Simpson?'

'Well,' said I, 'I am pretty well, how do you do?'

'I am well, thank you,' said he.

'But you have the advantage of me,' I said. 'I don't know you.'

'You don't know me? – you don't know Butler?' said he.

Said I – 'Yes, Sir, I know a great many Butlers, but I don't know you.'

Then he went on to tell me that he was a poor fugitive in 1853, and came to me in the office, and I assisted him, and although he had never seen me since, the moment he saw me, he knew me. He said I told him the best thing he could do was to go away into the country and see what he could do; that he did so, 'and now,' said he, 'I have got a little hotel and boarding-house in Hamilton, that I own myself, and my property amounts to some $1500.'

That was six years ago. He is a very skilful, sharp man, and has accumulated that, and I call it a very good beginning. Alfred Butler has been here eight years... He is a very energetic man; anything he undertakes he will go through with...

I have often wondered how in the world he could get customers, for Nature has unfortunately made him rather worse-looking than others. But there is something about him that engages the attention...

I have had a misfortune befall me in this city, and that was the loss of a number of books I had, and among them were the memoranda of conversations I had with fugitives or persons from the other side. I would not have lost that book for any money, because it was just verbatim what they had told me. But...I might say, just from the talk I had with them, that all those who came from the South here were men of superior mind – there is no question about that – energetic, bold men. The very fact of their coming here implies that...

EDITED BY JOHN LORINC

# THE ARRESTING CASE OF ANNIE WHALEN
CRAIG HERON

THE MAGISTRATE SWEPT into the courtroom, mounted the dais, and took his seat at the head of Toronto's Police Court. In his typically brusque fashion, Col. George T. Denison began to dispense with the drunks, vagrants, gamblers, thieves, and sundry other lawbreakers who appeared in the prisoner's dock opposite him. The next case involved the sale of liquor without a licence, and he was ready to see Maria or Jessie or Hattie or any of the many women who so often appeared to answer to this charge. This time, he raised an eyebrow and welcomed a familiar face. Annie Whalen was back in court.

It was not a long walk to the courthouse from Centre Avenue, where Annie lived. She must have been highly conscious of the law in her neighbourhood, with Osgoode Hall only two blocks south and the new armouries just a few doors away. But she made a living skirting the law by selling alcohol illegally to her neighbours in The Ward.

Alcohol bottles and a shot glass recovered from a privy behind bootlegger Annie Whalen's house at 15 Centre Avenue.

Back before 1876, the law had been easier on such activity. Tavern licences were cheap, and enforcement was lax. Many people in working-class neighbourhoods could expect to make a little extra income quietly by selling a bottle or two to a small number of customers they knew. Women might turn to this work, just as they might grow a few vegetables, raise a pig, take in laundry, or make space for a boarder. Some widows made bootlegging their major source of income.

Many middle-class Canadians were not happy with such easy marketing of alcohol. An aggressive temperance movement had reared up in the 1870s to challenge the availability of booze in Toronto, and Ontario's new liquor law of 1876 brought a much stricter regulatory regime. A provincially appointed liquor board for Toronto replaced the often-corrupt local officials, hiked up licence fees, and drastically cut the number of legal drinking establishments. In 1874, Toronto had 309 taverns and 184 licenced private liquor shops. In 1890, there were only 150 taverns and fifty private liquor shops. By 1915, on the eve of provincial prohibition, just 109 taverns and fifty shops remained. Toronto's population had, of course, increased massively over those years – jumping from about 180,000 in 1890 to almost half a million by World War I. Licensing officials were also pushing these watering holes out of residential neighbourhoods and concentrating them in downtown business districts, and they were required to close much earlier.

All these changes squeezed out people who wanted to sell alcohol, but also gave them opportunities. They could build a clientele among thirsty drinkers who no longer had a local pub to frequent or a nearby store where they could pick up a bottle. Many former licence-holders chose to continue selling illegally, and other enterprising workers took up bootlegging as an economic strategy in difficult financial circumstances. According to an 1877 Toronto police report,

[S]ome only attempt to do a Saturday night and Sunday trade, when the licensed places are closed up. The greater number of them do only a very small business, and sell only to those who they are well acquainted with. Many of these formerly did a considerable business openly. Some we have brought before the Police Court and fined are said to have followed the

business without license for 15 years. These remarks apply mostly to small shops in back streets.

15–17 Centre Ave., February 26, 1937. Annie Whalen's home is at right.

It is difficult to know exactly when Annie Whalen took to selling booze out of her house (above). She was born in Ireland in February 1848, and arrived in Canada twelve years later. Sometime around 1870, she married John Whalen, an Irish-Canadian who had learned the trade of iron moulding, and in the 1870s, they lived on Queen Street West, just beyond University Avenue. But in 1886 they moved into the house that Annie would inhabit for the next thirty-five years – 37 Centre Street (changed to 15 Centre Avenue after new armouries cut off the bottom of the street in 1893). It was a small, two-storey, semi-detached wood-frame structure. A driveway cut through the first floor into a cluttered backyard, where another small house stood with its own tenants. Like the great majority of Toronto workers, the Whalens were renters. When the census takers passed through in 1891, they found a twenty-year-old son, George, living with John and Annie. He worked as a steam fitter and plumber. Francis Simpson lived two doors south.

A moulder like John Whalen was a skilled worker who could make a good living, but he could also face lengthy bouts of seasonal unemployment. The heavy work in smoky foundries probably took a toll on his health, and men in the trade were also notoriously heavy drinkers. For all these reasons, John's wages may have been inadequate to support the family. Maybe Annie had begun to sell liquor to make some extra money before John died late in 1891, at age forty-seven, though she did not appear in the Police Court's Registry of Prisoners that year. Certainly, as Catholics, the Whalens would have had none of the devout Protestants' qualms about booze.

There is a common narrative of the poor, isolated widow who struggled to survive after her husband's death, yet Annie was not left alone. Their son, George, continued to live with her for the next decade, presumably practising the plumbing trade and at some point bringing a wife and at least one child into the household. It seems more likely that bootlegging was a family business, perhaps before John died but certainly afterward. In fact, in December 1891, it was George whom the police dragged into court on the charge of selling alcohol without a licence; he came away with a fifty-dollar fine (probably close to a month's wages). George, in fact, was caught in a major crackdown on bootleggers that saw a couple of dozen men and women in court that winter. Perhaps operating more cautiously, the Whalens avoided any more charges until October 26, 1892, when Annie and Police Magistrate Denison probably first got acquainted. Both she and George had to appear in court that day.

Being home most of the time, Annie likely ran the bootlegging operation on a daily basis, while John may have maintained the contacts with local brewers and distillers. They had a three-foot cellar under their parlour with a concealed trap door that was controlled by a secret lever in the floor across the room. A police raid in 1894 that finally exposed this contrivance found twenty-nine bottles of beer in a dark corner of the cellar. This was hardly a large stash and indicated the small scale of Annie's business. A few stray press comments suggest that she could be a feisty presence in her neighbourhood. She likely not only sold to her clientele, but allowed them to hang out in the parlour to enjoy a drink. The empties were no doubt dumped in the backyard, where many would be discovered during an archaeological excavation over a century later.

Starting in the winter of 1892–93, the police kept a close eye on Annie and George. Annie landed in court again in December 1892, in January and May 1893, twice in each of April and July 1894, in November 1894, four times in January 1895, and on and on. She must have put on convincing performances in the courtroom, since on all but two of those occasions (when she got fifty-dollar fines), the magistrate let her go. Denison was known for his quick intuitive judgments of the accused, yet once chose to believe Annie's dubious claim that she had not sold a woman two bottles but had given them as a present on Christmas Eve. George, however, had six charges by early 1895, and always received a stiff fine.

The family business faced a crisis in 1900, when George died. His widow, Frances, and their child continued to live with Annie for about four more years, until Frances either left the city or remarried. Annie was left with one co-resident, presumably a boarder. She nonetheless managed to carry on the bootlegging business on her own, still ending up repeatedly in court for selling illegally. Her street was now filled with Jewish families, who were not known as heavy drinkers, yet did not follow the teetotalling line of Protestant evangelicals. Her profits must have been substantial, since she was able to buy her house around 1906.

In 1916, Premier William Hearst's Conservative government introduced complete prohibition. Annie's bootleg business might have taken on new life. Certainly, she had to make a loud public denial in 1917 that she had supplied an elderly man with the booze that had killed him. But in 1920, at age seventy-two, she vanished from the city directory and assessment rolls – most likely she had died. The next year her old nemesis, Police Magistrate Denison, finally retired in failing health after more than four decades on the bench; he would die in 1925. His career has merited many biographical treatments, but we've heard far less about resourceful women like Annie Whalen, whose valuable, illicit service to her working-class neighbours brought her repeatedly into his courtroom.

Bootleggers deserve their place in history, too.

# A DRUGGIST FOR CHINATOWN: TOM LOCK

ARLENE CHAN

A T HIS STOREFRONT on Dundas Street, Tom Lock filled prescriptions and stocked his shelves with pharmaceuticals, personal care items, gift packages, and birthday cards. The enticing aroma of roasting peanuts by the cashier made them hard to resist. Folks lingered, waiting for medications, wandering the aisles, and chatting with Tom. In the 1950s and 1960s, his pharmacy was a Chinatown landmark.

Among the many household objects found in the nearby Armoury Street Dig, the archaeological team retrieved dozens of the day-to-day objects that would have been sold by druggists: medications, toothbrushes, syringes. While the excavated artifacts would have predated Lock's business, they illustrate that residents of this working-class, immigrant neighbourhood were consumers of the same products that would have been found in any household.

As Toronto's first pharmacist of Chinese descent, George Thomas (Tom) Lock must have had a prescription for an extraordinary life. Perhaps he was destined to be one-of-a-kind with the auspicious arrival of his mother to Toronto in 1909, seven years before his birth. At twenty years old, she appeared on the *Toronto Daily Star*'s front page with the headline 'Chinese Woman Comes to Toronto' – one of the first to settle in the city.

This was the era of the bachelor society, when the majority of the 1,099 Chinese in Toronto were men, many of them married but separated from their wives and children. The impacts of Canada's head taxes (1885–1923) and exclusionary legislation (1923–1947) were severe, deliberately deterring, then halting, Chinese immigration and preventing family life. The Locks were one of only thirteen Chinese families in the Chinatown area.

The youngest of four children, Lock had a unique childhood: hanging out at the YMCA on College Street, playing badminton at the Bay Street Mission on Elm Street, shooting hoops at the Chinese Young Men's Christian Institute on University Avenue, and joining the all-Chinese 128th Boy Scout Troop. Having Jewish friends who, like him, were often bullied and pushed around as outsiders, expanded his horizons. He learned Yiddish, carried out his friends' household duties during their Sabbath, and gained street smarts.

The Lock children had their share of responsibilities, especially after the untimely death of their father during the Depression years. Working at the family laundry honed Lock's expertise in sewing, cleaning, ironing, and mending cuffs and collars. Cooking was another chore, and his mother regularly sent him to Elizabeth Street to buy a live chicken. There were two Jewish poultry stores, owned by the competing Wasserman brothers. Lock was often caught in the middle for a sale, a brother yanking on each arm. These were not the only times he was pulled in two directions.

When Canada joined Britain and France in the war against Germany, the Chinese across Canada were strongly divided. Should they volunteer to fight for a country that treated them so poorly? On the other hand, the war opened a door for them to prove their patriotism and ultimately gain the right to vote. Lock's older brother Earl and his cousin and kung fu master Jimmy Lore were among the many to be turned away by recruiters who deemed them unsuitable because of their ethnicity. Lock's recruiter had a different opinion, and he enlisted without incident.

A turning point for the Chinese in Canada was the bombing of Pearl Harbour and Canada's declaration of war against Japan. Canada and

China were now allies against a common enemy. In 1944, conscription was expanded to include Chinese Canadians, who became regarded as assets in the Pacific war arena, where they could easily blend in behind enemy lines.

Lock went above and beyond the call of duty. Once again he volunteered, this time for a covert mission to sabotage, infiltrate, and spy behind enemy lines. Operation Oblivion was the code name, with a casualty rate projected at 80 per cent. Toughened on the streets during his youth, he was well-positioned for this elite guerrilla unit of Chinese Canadians. Intensive training, with a suicide capsule among the supplies, included jungle survival, demolition with explosives, parachute landing, and medic assistance.

Lock returned home safely after the war to the welcoming arms of his family at Union Station; however, he had one more battle to win. During his commando training in Australia, Lock had met and married Joan Lim On. They were now a stateless couple. Lock couldn't settle in Australia because of its White Australia policy, and his wife was not allowed into Canada due to the Chinese Immigration Act. A special Order in Council eventually granted her entry as a war bride, one of a handful of Chinese immigrants who entered Canada during the twenty-four years of exclu-

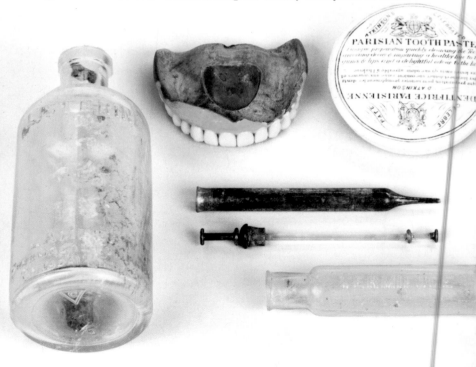

sion. Armed with impressive credentials and reference letters from two Nobel laureates, Dr. Frank Macfarlane Burnet and Toronto's Dr. Charles Best, a co-discoverer of insulin, she was immediately hired as a microbiologist at the Hospital for Sick Children.

With financial aid from the Veterans Rehabilitation Act, Lock enrolled at the University of Toronto, where he and his friend Sam Chin were the first Chinese graduates from the School of Pharmacy. The life-and-death precision of his wartime training had laid the groundwork for his chosen profession. Tom Lock Drug Store opened in 1954 at 136 Dundas Street West in the heart of Chinatown. Lock became Toronto's first pharmacist of Chinese descent, and proprietor of the first Chinese-owned pharmacy in Canada east of the Rockies.

He was even able to somewhat realize his pre-war aspirations of becoming an interior decorator or fashion designer with the store's startling colours of yellow, coral, and turquoise, rather than the typical black-and-white. What also distinguished Lock's drugstore was signage in English and Chinese, the small inventory of Chinese goods such as abacuses, tea, and herbal remedies, and services surpassing those of other pharmacies. Bachelor-society men, aging and still alone, relied on his bilingual fluency for filling out government forms, translating letters and doctors' instructions, and getting advice for aches and pains. Lock was the kind of person to lend a hand and serve his community.

Photo developing was a popular service, one that Lock particularly enjoyed providing in-house – he had a keen interest in photography. The customers were themselves a snapshot of the neighbourhood in the 1950s and 1960s: old-timers and new immigrants, travellers arriving at the Bay Street bus terminal, lesbians and gays who frequented the nearby Continental and Ford hotels, and prostitutes.

Across the street at the Kwang Tung Hotel, rooms were rented by the hour, and Lock kept an ample supply of condoms

Personal hygiene and medicinal products. Left: Glass Listerine bottle. Top left: Dentures. Bottom centre: Glass syringe and bottle of a deworming medication known as 'VERMIFUGE.' Top right: Ceramic lid from container of Atkinson's Celebrated Parisian Toothpaste. Right: Bone toothbrushes.

and aphrodisiacs to meet demand. His long workdays, from 10:00 a.m. until 8:00 p.m., had their slower moments. Lock would step outside and chat with passersby in English and Chinese, all the while keeping an eye on what was transpiring in the neighbourhood. His vantage point was ideal for watching the hotel, timing the sex-trade workers with their clientele, and noting, 'That didn't take long.' He was known for his observant quips about life in Chinatown; he called them his 'CDRs,' his complete detailed reports of the neighbourhood.

Another topic of Lock's CDRs was gambling, a prevalent pastime of the bachelor-society men in many establishments along Dundas and Elizabeth Streets. Lock witnessed frequent police raids, one resulting in furniture being tossed onto the sidewalk and smashed with axes. In the basement of his store, a steel door led to a gambling house in the adjacent building. The distinctive clatter of mah-jong tiles broke the silence whenever Lock made the trek downstairs to retrieve pop bottles from storage.

Fondly remembered as an outgoing personality with his own brand of humour and 'Lock-talk' expressions, he served his community at the drugstore for twenty-two years. Lock lived life to the fullest for eighty-eight years until his passing in 2003, leaving the legacy of a lasting impact on others. His first-hand experience, especially with the aging Chinese men living on the streets and in rundown rooming houses, strengthened his resolve to do more. He was a founding member and long-serving board director of the Mon Sheong Foundation, the first Chinese charitable organization in Canada. In 1975, the Mon Sheong Home for the Aged opened near Chinatown with sixty-five beds as the first residential facility in Ontario for Chinese senior citizens. This association coexisted with other institutions, such as the Chinese Christian Institute and the Chinese United Church, located down the street from Lock's pharmacy.

Lock's contribution lives on at the Mon Sheong Foundation, which has expanded its facilities to 457 beds in the Greater Toronto Area. And Chinese Canadians such as Lock, who enlisted in the armed forces during World War II, played a pivotal role in bringing about fundamental changes for the Chinese in Canada: gaining the right to vote, obtaining full citizenship, and seeing the repeal of the Chinese Immigration Act. Lock's prescription for life served him well to the benefit of his fellow Canadians.

# THE STONE IN THE GROUND: REV. THOMAS JACKSON

ROSEMARY SADLIER

W HEN I WAS a very little girl – a toddler really – I recall feeling special and safe in my own small area in the third pew from the front of the British Methodist Episcopal (BME) Church on Shaw Street. My mother and I always sat in the same seat, behind her cousin Marguerite Jackson. During the sermon, I was given blank paper and a pen and allowed to create anything I wanted, as this was when my innocent interest in speaking with my mother surfaced.

My capacity to hold a pen developed well before I attended Sunday school – or public school, for that mat-ter. I am sure I chiselled my way through many of Rev. Alexander Markham's sermons to the delight of all those who actually wanted to listen.

My mother's cousin, whom we called Aunt Marguerite, was the daughter of Rev. Thomas and Laura Jackson. She played the organ, read announcements, served as the church clerk, and fulfilled any other duty that arose. From an early age, Aunt Marguerite was enmeshed in the workings of the church. Reverend Jackson, like most BME ministers, was an itinerant pastor during his youth;

BME Church, 1953.

he and his family frequently moved to serve any one of several BME churches across the province, including the BME Church on Chestnut Street. The church and its rituals were comforting and familiar for Aunt Marguerite; it was her home.

While the minister was a man, the other church work was done by women: choir director Grace Price-Trotman, the members of the Missionary Society, the Sunday school teachers, and the ladies who organized dinners and events. It was a special place where I saw Black people of every hue, and Black women working toward a meaningful whole in a way that I did not see in my own neighbourhood, nor reflected on television.

My mother, Aunt Marguerite, and many congregants shared a special bond that was most fully appreciated within the confines of the BME and not recognized in any other space. They were the descendants of those who had come to Canada on the Underground Railroad, as well as Black people who had secured their own freedom and settled in Windsor, London, Woodstock, and Brantford, and later moved to Toronto for better employment prospects. Some had family who had lived in Canada for decades, and moved from other towns to the big city. Others were second-generation, born in the West Indies or the United States. The church population boasted a diverse group, with professionals and working-class people worshipping together with newcomers from the Caribbean.

To get to the Shaw Street BME, we took a long trip on public transportation, as did many attendees. However, when my mother was a little girl, she lived in the Spadina/College area, close enough to all the Black churches in downtown Toronto that she could walk. Her neighbours then included Leonard Braithwaite, who went on to become the first Black Canadian elected to a provincial legislature, and George Carter, later the first Black Canadian judge.

But when my mother was a girl, in the 1940s, most of those in the Black community did not live near the BME on Chestnut Street. Factors like available housing outside of the downtown core and greater affluence pulled Toronto's Black community in many directions. In fact, when my parents bought their first home in north Toronto, they were

the only Black people in the neighbourhood – I was one of perhaps two Black kids in my school.

Marble inscription stone that once adorned the front of the 1871 British Methodist Episcopal Church on Chestnut Street.

This was part of the reason the BME on Chestnut Street finally moved to Shaw Street by 1955. Though centrally located, the BME on Chestnut proved to be too small, despite several additions, to provide the parking and the banquet space so necessary for raising funds to sustain the church. By World War II, the church was in the middle of a growing Chinese community whose members had set up restaurants, laundries, and fruit markets nearby. When, in the early 1950s, the larger Afro Community Church on Shaw Street indicated it was amenable to a merger, Reverend Thomas, the last Chestnut Street BME minister, negotiated the arrangement with his counterpart at Shaw Street, Reverend Markham. The Chestnut Street location was sold to the United Church of Canada, which established it as the first Chinese congregation with a dedicated building.

When I went to City Hall in 2016 to advocate for the retention of the BME Church foundation, which was uncovered the previous year during the archaeological excavations of the Armoury Street site, I received a standing ovation for my remarks on the significance of this place. According to the Provincial Policy Statement, which guides planning in Ontario, 'significant built heritage resources and significant cultural heritage landscapes shall be conserved.' Section 2.6.2 of the PPS also states that 'development and site alteration shall not be permitted on lands containing archaeological resources or areas of archaeological potential unless significant archaeological resources have been conserved.'

I, and others, had hoped the BME foundation would be retained as part of the new Toronto courthouse. While we were unsuccessful, it is nevertheless important to ensure that the background, the history, the experience, the impact, and the interpretation of the artifacts be made known. According to the archaeologist's report on the site,

> The remains of the BME church represent a significant archaeological and heritage resource as an important place of worship and advocacy for the abolition of slavery. The church served as a platform for political activism, was one of the last stops on the Underground Railroad, represents the struggle for freedom for people of African descent and remains an important tangible reminder of the presence of a sizeable, early Black community in Toronto.

But before I advocated for the retention of this site, I had the opportunity to visit it and see for myself the outline of the church, the various segments, and a simple stone tablet that marked two key events in the life of this building.

On a warm, sunny day in mid-2015, Abbey Flower, a heritage specialist with Infrastructure Ontario, and consulting archaeologist Holly Martelle ushered me carefully through the site. Though the ground was rough and muddy, there was an energy I could not identify, as well as a restlessness. When Holly descended into the bowels of the BME Church footprint, my eye was drawn to a stone sign. She described it as a date stone for the building. I needed to get closer to it, and as I did, I was not content with photographing the stone – I had to touch it.

ROSEMARY SADLIER

The stone was inscribed with the following words:

BMEC

Founded 1856

Rebuilt 1871

Originally affixed to the exterior, the stone marker had been removed and embedded in concrete in the floor of the BME's basement during an expansion of the building in the 1890s.

I felt a warmth – a comforting presence. I looked up, and the sky just seemed so very blue. It was a beautiful feeling, as if I was in the presence of others. I felt surrounded and supported by the ancestors, my ancestors. The feeling was brief and surreal, but palpable.

The stone holds a great deal of significance. It symbolized the permanent nature of the BME's purpose in creating and supporting a loyal, committed society based in faith and furthered by the work of the Church. This marker not only placed the BME foundation in time, it served as an emblem of the hard-won struggle for freedom of formerly enslaved Africans. The stone also displayed this structure's connection to other BME churches in Ontario, in Canada, and internationally (i.e., that the BME was established as an independent denomination in 1856 at a conference in Chatham, Ontario) and celebrated the Chestnut Street congregation's own growth (i.e., rebuilt 1871).

Lastly, the stone speaks to the ongoing significance of writing and education – from the early conference-wide efforts to create educational institutions for their ministers to the importance the BME placed on literacy for the general uplifting of a diverse Black community that included those who came to serve, lead, and chisel out ways to live in a society that both offered and denied many freedoms. For me, that engraved stone ultimately reflects the hopeful time in which the church was built, and the reality of life for the many who made their way to The Ward and the BME Church on Chestnut Street.

# FROM PUSHCART TO PROPERTY MAGNATE: HENRY GREISMAN

ELLEN SCHEINBERG

Around 1916, Henry Greisman, a prosperous garment manufacturer and real estate investor, decided to knock down a row of old workers' cottages on Chestnut Street to make way for a substantial new building that, he imagined, would transform a corner of The Ward, where he'd lived many years earlier. Greisman owned a number of properties on the block, but assumed that he could find large commercial tenants for this new property.

His hunch, as usual, turned out to be accurate: soon after construction was completed, the T. Eaton Company became his first tenant, leasing the entire facility for its tent and awning production. It was an unlikely partnership. After all, Eaton's had famously prevented The Ward's Jewish residents from working in its department stores, relegating thousands to the sweatshops that operated in its large factories in The Ward.

Greisman's rise to prominence and success within The Ward and the City of Toronto was remarkable, particularly considering he was a first-generation Jewish immigrant who came to the country with no material assets. He was born in 1867 in Galicia – then part of the Austrian Empire – to Selig and Fegel Greisman. He married his wife, Fanny (née Garten), at the age of seventeen in 1884. The couple had three sons and two daughters – Pearl, Morris, Louis, Samuel, and Gertrude. The two eldest children were born in the old country and the last three in Ontario. Tragically, in 1902, the couple lost a son, Abraham, due to a mistake made by the rabbi who performed his circumcision.

Henry came to Toronto in 1888 with his older brother Joseph and younger brother Israel. The rest of the family – their spouses, children, remaining six siblings, and parents – were brought over between 1889 and 1898. They looked after one another and mostly settled on Chestnut Street. In 1901, Henry was living with his wife and four children, along with his youngest siblings, Sarah (fourteen years) and Louis (eleven years).

Henry and several of his family members worked as peddlers during the early years to support their families. Many early Jewish settlers adopted this job, since it afforded them a degree of autonomy and required minimal capital. In her 1993 article in *Canadian Jewish Studies*, 'A Social Profile of Peddlers in the Jewish Community of Toronto,' Deena Nathanson writes that 'many Jewish immigrants used street trading as a threshold occupation from which to launch their careers.' This was indeed

Henry Greisman, 1926.

the case with the Greisman brothers: Jacob and Joseph went on to become grocers on Chestnut Street, and in 1901, Henry set up the Canadian Suspender Company in his home at 72 Chestnut, at Armoury. His oldest son, Morris, soon joined him in this enterprise.

Around 1909, Greisman changed his company's name to the King Suspender Company and relocated his home and business to 99 University Avenue, just north of Wellington Street West. Three years later, he secured a factory at 68 Adelaide Street East and ran his company from that location. Business was good – by the 1920s, the family was enjoying an upscale lifestyle, residing in a grand residence on Admiral Road in the Annex, with a servant to assist them with household tasks. Henry's business produced both suspenders and neckwear, made in large factories at 210 and 240 Richmond Street West. The latter was six storeys high, with 60,000 square feet of floor space. His sons all actively helped him run the firm. Suspenders enjoyed a fashion revival at this time, boosting the fortunes of the Greisman family.

Besides his success in the garment trade, Greisman also became a major property owner in the city, making his first investments within a decade of arriving in Toronto. In 1897, he had purchased a row of homes on Chestnut Street – 45 to 57 (he was renting the latter). Over the next decade and a half, he acquired several more Chestnut Street properties, including numbers 74, 80 to 90, 109, 111, and 133. It was the row houses at 86–90 Chestnut that he redeveloped and rented to Eaton's a year later. (The building was subsequently sold to the Fashion Hat and Cap Company in the early 1940s.)

Greisman later expanded his property holdings outside of The Ward once the shmatte industry began to move to the Kensington Market area in the 1920s. A couple of the important and imposing factory buildings he constructed during that period included the Reading (116 Spadina Avenue) and the Spadina (129 Spadina Avenue). He commissioned a local Jewish architect, Benjamin Brown, to design these two edifices, along with several other structures he developed during the late 1920s and early 1930s.

Beyond his commitment to family and business, Greisman was a devout man who helped set up a synagogue on Chestnut Street for his family and landsmen (people from the same town or region in Eastern Europe). Shomrai Shabbos, or the Galitzianer Shul, was established around 1888 and initially held services in Greisman's house at 61 Chestnut. The congregation eventually purchased a synagogue at 109–111 Chestnut Street – on the east side, a few steps south of Dundas – which was dedicated in 1900. Greisman funded the land and renovations, and served as president for eight years. The congregation hired Rabbi Joseph Weinreb, who was brought over from Galicia. The cantor at that time was another founding member, Moses Brody.

Greisman also invested much of his time, energy, and wealth into the Jewish community. He served as vice-president of the Federation of the Jewish Philanthropies of Toronto (now UJA Federation) and was an

honourary VP of the Brunswick Talmud Torah. What's more, Greisman actively supported

Shomrai Shabbos Synagogue at 109–111 Chestnut Street, 1926.

community institutions such as the Jewish Old Folks Home and the Jewish Orphans Home. Finally, he was an ardent Zionist who served as honourary vice-chair of the United Palestine Appeal Campaign.

When Henry Greisman died in 1938 at the age of seventy-one, he left a sizable estate amounting to $120,000. He instructed his executor to evenly split his fortune between his family and the United Jewish Welfare Fund. The donation to the Jewish community financed a community building on Beverley Street, where a large portrait of him hung on the main floor in recognition of his contribution.

In the four decades that Greisman lived in Toronto after immigrating from Galicia, he achieved wealth, mobility, and commercial success. He went further than most Jewish immigrants of his time, rising from the ranks of a peddler to become a highly influential community leader. And even though he'd moved out of The Ward by 1908, some twenty years after he first came to Canada, Greisman left his mark on Chestnut Street for years to come.

Red brick with mortar, marked J. Price. Between 1912 and 1962, the John Price brickyard on Greenwood Avenue in Scarborough produced a soft mud brick popular in residential construction. After 1962, the Price brick-making machine was moved to the Toronto Valley Brickworks. It is currently on display at Evergreen Brickworks.

# THE ARCHAEOLOGICAL LIFE

# BOMB SCARE

### HOLLY MARTELLE

'YOU FOUND *WHAT*?'
I'd already had a long, dreary day, and heavy rain was approaching. It was the end of October, the time of year when an archaeologist's patience wears thin from working in Ontario's unpredictable fall weather.

'A bomb!' said an excited digger, dressed in fluorescent-orange safety gear and holding his hard hat, now short of breath after running across the site to find me.

Puzzled, I made my way over to where the crew was excavating a series of very rich and very ripe wood-lined privies, unearthed below a 1940s cinderblock storage building and garage that once stood behind the Pearl Furniture Company. I was highly skeptical. What would a bomb be doing in an early Toronto working-class neighbourhood – and in an outhouse, no less? I was prepared to dismiss the find. Clearly someone had an overly active imagination.

I neared the excavations, and my heart began to beat a little faster as the startling outline of the curious object came into view. There it was in plain sight, now undeniable. After inching closer, I was able to make out the familiar shape of an artillery shell of modest size, roughly twenty centimetres long and eight centimetres in diameter. It had a rounded cap and a long, grooved body that had been partially cleaned of the damp, putrid-smelling night soil it had been buried in.

My mind was racing. How did it get here? Who would have ever disposed of it in an outhouse, and why? What were we going to do with it? And, most important, was it dangerous? While this certainly qualified as one of the most intriguing and bizarre finds of my career, it was also potentially the most concerning. Putting my archaeological curiosity aside, I took a photograph of the shell and sought expert advice.

Most popular depictions of archaeology portray it as an adventurous endeavour. But beyond Indiana Jones's snake pits and booby-trapped temples, the safety hazards of our profession might not be obvious. We often encounter dangers such as contaminated soils, deep excavation pits, weather exposure, and the discovery of volatile objects and substances. Health and safety training is a big part of the 'business' of archaeology as it is practised today. Crews are versed on the correct use of personal protective equipment, identifying poisonous plants and harmful substances, and even how to evacuate or secure a site should any threats to safety occur. Yet our training can't prepare us for every dangerous situation we might encounter.

Luckily, our firm had been involved in the environmental cleanup and archaeological assessment of Camp Ipperwash and Ipperwash Provincial Park, where the former use of the land as a World War II army training facility made the presence of unexploded ordnance (UXO) a major concern. I sent the photograph of the artillery shell to a colleague with UXO expertise, who offered quick and stern advice: 'Call the local bomb squad.' While I was confident that the munition was not at risk of exploding, due to its incomplete casing, it seemed better to be safe than sorry.

The excavation crew had all returned to the hotel while I tried to sort out what to do next. I spent some time scrolling through the Toronto Police Service (TPS) website, trying to establish whom to contact. The 'local bomb squad' isn't a phone number archaeologists typically have on hand. My searches for 'bomb squad,' 'munitions,' 'explosives' all turned up blank, so I resorted to calling the main switchboard number. I dreaded the thought of having to tell my unbelievable story over and over again, first to the nice lady with the pleasant voice who answered all general inquiries, and then to a seemingly endless number of detectives and department heads, until I was connected with someone who could handle this unique situation. Finally, I heard the reassuring words, 'We'll send someone over.'

After just short of an hour, I was greeted by a young constable. 'Today is your lucky day,' I said sarcastically. He was clearly unsettled, uncertain of what to do. I'd seen this before. From time to time, I've had to report human-remains discoveries to the local police, and the stories of our finds and what we do for a living are always met with quizzical looks and questions – lots of questions. Appreciating that this was not everyday police business, I showed the officer our bomb, offered my account of finding the piece, gave a layperson's identification, and did my best to explain why we were digging on the property in the first place. Admitting that he was just a 'regular street cop,' the officer brought out his phone and initiated a round of calls, looking for assistance.

Eventually, word came that experts from Canadian Forces Base Borden had been called to examine and collect the find – the Toronto Police Service's procedure in situations where old munitions were found. 'Ma'am, you'll need to evacuate the site,' the officer said. 'I've been advised to shut down the area until this thing is resolved.' With a feeling of guilt about creating such an inconvenience, I quickly left the site to await further news in my hotel room.

As I walked down Armoury Street, I did my best to stay out of the way as barriers and caution tape were set in place. Police cruisers had surrounded the site. Curious reporters, assembled at the adjacent courthouse to collect their daily news, conveniently turned their attention to the north side of Armoury Street and began asking questions. After all, our discovery had shut down the entire city block, from Dundas Street to Armoury and between Chestnut Street and Centre Avenue. The police had turned vehicles away, causing a traffic nightmare, and asked pedestrians to vacate the block. Students from the University of Toronto's Chestnut Street residences were late for class. Judges and lawyers from the courthouse had to return to their building, probably annoyed by the archaeological work for their soon-to-be-new, state-of-the-art facility. It was already enough of a hindrance to have lost their most convenient parking lot in a congested neighbourhood.

Thankfully, the hotel I was staying in was directly beside our excavation site. As I approached, the bellman was waving his arms frantically.

HOLLY MARTELLE

Late for their outings, guests were shouting in concern, and a crowd gathered outside to peer down the street, hoping to get a glimpse of what was happening. I

Circa 1860s munition likely from a 20-pounder Armstrong gun used by the Canadian militia. Recovered from a privy behind 29 Centre Street, alongside several pistol rounds.

darted through the door and hung my head sheepishly while scurrying to the elevator, knowing I was in some way responsible for all the commotion.

Entering my room, I threw off my drenched outerwear, and quickly turned on the local news. There we were. 'Breaking News: Military artifact uncovered downtown' – our first ticker-tape news coverage! A short live story followed with a promise of 'more to come.' But that promise went unkept, for just a few moments later it was announced that former Toronto mayor Rob Ford had cancer. Our bomb's fifteen minutes of fame had been trumped by a tumour. Nonetheless, its brief coverage had heightened my awareness of the severity of the disruption. CTV's John Musselman had reported, 'People are being told to stay away from the windows.' The north side of the courthouse at 361 University Avenue had been evacuated. Toronto's chemical, biological, radiological, and nuclear defence team had been called in to manage the scene. With a name like that, it is no wonder a quick search of the TPS website was unhelpful! All the precautions were in keeping with police protocols to ensure everyone's safety. That was reassuring.

Eventually I received a call saying our site was all clear. The police informed me that the military folks had taken the bomb away for disposal.

That was it. No identification, no helpful information to quell my curiosity. I let my imagination run wild. Perhaps it was a wartime trophy of an elderly British or Canadian veteran who propped it up on his mantel in memory of friends lost on the battlefield, despite significant protest from his wife. She wanted no visible reminder of the time she was without her husband and felt the munition was too dangerous to have in the house. It was only upon his passing that she felt it was finally okay to dispose of it.

The most plausible explanation I could offer for the find was the historical presence of the Armouries nearby. Built between 1891 and 1893 as a training site for soldiers and militia, the Armouries had been demolished in 1963, replaced by the 361 University Avenue courthouse that now stands on the south side of Armoury Street. It's possible someone took the bomb from the armouries to a lot across the street. What if it was the plunder of a mischievous teenager, dared by friends, who later disposed of the evidence, fearful of the consequences of getting caught?

But as sometimes happens in archaeology, the inevitable speculation arising from hard-to-explain artifacts yielded to new information that surfaced more than two years after we stumbled across this object.

HOLLY MARTELLE

Recruits doing artillery training with an 18-pounder drill at the Armouries.

In February 2018, our office received an email from Eric Fernberg, an arms and technology specialist at the Canadian War Museum, to whom we had sent images of the shell and questions about its provenance.

Fernberg's initial hunch, as he explained, was that it was a lead-coated munition used in 20-pounder Armstrong guns by the Canadian militia. 'I will let you know when I find out more,' he wrote.

A few days later, Fernberg sent a follow-up. 'My hunch was right,' he began. The shell wasn't an explosive at all, but rather a solid artillery shot dating to the 1860s – a detail confirmed by the ribbing pattern on its exterior. He couldn't, of course, explain how it had ended up buried in a privy in a working-class neighbourhood in downtown Toronto. But we learned that the bomb squad never really had anything to worry about.

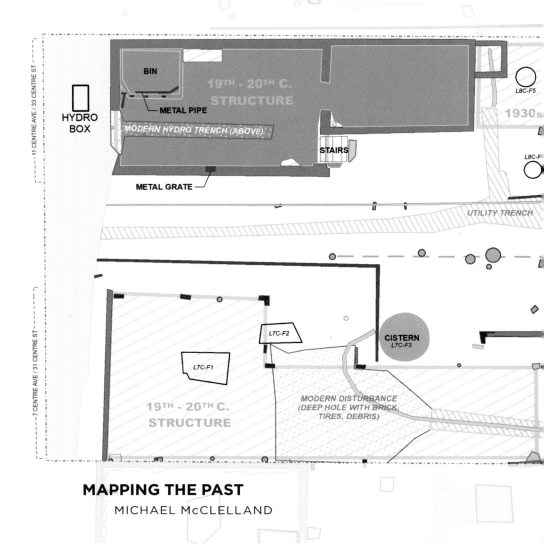

## MAPPING THE PAST

MICHAEL McCLELLAND

EVERYONE KNOWS THAT archaeologists dig up artifacts. But the maps they produce during an excavation – everything from working drawings made in the field to highly detailed schematic diagrams constructed with specialized software – are also artifacts, though in a more abstracted form.

The maps on the following pages tell stories about both the dig and the complex process of making sense of an archaeological site. When Holly Martelle and her colleagues began peeling away the asphalt and

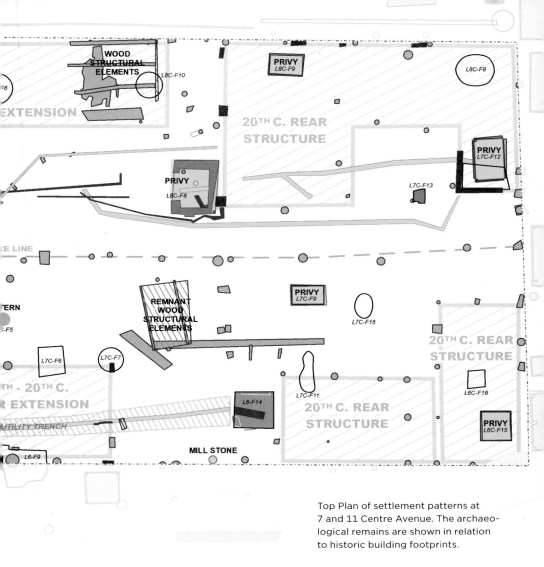

Top Plan of settlement patterns at 7 and 11 Centre Avenue. The archaeological remains are shown in relation to historic building footprints.

compacted soil on the Armoury block, they encountered layers of muck and debris, pits full of human refuse mixed with trash, collapsed foundation walls, and snaking handmade drains, all of it presented as a confusing, smelly, and often soggy jumble.

Archaeologists map out such sites in exacting detail to tease broken narratives out of the ground, much in the way that heritage conservation architects decipher historic buildings that have accumulated layers of renovations. Whereas heritage architects seek out both the original

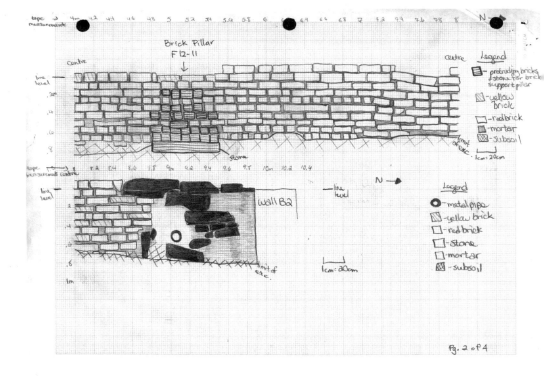

Brick Pillar
F12-11

Centre

line level

.2m

.4

.6

.8

Centre

Legend
- protruding bricks / stones for brick support pillar
- yellow brick
- red brick
- mortar
- subsoil
1cm: 20cm

stone

limit of exc.

tape measurement centre

line level

2

.4

.6

.8

1m

7.2 8.4 8.2 8.8 9m 9.2 9.4 9.6 9.8 10m 10.2 10.4

Wall B2

limit of exc.

line level

N

1cm: 20cm

Legend
- metal pipe
- yellow brick
- red brick
- stone
- mortar
- subsoil

Fig. 2 of 4

designer's intent and the values revealed by later alterations, archaeologists are like forensic investigators who record and interpret fragmented evidence left by the people who inhabited the same piece of turf at different times, often with no awareness of one another's presence.

Consider the map on pages 246–247, which indicates that a well sat scarcely a few paces from a privy. Which came first? Did residents dig the well despite the presence of the outhouse? Was the privy constructed in defiance of the water source? Or perhaps the outhouse appeared many years after that well had gone dry.

By contrast, the church site (pages 250–251) was highly ordered with readily identified features, while the other lot was strewn with all sorts of elements, from cisterns to a nearly intact basement.

These maps also reveal much about the professional archaeologist's technique. The hand-drawn sketch of a foundation wall (above) reveals not only the recording of granular details, but also the training that permits the archaeologist to see and observe with great acuity. Heritage

MICHAEL McCLELLAND

## Lot 7 Chestnut Street Feature 9 (Privy) Profile
### - South Wall of North Half

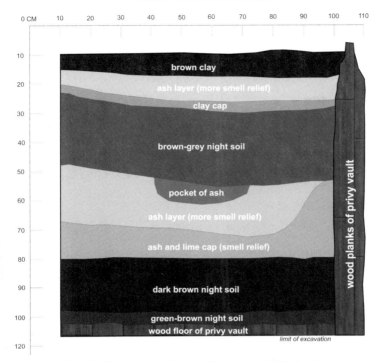

## Lot 7 Chestnut Street Feature 9 (Privy)
## Partial Top Plan

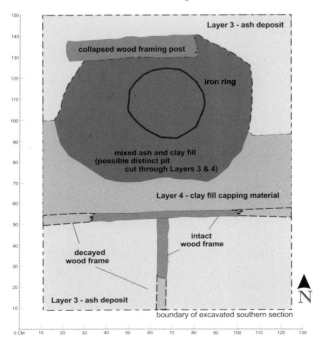

Sample rough and finished drawings of archaeological features.

20TH C. CHINESE UNITED CHURCH REAR ADDITION (INCORPORATES FOOTPRINT OF 19TH - 20TH C. REAR ADDITION AND MEETING HALL OF BRITISH METHODIST EPISCOPAL CHURCH)

EARLY 20TH C. REAR ADDITION W

LIGHT STANDARD XCAVATION BAULK

L12-F18   L12-F17   L12-F14
L12-F15

BUILDER'S TRENCH

1957 REAR ADDITION

Top Plan of settlement for the British Methodist Episcopal Church/Chinese United Church.

architects must approach projects in the same way, and we often bring pencil and paper to work sites because we know that we will learn about what made a building tick through the act of drawing it.

Finally, the plan and section of a deposit on Lot 7 (page 249) evokes some kind of geological bore-hole. But what these drawings describe are pits full of shit and ash and 'filth,' which, apparently, is different from 'night soil.' These strata remind us that waste disposal is, and always has been, one of the most fundamental tasks of urban life, and

MICHAEL McCLELLAND

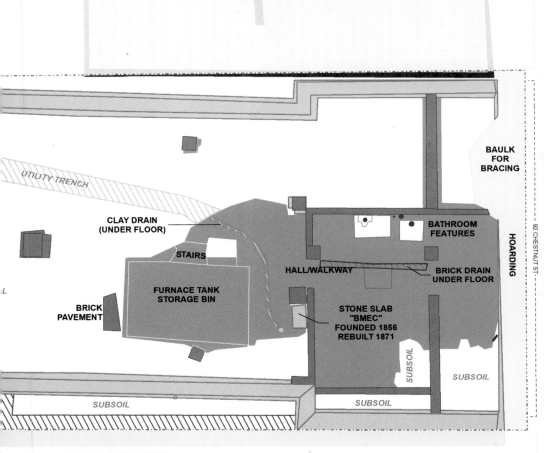

UTILITY TRENCH

BAULK
FOR
BRACING

92 CHESTNUT ST

HOARDING

CLAY DRAIN
(UNDER FLOOR)

BATHROOM
FEATURES

STAIRS

HALL/WALKWAY

BRICK DRAIN
UNDER FLOOR

FURNACE TANK
STORAGE BIN

BRICK
PAVEMENT

STONE SLAB
"BMEC"
FOUNDED 1856
REBUILT 1871

SUBSOIL

SUBSOIL

SUBSOIL

SUBSOIL

71 CHURCH FOOTPRINT

1894 CHURCH FOOTPRINT

also point to the evolving ways in which people living in close quarters sought to isolate themselves from their own waste (lime, clay, etc.).

These disgusting pits, as Martelle discusses in 'Daily Life,' yielded many of the site's most valuable and intriguing discoveries. But as the diagrams indicate, their precise dimensions and layers have also been recorded in minute detail so that future historians may have the opportunity to consider all the evidence as they construct as-yet-untold accounts of the histories of these buried neighbourhoods.

# WHY WERE ARCHAEOLOGISTS WORKING IN THE WARD?

RONALD F. WILLIAMSON & DAVID ROBERTSON

I F YOU HAD been walking along Armoury Street near Chestnut Street north of city hall in 2015, you may have glimpsed dozens of archaeologists who invaded the area for months. The obvious question: what were they doing there?

The answer can be traced to the response of government officials in the twentieth century to staggering losses to the archaeological record of Ontario. Over 8,000 archaeological sites were destroyed in the 1950s and 1960s within the Greater Toronto Area alone as a result of private and public land development. At least 2,000 of these likely merited some degree of archaeological investigation – they could have contributed meaningfully to our understanding of the past. While most of this archaeological site loss can be traced to the conversion of farmland to residential and industrial subdivisions, colonial sites within Toronto were also lost as the city developed parking lots and parks, and old buildings and neighbourhoods underwent urban renewal.

This site destruction was not lost on 1970s land-use planners and policy-makers. Ontario now boasts some of the most comprehensive legislation in North America related to archaeological resource conservation during the land development process. The Ontario government first enacted the legislative basis for this mandate, like much environmental protection regulation, in the 1970s, and the policy framework has since increased steadily in effectiveness. In particular, the Ontario Planning Act and the Ontario Environmental Assessment Act now require that archaeological surveys, as well as built heritage and cultural landscape analyses, be carried out in advance of land-disturbing activities, whether these are private developments or public initiatives, such as infrastructure projects, or, as in this case, a provincial courthouse.

But local governments also play an important role since locally approved developments comprise the majority of land-disturbing activities in the province. Municipalities review development applications and determine the need for archaeological assessments. Once these applications are completed to the satisfaction of the provincial archaeological regulators, proponents are free to carry on with the development, provided they meet all other approval conditions. Some municipalities with trained heritage staff also review these assessment reports, as they are often more familiar with local history.

The authority for municipalities to manage this process derives from the Ontario Planning Act and the Provincial Policy Statement (PPS), which guide all provincial and local planning authorities in their decisions. With respect to archaeological resources, the PPS states that development and site alteration shall not be permitted on lands containing archaeological resources or areas of archaeological potential unless significant archaeological resources have been conserved. In other words, these resources are identified and managed so as to ensure their cultural heritage value or interest survives the development. The legislation enables municipalities to require that archaeological assessments be completed on public or private lands prior to the approval of a planning application.

In some cases, provincial or municipal officials require builders or agencies to submit the assessments with the application in the hope that development proponents would have ample time to plan for archaeological site protection, rather than mere salvage excavation, by considering alternative site-plan designs. There is no Ontario legislation that compels land developers to protect sites in their plans – such legislation exists nowhere in Canada or in the U.S. or Europe, although most jurisdictions have federally or regionally designated historic sites protecting them from encroachment.

Municipalities do have the opportunity for enhancing this policy by establishing tailor-made heritage conservation guidelines within their official plans. The City of Toronto's Official Plan articulates a vision of heritage conservation in the context of well-designed development that protects important heritage attributes on heritage properties and raises awareness throughout the neighbourhoods of the city. The archaeological policies, while laying out the process for assessment in areas with archaeological potential, also encourage protection as the preferred option to mitigate the impacts of proposed development on any archaeological feature. They do acknowledge, however, that this is most feasible in greenfield contexts and those situations where the discovery is on publicly owned land.

Policy-makers also need to revisit the definition of 'significant.' In the PPS, 'significant archaeological resources' are defined as those that have been determined to have cultural heritage value or interest for the important contribution they make to our understanding of the history of a place, an event, or a people. But the very people whose history might benefit from that enhanced understanding rarely have a role in defining the significance of a resource – about 80 per cent of archaeological sites in Ontario are Indigenous in origin. While the identification and evaluation of such resources are based on data gathered during archaeological fieldwork, regulations have only recently been instituted requiring archaeologists and proponents to actually engage with the relevant Indigenous communities prior to salvage excavations – an initiative that will soon be extended to other peoples.

Many municipalities where the pace of development has been intense have commissioned detailed archaeological management plans (AMPs) or archaeological potential studies to acquire a more accurate means of determining archaeological potential and the need

for the assessment of specific properties or land areas. In 2004, City of Toronto officials retained Archaeological Services Inc. to develop an AMP that would effectively offer a road map laying out the locations of the city's known and unknown archaeological resources. (The original AMP report is available at https://www1.toronto.ca/city_of_toronto/city_planning/urban_design/files/pdf/masterplan_arc.resources.pdf.) An archaeological potential model was required since one of the major problems in planning for site conservation is that we don't know where all the sites are located. Comprehensive surveys of entire municipal jurisdictions are clearly not feasible. As an alternative, planners and managers must depend on predictive site location models designed specifically for the lands over which they have control.

While modelling must be done for both Indigenous archaeological sites and those that date after the founding of York, the AMP research team developed the locations of latter-period sites through primary and secondary source research, beginning with the identification of historical themes related to the growth and development of the cross-road communities or settlement centres that amalgamated to become Toronto. The researchers overlaid historical maps, in particular, to compile an inventory of features of archaeological interest and to identify areas of large-scale development that have clearly resulted in deep subsurface disturbances (e.g., foundation and basement excavations) or alteration of the original topography (e.g., burying of former creeks) that likely removed any archaeological deposits that were present.

These zones are then excluded from the archaeological potential layer. The only exceptions tend to be the historic cores of settlement centres, which may retain significant deposits among the existing

Left: A candle snuffer and wick trimmer.
Below: Reeds from a harmonica.

structures but cannot be identified in detail within the context of a municipal archaeological potential model due to the effort required. Within these settlement centres, far more detailed assessments of individual properties, involving the development of comprehensive land-use histories and the compilation of large-scale nineteenth- and twentieth-century map sources, are completed by archaeological consultants as well as any necessary fieldwork prior to land redevelopment.

In the case of Toronto, despite considerable late-twentieth-century urban-core redevelopment, 28 per cent of the city still has archaeological potential, and its mapping is used by municipal planners to identify those land developments that may impact archaeological sites. If any portion of a planning application – for a housing subdivision, condominium, new hotel, or other commercial, industrial, or recreational use – includes an area of archaeological potential, it will be subject to assessment prior to land-disturbing activities. Toronto planners review about three hundred development applications every year for archaeological potential, not including the many reviews of city activities such as parks projects.

Infrastructure Ontario's (IO) Environmental Management team is responsible for ensuring archaeological concerns are addressed during major construction and infrastructure initiatives, land dispositions and acquisitions, land development and planning, and day-to-day operations of facilities and lands. When plans for the new Toronto courthouse were initiated, archaeologists at IO undertook a preliminary screening process that included review of the AMP and other property features that established the property had archaeological potential. Based on IO and provincial regulatory processes, an archaeological assessment was required and background research was commissioned to determine if field investigations were necessary and if so, where they might be targeted. As followup testing established that significant archaeological resources were present, IO commissioned excavation of the property. Since municipal approvals were also required prior to the construction of the new courthouse, the initial background assessment report was submitted to the City when IO filed

RONALD F. WILLIAMSON & DAVID ROBERTSON

the planning application for the project. IO subsequently worked with City and provincial staff as the archaeological excavation continued to ensure all necessary investigations were undertaken. This explains why those archaeologists spent months in that parking lot.

Due to the design requirements for the new Toronto courthouse, particularly the need for significant underground operational and parking space, the protection of archaeological features on the site – e.g., foundations of nineteenth-century buildings, cisterns, etc., – was not possible. This is a common challenge for large-scale developments on smaller downtown properties.

The archaeologists working on the site salvaged all the artifacts and other features through extended excavation and conservation of the archaeological record. It is an axiom of cultural resource management that archaeology conducted in advance of development is in the public interest – it preserves knowledge of the past that would otherwise be lost and provides the opportunity to disseminate the results to the public.

The City of Toronto, in its archaeological management role, has embraced the concept of public interpretation of archaeological excavations. In recent years, the City has begun routinely requiring development proponents to fund and maintain permanent commemorative and interpretive displays related to the history and archaeology of their properties. These include displays at the TIFF Bell Lightbox, built on the site of the first Toronto General Hospital, and the Bishop's Block, a cluster of nineteenth-century Georgian row houses excavated and restored during the development of the Shangri La hotel and condos at University and Adelaide.

The initiatives completed to date have all been paid for by the proponents and typically include panels and signage, or artifact displays in public spaces. The integration of the foundations of a barracks in Exhibition Place for a new hotel is one of the first instances of full protection for archaeological features in the city. While this was not possible in the case of The Ward, its rich archaeological history will be interpreted. This book is testimony to the considerable interest in the project stimulated by media coverage and the stories that lay hidden in that archaeological record.

# WATER TABLE: HOW THE ORGANICS SURVIVED

ABBEY FLOWER

T HE PRIVIES FOUND at the Armoury Street Dig were especially well-suited for preserving some of the most fragile organic materials, like newspaper. To our amazement, several pieces of newspaper survived well enough to not only be excavated but also remain legible. Finding newspapers at the homes of those Ward residents who likely read them offers a powerful connection to the everyday life of a past community.

A sample of newspaper preserved in a privy. This particular fragment contains instructions on how to make Rhubarb Chiffon Tarts. Newspaper was often used as toilet paper.

These weren't the only paper products found on the site. Equally exciting was standing on an archaeological site and holding bits of wallpaper in my hand. These small fragments provide a rare first-hand glimpse of the interior decor of the cottages and row houses that once stood on that block. The colours on these scraps serve as a poignant contrast to the hundreds of grim archival photos of Ward interiors. The crowded neighbourhood garnered the attention of reform-minded city officials in the early twentieth century – photographers Arthur Goss, who worked for the city, and William James, a freelancer, extensively documented the interiors to project an image of rundown homes, their poor occupants, and the area's dismal living conditions.

But the people of The Ward did not live in black and white. Seeing this wallpaper, with its soft blue-greens and whites with tiled floral designs, adds vibrant colour to the way we regard this past and the people who lived it. Those homes were not the dark and monochromatic spaces that the written and photographic records have long suggested.

How did these paper scraps manage to survive underground for a century? Shouldn't they have disintegrated long ago?

Southern Ontario's climate cycle – freeze, thaw, warm, dry, freeze again – doesn't bode well for the survival of organic materials in the ground. With the exception of tougher organics, like bone and antler, the freeze-thaw/wet-dry cycles, combined with an active soil environment, wreak havoc on less hardy materials like leather, fabric, and wood. Compared to arid desert conditions or the deep cold of the north, southern Ontario conditions accelerate organic decay. As a result, archaeological sites in this region tend to be dominated by objects made of stone, ceramic, metal, bone, and glass.

Yet sometimes we get lucky. If just one of those cycles can be broken, the decay of organic materials is slowed considerably. As it turned out,

Preserved painted wallpaper fragment with floral and geometric design.
Recovered from mixed demolition layers immediately beneath the asphalt of the parking lot.

the Armoury Street site provided nearly ideal conditions for the preservation of objects we rarely see in the archaeological record in southern Ontario. Three specific factors were key.

*An excess of water.* The property is located in a part of downtown Toronto with a particularly high water table. Prior to the mid-nineteenth-century surge of development, a watercourse – Taddle Creek – ran near the north end of the property. Even after development and burial of the creek altered the topography, the groundwater still followed past routes. What's more, the Armoury Street site is surrounded by towers with deep footings and underground parking, which serve to elevate the water table, insulate a bit against cold, and restrict the flow of groundwater.

*The lack of drainage.* At no point during the decades-long lifespan of the parking lot was below-ground drainage installed. Unlike contemporary parking lots, this one had no catch basins, stormwater sewers, or ties to city drains. The lack of waste-water infrastructure kept the water-saturation levels consistently high. Consequently, water was trapped in the many artifact-rich wells, privies, and cisterns across the site.

*An absence of development.* Not only was this organics-rich site saturated, it also didn't change much. Despite its downtown location, the property remained undeveloped for over fifty years. As the automobile began to dominate personal transportation in the mid-twentieth century, the need for parking grew. During the 1950s, 1960s, and 1970s, the houses, churches, and businesses on the property were gradually demolished to make way for surface parking. Moreover, when structures were removed, they tended to be razed only to ground level, with foundations filled in. Passersby may remember the substantial change in elevation from the sidewalk up to the level of the parking lot. The reason? The parking lot was built up from the previous street level, with many of the buildings cut off at the knees and sealed from above under multiple layers of asphalt.

From the time when the last buildings were removed (1988) until archaeological excavations began (2015), the site went largely undisturbed, sealing in a wonderful, waterlogged world ripe for preserving organic materials such as leather shoes, wood items, felt hats, textiles, and paper.

Ironically, the property probably had better drainage in the past, including the period in the early twentieth century when the entire Ward was disparaged for overcrowding, fetid privies, and a lack of fresh water. At the time, wood-lined box drains were common on such properties to help manage rainwater. These modest channels survived for decades underground, well below the parking surface. Amazingly, after the layers of dirt fill were excavated, those uncovered nineteenth-century box drains went right back to work, channelling groundwater around the site. The pattern of the drains also shows that the people who built them sought to direct dirty water away from their homes, workspaces, and well-travelled paths. These drains reveal active planning and engineering by both individuals and the community.

Other wood-lined amenities found on the site sought to store water instead of getting rid of it. Barrel-like cisterns were abundant in the nineteenth century and even the early twentieth century. Often built from cedar, these cisterns collected rainwater, which was essential for cleaning, laundry, keeping small animals, and more. The importance of these cisterns is emphasized by the number of them that persisted on the Ward site, located in the multi-purpose rear yards where space was at a premium.

From an archaeological perspective, wooden cisterns barely survive in southern Ontario's climate. At most sites, we might find fragments of the wood staves clinging to metal bilge hoops; these wood pieces tend to disintegrate soon after being excavated. But on this site, the cisterns survived completely intact.

One in particular I will never forget. The archaeological crew had just finished cleaning it, removing by hand a century's worth of packed dirt. The wood staves were not only beautiful and rich in colour, but an overpowering cedar scent wafted out of that cistern, transporting us back in time to the community it once served. Built in the 1800s and unearthed in 2015, that wood cistern, preserved by a confluence of unplanned soil and water conditions distinctive to this spot, smelled like it had been made yesterday.

# THE MYSTERY OF THE HIDDEN CROSS

## HOLLY MARTELLE

O NCE IN A while, archaeologists unearth objects that defy easy explanation and demand detective work. Some seem entirely out of context, and accounting for their presence on a dig site demands imagination. Others are so unusual they remain a mystery forever.

One such find was the large iron cross we recovered from the lower levels of a nineteenth-century privy on Centre Avenue. My team found it in three parts: a long, main shaft with a deep bend at one end; a cross piece; and a top end. When assembled, this cross was at least eighty

Iron cross recovered from a privy on Centre Avenue, measuring just less than a metre in length and weighing 7 kg.

centimetres long, about forty-five centimetres wide, and weighed nearly seven kilograms. In both material and form, it was a sturdy object.

As with everything we found at the Armoury Street Dig, we had to figure out what this artifact was, and then determine how it ended up buried in a corner of The Ward. While some information has been gathered to date, solving the riddle of the cross will take much more sleuthing.

To identify it, we first considered its unique characteristics. While it is obvious this object is a cross, the type, origin, and purpose were still unclear after months of investigation. We first sought comparisons, scouring books and online images. After doing some visual research, we felt fairly confident that the object was a cross, although we still didn't know its function or meaning. As we routinely do with mysterious finds, I canvassed some other archaeologists and experts in fields such as religion, history, and cemeteries. While outreach can often lead to the positive identification of an object, for this cross it only created more questions and opened up new potential explanations.

Here's what is known to date:

In form, the piece is a budded cross, with a straight shaft and cross piece that have small buds at the ends, consisting of three overlapping circles or discs. While there are varying interpretations of the religious symbolism, the three buds may represent the Holy Trinity. Some experts see a resemblance between the budded cross and Celtic cross, where the circles represent earth, sky, and sea.

While the budded cross is present in various Christian denominations, it is a common Greek Orthodox symbol. Did the cross we found come from a Greek Orthodox church in Toronto? Unlikely, as it turns out: Toronto's first Greek Orthodox church was established decades *after* the period when the cross would have been deposited in the privy.

The symbols on the cross are also curious.

On one side, the centre of the cross bears intertwined alpha (→ and omega (..) symbols. These are common elements of Christian iconography, deriving from the Book of Revelation in the New Testament, and are regularly found in churches and on grave markers. What's odd is that the symbols are turned sideways.

On the other side are four intertwined letters: *I, H, S,* and *V.* The first three are regular elements of Christian iconography, representing the symbol of the holy name of Jesus. The addition of the *V* is more difficult to explain and potentially changes the meaning. The acronym IHSV is often taken to be a short form for the Latin *in hoc signo vinces,* which translates to 'in this sign, you shall conquer.' The phrase occurs regularly with the symbology of the Knights of Templar, a twelfth-century Catholic military sect. We consulted religious and historical experts, cemetery caretakers, and others who might have some insight, but no one could explain these symbols.

The weight of the cross, and the threading on the end, suggests it was not portable but rather mounted on a base, probably made of metal, stone, concrete, or wood. These clues most likely mean the cross was an architectural ornament (an exterior or interior furnishing) or perhaps a grave marker. Crosses of similar size and shape are found in cemeteries across North America. However, none have yet been identified in Toronto's early cemeteries, including the Necropolis in Cabbagetown.

A more plausible interpretation is that the cross was an architectural piece that topped a church spire or steeple. Yet if it was from the top of a church, how would someone have gotten their hands on it? What's more, how did it become so disfigured? The strength of the iron suggests that a significant downward force had to have been applied to the cross to cause it to bend and then break.

While the true story of the cross cannot yet be told, if ever, it's fun to ponder other explanations. I imagine a group of young, boisterous men walking along the street after a long, ale-filled night. As they approach a neighbourhood church, they spot the outline of a cross glimmering in the moonlight. Someone throws out a drunken dare. Taking up the challenge, two energetic and confident lads stealthily climb up to the roof and together tug on the top of the cross, eventually splitting its mortar-and-stone base, and sending the broken ornament into the bush below. Not wanting to be caught, they swiftly gather up the evidence and run home to Centre Avenue, where they dispose of it in the one place that no one will ever look: a wretched-smelling loo.

HOLLY MARTELLE

# THE LAYERED CITY: THE PROMISE OF URBAN ARCHAEOLOGY

JOHN LORINC

I N 1991, CONTRACTORS hired by the U.S. General Services Administration (GSA) began excavating a pair of properties in Lower Manhattan slated for the development of two large new federal structures: an office building and a courthouse. One was to be built on the location of a parking lot near Foley Square while the other would be situated at 290 Broadway, just a block north of New York's ornate 1812 city hall.

Both sites, just a few metres apart, were located in an area once known as Manhattan's Five Points, a storied slum infamous not just for its gang rivalries and teeming tenements but also as the prime organizing turf for the notorious nineteenth-century New York ward heeler, Boss Tweed. The area grew up around a fetid pond, Cow Bay, and came to be settled by waves of Irish, Italian, German, Jewish, and Chinese immigrants, as well as African Americans. Nearby Lower East Side streets, such as Mulberry and the Bowery, were known for their extreme crowding and raucous taverns. These places eventually became a destination for slum tours, missionaries, and social reformers like Jacob Riis, whose photos of the area's extreme poverty, collected in the 1890 book *How the Other Half Lives*, captivated civic authorities.

While Five Points has a deeper and more complex history rooted in New York's centuries-old mercantile culture, the parallels to The Ward are evident, especially the immigrant settlement patterns, the crowding, and the stigmatization of the generations of people who lived, worked, and died there.

New York City's *Five Points,*
*1827*, George Catlin.

By the time the construction crews arrived in the early 1990s, the Lower East Side near city hall had evolved into Little Italy and Chinatown, still teeming but far removed from the notoriety that emboldened missionaries and produced tales such as *The Gangs of New York* (Herbert Asbury's sensationalist and mythologizing 1927 bestseller that begat the 2002 film).

Soon into the excavation, crews discovered that the sites contained vast archaeological deposits. The site designated to become a courthouse comprised a nineteenth-century city block with the foundations of houses, taverns, brothels, and breweries, as well as privies packed with the detritus of the people who lived there.

An archaeological team led by Rebecca Yamin, of John Milner Associates, a Philadelphia firm, eventually excavated a million artifacts. In the subsequent outpouring of scholarship about the dig, Yamin and her colleagues reconstructed the many elements of Five Points' history, but also offered an important counter-narrative to more accepted accounts. While the area had long been vilified (including by celebrity visitors like Charles Dickens), Yamin's work suggested that this enclave functioned for years as a diverse working-class neighbourhood 'where newly arrived immigrants and native-born workers struggled to find their way.'[1]

JOHN LORINC

The other site revealed an equally compelling story. About eight metres beneath ground level, construction crews found human remains – skeletons in much-decayed coffins, with no identifying marks or headstones. Eventually, the consulting archaeologists discovered and carefully removed the bones of 419 individuals. As they began studying the site's deep history, they discovered a 1755 map entitled 'Negros Burial Ground,' as well as other evidence suggesting that thousands of people – both enslaved and free, as well as some likely born in Africa – had been interred there in the seventeenth and eighteenth centuries.[2]

While the GSA initially insisted on proceeding with its plan to move the bones, mounting protests from New York's Black community prompted the government to hit the pause button. 'The evidence [of the burials] created a conceptual quake, transforming how New York history is understood and how black New Yorkers connect to their past,' observed the *New York Times*' Edward Rothstein.

Although construction on the thirty-four-storey tower did proceed, the African Burial Site itself was declared a National Historic Landmark in 1993, two years before the project was finished. Then, about a decade later, the site was formally designated a National Monument, to be managed by the National Parks Service. An austere black-marble memorial plaza was installed in a courtyard behind the tower, while a visitors centre opened on the ground floor. The exhibit offers eye-opening details about the extent of slavery in New York and includes a thorough account of the passionate and contentious fight over how to preserve the site.

The remains of all 419 bodies were reinterred in the memorial plaza, a remarkable example of commemoration. As an inscription carved into the memorial's wall tells visitors, 'You are standing where thousands of Africans buried their loved ones during the 1600s and 1700s.' The memorial opened formally during Black History Month in 2010.

The drawn-out development of the African Burial Site stands in stark contrast to the fate of the Five Points block that had been excavated nearby. The giant twenty-seven-storey courthouse opened on the site in 1996, and the vast assemblage of artifacts was placed in a GSA storage facility in the World Trade Centre. Almost the entire collection, except for a handful of artifacts out on loan, was destroyed on 9/11.

THE STORIES OF these two New York digs vividly illustrate the challenges associated with the discovery of extensive archaeological sites in the cores of big cities. These zones are often the oldest areas, but also the busiest and densest, and have seen the most destructive redevelopment. In many places, waves of redevelopment took place well before governments sought to protect archaeological assets using policies that govern excavation and artifact stewardship. In fact, the sites that survived often did so by chance and the vagaries of the development industry. The Armoury Street Dig faced all these same issues.

In many European and Middle Eastern and some Latin American cities, urban areas have grown up over centuries around the often-extensive remnants of antiquity – fora, citadel walls, temples, etc. Subways in Rome had to be designed around Roman ruins, while other cities, like Lisbon, have incorporated ancient elements – foundations, catacombs, amphitheatres, etc. – into the urban fabric (including, in one case, beneath the Plexiglas floor of a downtown H&M outlet).

For generations, builders in London have unearthed archaeological sites and artifacts from various periods in the city's 2,000-year history. Antiquities legislation enacted by the British Parliament and municipal officials in London date to the nineteenth century. After the bombing of London during World War II, many ancient sites were exposed, resulting in a growing number of excavations and, by the 1970s, the appointment of a chief archaeologist for the old City of London.

Among the latest discoveries are an extensive cache of items found as contractors built the Crossrail subway tunnel. 'Since construction of the Elizabeth line began in 2009, over 100 archaeologists have found tens of thousands of items from 40 sites, spanning 55 million years of London's history and pre-history,' notes a website with a virtual exhibit of Crossrail archaeology.

The discoveries ranged from human remains to Roman coins, Victorian-era ceramics, and prehistoric bison bones. Because in situ preservation wasn't possible – the material was found deep beneath city streets – a selection of the artifacts was installed in the Museum of London Docklands and displayed online.[3] The excavation process also gave rise to a small library of academic reports and trade books.

A completely different story played out with a much larger Roman ruin – the foundations of a temple discovered and excavated in the mid-1950s. Identified as the Temple of Mithras, a mysterious Roman sect named for a bull slayer, the site, near the Bank of England in the old City of London, became a mass sensation in the 1950s, attracting tens of thousands of curious onlookers.

The public response, observed archaeologist Ivor Noël Hume in 1961, offered a measure of the 'immense popular interest in archaeology which, thanks to the power of television, has grown up in England since the war.'[4] London property owners, Hume noted, began putting 'antiquities clauses' in leases, requiring construction crews to halt work if they encountered artifacts. Winston Churchill himself waded into the fray, halting redevelopment of the site. The temple foundation was dismantled, placed in storage, and reconstructed about a hundred metres away in the early 1960s – a sloppy and historically questionable process that led to the destruction of some of the salvaged material.

Four decades later, however, the Temple of Mithras re-emerged from London's substrata. The original site had passed into the hands of Michael Bloomberg as a location for Bloomberg's European headquarters. The billionaire former New York mayor hired Sir Norman Foster to design both the office building and a new on-site exhibit space for the temple and six hundred of the 14,000 artifacts excavated from the dig. The London Mithraeum Bloomberg SPACE, situated seven metres beneath street level, opened in the fall of 2017.[5] (Another example of this kind of past-present pairing is Liverpool's Old Dock, an eighteenth-century wet dock that has been reconstructed beneath a sprawling shopping mall.)

Such examples, of course, are outliers – in this case, the confluence of London's unique archaeological heritage and Bloomberg's distinctively urban-minded brand of philanthropy. Other cities and regions in recent years have developed more accessible tools and policies intended to allow the public to engage with archaeological discoveries in a range of ways.

Among these are public archaeology programs that allow volunteers or schoolchildren to participate in digs and learn about the process of discovery.

In the early 1980s, for example, the Foundation for Public Archaeology brought thousands of schoolchildren to Indigenous sites in London, Ontario, the nineteenth-century Schneider Haus in Kitchener, the Waterloo County Gaol, and Upper Canada's third parliament buildings (under the current CBC building in Toronto).

In 1985, an archaeological team headed by Karolyn Smardz Frost excavated the former home of Thornton and Lucie Blackburn on behalf of the Toronto Board of Education. A formerly enslaved Kentucky couple, the Blackburns fled to Canada in the 1830s, settled in Toronto, and founded the city's first cab company. In 1985, the foundations of their small house and barn were found on the grounds of the Inglenook Community School, on Sackville Street. During excavations, thousands of schoolchildren visited the site and learned about the archaeology being done there.

In Boston, where colonial sites surface frequently, municipal officials, beginning in the 1980s, created an ambitious public archaeology program for volunteers, children, and graduate students. But from the early 1980s, Boston became the hub of one of North America's richest archaeological digs, due to the tunnelling required for the Central Artery (a.k.a. Big Dig), a massive highway burial scheme that became one of the costliest infrastructure projects in American history.

The route, which passed through central Boston, was dubbed the 'highway to the past' by the Massachusetts Historical Commission. Among other discoveries, the commission's project archaeologists unearthed 7,000-year-old Indigenous artifacts, wharfs, the rich contents of colonial-era privies, the foundations of the popular eighteenth-century Three Cranes Tavern, and remnants of the city's nineteenth-century glass industry.

The artifacts and related historical documents were exhibited in the Commonwealth Museum in Boston, and have become the subject of educational materials,[6] scholarly research, and a permanent online exhibit.[7] The tavern's foundations were reconstructed in one of the public parks created by the burial of the highway.

The most expansive examples of public and in situ urban archaeology in Canada can be found in Quebec. Following extensive archaeological excavations in the 1980s, the Montréal Museum of Archaeology and History (now the Montréal Archaeology and History Complex) opened in 1992 on Pointe-à-Callière, the site of the city's earliest settlement, and later a customs house, market, and collector sewer that was once the Saint Pierre River, a Saint Lawrence tributary.[8] To celebrate the city's 350th anniversary in 2017, the museum opened the collector sewer to the public and began publishing a series about Montreal's history, both moves that show how public interest in archaeology can be leveraged to generate further scholarship about local history.

Quebec City, a popular tourist destination, has also sought to leverage the archaeological assets in its Old Town neighbourhood, which include some of the oldest post-colonial communities in Canada as well as the remnants of Saint-Louis Forts and Châteaux, located beneath the iconic Dufferin Terrace outside the Château Frontenac hotel. Beginning in 2005, Parks Canada began stabilizing parts of the structure, in the process retrieving tens of thousands of artifacts. Many were put on display in the late 2000s, an exhibit that attracted half a million visitors; a permanent crypt space was constructed more recently, as well as viewing portals that allow pedestrians strolling along the terrace to peer down at the foundations of the fort.[9]

In the Old Town, the Auberge Saint-Antoine, a luxury hotel built atop an old wharf and warehouse property known as the Hunt Block, showcases the thousands of artifacts found by archaeologists who excavated the site prior to the multi-phase construction that began in 1992. The objects – everything from cutlery to bottles, ceramics, locks, and tools – have been displayed in illuminated cases throughout the hotel, both in its common/public areas as well as in individual rooms.[10] These displays, notes archaeologist Ron Williamson, 'are more akin to art installations than didactic history and heritage treatments.'

According to William Moss, Quebec City's former chief archaeologist, the hotel project emerged from the municipality's heritage preservation policies, which included a research partnership between the city and Université Laval that focused on Hunt Block excavations prior to the development of the hotel. 'Though this was entirely a private sector initiative,' notes Moss, 'both the City and the Province worked closely with the developer to ensure the harmonious integration of the new construction into the historic fabric of the Old Town.' Indeed, Laval researchers continued to advise on the project during an expansion in 2000.[11]

As of 2018, no comparable examples can be found in Toronto. There are still many archaeological sites, including dozens of extensive Indigenous settlements, in and around the city, with no shortage of unexpected finds that trigger widespread public interest, such as the discovery of a portion of a nineteenth-century ship's hull found during a 2015 waterfront construction project.[12] The ship had been moored near the historic Queen's Wharf, which extended into Lake Ontario south of Fort York, and eventually became subsumed by railway spurs and lake-filling. While excavations in the early 2010s revealed an 1850s railway engine house and the Garrison Creek channelization infrastructure built next to the wharf, there are not yet any public space markers or interpretive panels indicating its presence and role.[13]

Yet as Ron Williamson and David Robertson note in 'Why Were Archaeologists Working in the Ward?' (pages 252–257), archaeological policies adopted since the mid-2000s have begun to change this narrative. Two large downtown developments (TIFF Bell Lightbox and the Shangri-La Hotel) include permanent (though modest) on-site artifact displays. Meanwhile, the exposed foundations of Fort York's Stanley Barracks are featured prominently in front of a new hotel at Exhibition Place. Dating to the 1840s, the foundations will be displayed under a glass covering, footbridge, and interpretive canopy that adopts the shape of the two-storey structure that stood there until the 1950s.[14]

Moreover, city council's heritage-interpretation plans for two new projects – the North Market and the new Toronto courthouse, which will rise on the site of the Armoury Street Dig – include a significant

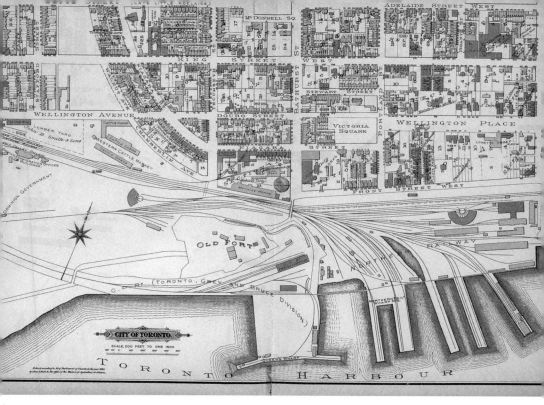

focus on historical commemoration and archaeological interpretation within the public spaces in the buildings, as well as displays of recovered artifacts and foundation or sub-grade elements.

Queen's Wharf. Goad's Toronto Fire Insurance Map, 1890.

Likewise, the remnants of Upper Canada's first Parliament buildings were identified in 2000 under a downtown car-wash parking lot at Front and Parliament Streets. The site later housed a jail, from 1840 to 1846, and then a sprawling gasworks plant from the 1890s to the 1960s. The City of Toronto and the provincial government secured the property, and, as of 2018, have embarked on a process for determining how to create public access and interpretation around this site.[15]

As the experiences of numerous other cities have demonstrated over many years, the effort and resources invested in such projects will almost certainly be met by the public's enduring fascination with urban archaeology.

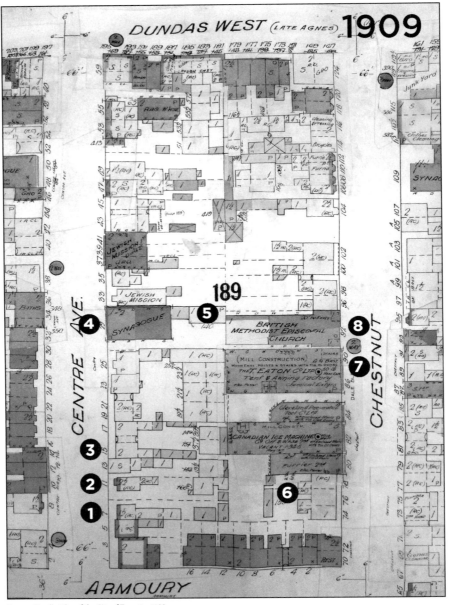

Source: Goad's Atlas of the City of Toronto, 1909

1. Francis Simpson's House
2. Cecelia Holmes's House
3. Annie Whalen's House
4. Shaarei Tzedec Synagogue
5. Israel Lerman Privy
6. Projectile Point
7. Eaton Tent & Awning Factory
8. BME Church

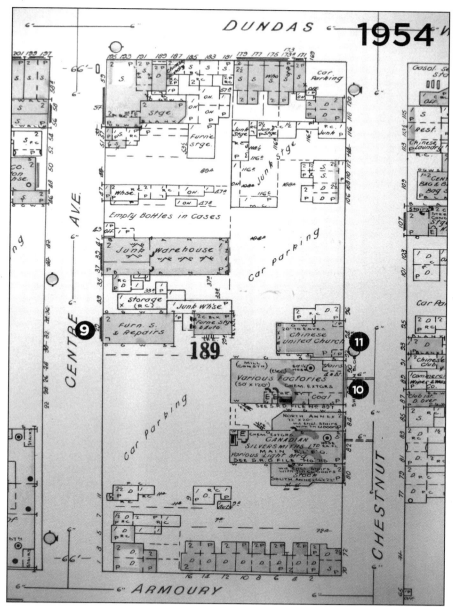

Source: Goad's Atlas of the City of Toronto, 1954

9 Pearl Furniture

10 Sheridan Building/
Fashion Hat & Cap Co.

11 Chinese United Church

# DRAWING CONCLUSIONS

### HOLLY MARTELLE, MICHAEL McCLELLAND, JOHN LORINC, & TATUM TAYLOR

**MAKING PLACES FOR ARTIFACTS**

AS AN ARCHAEOLOGIST, I get excited about the past. My heart beats a little faster when I see an artifact being uncovered or when I get to hold it in my hand. Such items offer a tangible link to a distant past I can only begin to imagine. Stories and plot lines immediately begin to form in my head as I think about the meaning of the objects, their origins, owners, makers, and functions, as well as their contributions to the place where they were found.

But archaeologists aren't the only ones who are fascinated with artifacts. Scholars and laypersons, adults and children, all have unique and varied interests in the past and in the materials that tell its stories. Beyond the public's curiosity, Indigenous and descendant communities whose ancestors created the sites that archaeologists dig up have an inherent right to participate in archaeological decision-making, interpretation, and artifact curation. These communities also see value in artifacts for, among other reasons, their ability to help tell stories to future generations and ensure the past will never be forgotten.

For historically marginalized groups like Canada's First Nations, Metis, and Black communities, storytelling opportunities have been limited within a colonial rubric that has minimized their contributions to this country. Archaeology can help tell the stories of groups that were long omitted from national historical narratives. With increased political activism on the part of descendant communities, archaeology done by and for archaeologists is becoming a thing of the past.

As part of an archaeological firm committed to promoting and practicing Indigenous engagement and public outreach, I have witnessed firsthand the benefits of active participation of descendant communities and the public in archaeology and the educational value of archaeologically based storytelling. And as the lead archaeologist on the excavation of the Armoury Street Dig, I am overwhelmed by the exciting public- and community-outreach opportunities this site and its incredible artifact collection afford. The outpouring of descendant, public, and scholarly interest in the project is testimony to the power of archaeology in reconnecting modern and historic communities, and in their desire to see, experience, write, and know the past. As a first step, this book speaks to those aspirations. Archaeology and artifacts play a role in place-making, and in the forging of identities (individual, local, national). This is why it is imperative that the artifacts from the Armoury Street Dig – forming part of the historical heart of Toronto – ultimately find a repository in the city.

The archaeological remnants of The Ward are invaluable to all of us. As an archaeologist, I find nothing more professionally or emotionally rewarding than to share these unearthed objects and their stories with descendants, the public, and schoolchildren. There is, in fact, an unparalleled opportunity here: the Armoury Street Dig yielded one of the richest and most distinctive artifact collections in Ontario; its educational merits are endless. For archaeologists, meanwhile, it is an incredible research and comparative resource, not just for the province but for all of North America. Historians are already elated by the opportunities to learn more, through archaeology, about the earliest periods of Toronto's past, and about many of the early Black settlers whose identity is defined by not much more than a name written on a map, a deed, or a tax assessment.

Descendant communities have looked to this collection seeking affirmation of their contributions to the City of Toronto. For them, these artifacts help illustrate, in three dimensions, the lives of known historical figures whose fortitude, resolve, perseverance, bravery, and entrepreneurialism offer salient models for us today. – *Holly Martelle*

## HOW MUSEUMS LEARN

MUSEUMS ARE NOT static; they act like living organisms, nurtured by context. In Toronto, the notion of exhibiting collected objects began in the nineteenth century with wealthy patrons sharing their private assemblages with the public as cabinets of curiosity. Collections were part of the intellectual mania of Victorian times, and sharing them followed the same philanthropic reasoning as creating public libraries. Knowledge was the path to self-improvement, and education was beneficial for all.

The Royal Ontario Museum (ROM) opened in 1912 with similar noble ambition – to assemble the treasures of the world. Reflecting broader museological trends, it changed its focus with each generation. During the Great Depression, the ROM was the 'palace of the people' with its beautiful gold mosaic rotunda, lifting spirits and welcoming all. When focus shifted to professionalism in museums, money was spent building up the curatorial wing and other back-of-house spaces. Then the museum adapted to new fascinations with the 'black box,' controlled environments, and immersive experiences – think of the Bat Cave and the blanking out of windows to control light levels. Later the complex introduced restaurants, retail shops, and event spaces, meant to compete with other commercial attractions by drawing visitors and tourists. Each shift was a rethinking of how the ROM was understood and what it contributed to the city and the province. Remarkably, it has retained all of these accumulated facets. Its Crystal transformation of 2007 and current works are positioning the ROM as increasingly urban, transparent, and engaged with its surroundings.

If the ROM reflects an ongoing evolution in the approach to museums over the past century, what is the next stage in that trajectory? If a museum were to open that exhibited the Ward artifacts, what sort of a museum would it be? It might have an approach somewhat like this book, which brings together a variety of voices, providing diverse narratives and even different conclusions, yet always leaving open the possibility that there are stories yet untold. And these stories go far beyond the boundaries of The Ward. The neighbourhood's DNA has spread widely to define the character of the diverse, multicultural city we now live in.

In a contemporary museum for Toronto, the humble artifacts of The Ward could appear alongside objects from the city's holdings, currently stored away in a Liberty Village warehouse. These collections are the tangible evidence of our past – a past that held much in common with our present, but of which little built fabric remains. A Toronto museum for the twenty-first century would tell the stories of our past to new generations, who face the task of continuing the building of this city. – *Michael McClelland*

## WHERE PATHS CROSS

THIS BOOK'S PREDECESSOR, *The Ward*, was inspired by a family trip to the Tenement Museum in New York's Lower East Side in 2013. That institution uses the vehicle of the long-condemned apartment buildings at 97 and 103 Orchard Street to unpack the social history of a notorious New York 'slum.' Like so many other visitors, I found the museum enthralling for its eclectic, intimate rendering of the area's past. Upon returning to Toronto, I wrote a feature for the *Toronto Star* about our own long-forgotten immigrant enclave, St. John's Ward. Noting the success of the Tenement Museum, the article pointed out that there were almost no Ward-era buildings left.

For the *Star* story, I interviewed heritage architect Michael McClelland, who offered an insight into the source of our historical amnesia. When society selects which buildings should be preserved for their heritage or architectural value, he observed, we mostly choose venerable institutional structures or those associated with the rich. Poor areas packed with derelict row houses and rundown commercial buildings tend to be bulldozed, even though such communities have produced complex and important histories of their own. When an area's built form is erased, the collective memory of what occurred there soon follows.

After the article came out, Michael and I began talking about creating a Ward Museum – a conversation that expanded to include heritage planner Tatum Taylor and historian Ellen Scheinberg. Lacking funds, a building, or stuff to put in it, we decided to publish a book instead.

As this sequel attests, a huge quantity of material evidence of life in this arrival city came to light, literally, around the time *The Ward* was

published, in 2015. The sequel anthology, in turn, surfaces as municipal officials begin to plan a Toronto Museum, to be located in old City
Hall, which was built in The Ward in 1899 and then loomed judgment-
ally over this stigmatized neighbourhood for almost sixty years.

In spite of their familiar buildings, distinct geographies, and signature
public spaces, cities are essentially unknowable as social spaces. At the
same time, like any city museum, the Toronto Museum must aspire to
relate the story – or, more accurately, *stories* – of this place. These two
observations may seem irreconcilable, yet The Ward's kaleidoscopic
history, and now its rich archaeological legacy, provide some valuable
clues about how Torontonians can begin to confront a formidable curatorial challenge.

As the city's first immigrant neighbourhood, The Ward was a place
with many narrators offering conflicting accounts of what transpired
there, a truly urban drama. The telling involves an almost forensic
search for palimpsests amid the erasure that decimated not just The
Ward, but huge swaths of Toronto's built heritage after World War II. So
a key mandate for this new museum will be accounting for these dis-
continuities, and revealing why and how they occurred.

Not unrelated is the fact that Toronto's future emerges from decades
of mass immigration, which has created a sprawling, forward-looking
metropolis with a higher proportion of newcomers than any other
global city, but little shared memory. More than any other political,
cultural, or commercial capitals, Toronto's defining trait is its abundant and bracing diversity – a demographic feature that traces, in some
ineffable way, back to The Ward. This, then, is the new museum's main
task: to relate a fundamentally social story about what happens when
paths cross. – *John Lorinc*

## UNCOVERING THE STORIES

AS I PORED over the Armoury Street Dig archaeological reports, in
which Holly and her team had begun to catalogue thousands of
artifacts, a familiar image caught my eye. It was a milk bottle – one of
hundreds recovered from the site. I recognized this particular silhouette and the letters in the cloudy, iridescent glass as being identical to a

bottle I keep on my desk. I bought mine at a vintage store, and it sits here unassumingly, brimming with wilted flowers. Meanwhile, its twin lies boxed in a London, Ontario, warehouse, awaiting its turn in the spotlight as a subject of archaeological study or a feature in a museum display.

The two bottles surely embarked on similar paths, manufactured and sold by the local Farmers Dairy in the 1920s. But at some point, their lives diverged, leading one across the decades to my desk and the other to the purgatory beneath a parking lot. Now my bottle is a curio that cost ten dollars; the excavated bottle is an artifact, priceless by virtue of its having been dug up from a privy. And yet, had this object never been unearthed, it would have no worth at all. We would continue to park our cars several feet above it, never knowing it was down there.

So what gives the artifact bottle value, so much more than my shabby-chic vase? Perhaps it is the story it represents as part of the dig, and part of The Ward.

The complex arithmetic of an artifact's cultural value includes many variables. An object begins with a simply commercial cost, accumulates sentimental value to its owners, loses this value and gets discarded, is rediscovered with accrued archaeological value, and gains new resonance if shared with the public. Even when archaeology has restored value to once-buried items, there is a tension between the artifacts' tangibility – their existence as hard, three-dimensional historical evidence – and the fact that they're still mostly unseen and transient. Their time as the object of a gaze, usually that of an archaeologist, is often fleeting. When they're not being studied, these artifacts are usually in storage.

Storage can be another form of burial, and not necessarily as secure as we assume. The terrorist attacks of September 11, 2001, destroyed nearly a million stored artifacts from the Five Points archaeological excavation in New York City; the only survivors were eighteen items out on loan for future display at a museum. Much like the findings from the Armoury Street Dig, these objects once belonged to early immigrants in New York. Though many field photographs were also ruined, the Five Points archaeologists had retained extensive documentation and analysis of the artifacts; the physical things were decimated, but not the information they yielded. Most New Yorkers knew nothing about these discoveries when they were stowed in the basement of Six World Trade Center, and had no chance to view them. After 9/11, they never will. How, then, to calculate this loss?

To the general public, an unseen artifact is perhaps like the proverbial tree falling in a forest. Its value is largely limited to the archaeological information it has yielded. That usefulness should by no means be discounted. But an artifact's meaning magnifies immeasurably through interpretation and public access. If objects acquire value through story, those stories need to be told to someone. We – the heritage professionals and writers privileged to work with these materials, but also the city and its officials – have a social imperative to share these narratives.

This responsibility raises questions: Who should be telling these stories, and to whom? Who 'owns' these artifacts? And whose heritage do they represent? Within my field of heritage conservation, a debate about the connotations of *heritage* versus *history* has continued for decades. Some say that heritage, through its etymology, implies inheritance; it is different from an all-encompassing history, in that heritage gets bequeathed to an exclusive group. Others say that heritage is not a cultural heirloom but rather an ongoing process of engaging and negotiating with a multiplicity of histories, memories, and identities. I find this latter viewpoint to be potent guidance in understanding the value of the Armoury Street Dig and its exhumed objects. We need to create public spaces to hold these artifacts. And when we do, we must also make space for their stories, told by multiple narrators. The objects may not belong to all of us, but their stories do. – *Tatum Taylor*

# NOTES

## INTRODUCTION

1. In the summer of 1847 alone, some 38,000 Irish migrants arrived in Toronto, a figure that exceeded the city's entire population.
2. Constance B. Backhouse, 'The Sayer Street Outrage: Gang Rape and Male Law in 19th Century Toronto,' *Manitoba Law Journal* 46 (1991).
3. Under Ontario law, all developers are required to complete archaeological assessments of a site before building on it. But it's probably safe to conclude that only a public agency would have been prepared to invest the time and resources necessary to thoroughly excavate a site like this one.
4. For further discussion about the agency of objects, see Aleshia Westgate (Bailey), The Object Agency (blog), https://theobjectagency.wordpress.com/2014/08/20/object-agency-and-object-biography/; and Torill Christine Lindstrøm, 'Agency "in Itself": A Discussion of Inanimate, Animal and Human Agency,' *Archaeological Dialogues* 22 (2015): 207–238, doi:10.1017/S1380203815000264, http://www.uib.no/sites/w3.uib.no/files/agency_ard_ard22_02_s1380203815000264a.pdf (accessed March 5, 2018).

## PARK LOT 11

1. S. R. Mealing, 'Powell, William Dummer,' in *Dictionary of Canadian Biography*, Vol. 6, University of Toronto/Université Laval, 2003 (accessed December 31, 2017), http://www.biographi.ca/en/bio/powell_william_dummer_6E.html.
2. Stage 1 Archaeological Assessment, Infrastructure Ontario, Toronto Courthouse. Timmins Martelle Heritage Consultants (February 2015). Submitted to the Ontario Ministry of Tourism, Culture and Sport. Page 9.
3. Indian Claims Commission: Mississaugas of the New Credit First Nation Inquiry, Toronto Purchase (June 2003). http://maps.library.utoronto.ca/datapub/digital/NG/historicTOmaps/newcreditlandclaim-eng.pdf.
4. Ronald Williamson (ed.), *Toronto: An Illustrated History of Its First 12,000 Years.* (Toronto: Lorimer, 2008), 42.
5. Historical Maps of Toronto, http://oldtorontomaps.blogspot.ca/2013/01/1787-1805-toronto-purchase.html.
6. The Ontario government completed a land-claim settlement with the Mississaugas of the New Credit in 2010, offering compensation of $145 million, a figure that reflected the commercial value of the Toronto Purchase as of 1805, adjusted to current dollars. https://www.thestar.com/news/gta/2010/06/08/shrugs_greet_historic_145m_toronto_land_claim_settlement.html.

## COCONUTS IN LATRINES!

1. *Coco* is the scientific name given to the tree by Carl Linnaeus in the eighteenth century; however, *coconut* is sometimes incorrectly spelled *cocoanut* (especially in old cookbooks), an error dating back to Dr. Samuel Johnson's entry for the fruit in his 1755 dictionary. Alan Davidson, *The Oxford Companion to Food* (Oxford University Press, 1999), p. 199.
2. Alexandra Greeley, 'Coconuts,' in *The Oxford Encyclopedia of Food and Drink in America,* ed. Andrew F. Smith (Oxford University Press, 2004), Vol. 1, p. 265.
3. 'Notes from the Capital,' *Globe,* October 28, 1881, p. 9.
4. *Globe,* October 13, 1864, p. 4.
5. *Globe,* December 31, 1887, p. 16.
6. *Globe,* August 13, 1898.
7. *Globe,* May 1, 1860, p. 2.
8. *Globe,* April 24, 1868, p. 2.
9. *Evening Star,* January 25, 1894, p. 4.
10. Cocoanut Pudding, p. 171; Kiss Pudding, p. 194; Cocoanut Pie, p. 209, and two recipes for Cocoanut Pie on p. 217; Cocoanut Puffs, p. 224; Cocoanut Drops, p. 263; Cocoanut Cake, p. 306, p. 324, and two Cocoanut Cakes on p. 329 (coconut seems to go in the batter); Cocoanut Cake, p. 310, p. 313, and p. 333 (coconut as part of the icing); Plain Sponge for Jelly or Cocoanut Cake, p. 311; Sandwich Cake, p. 320; Cocoanut Cake Made as Jelly Cake, p. 329. The spelling *cocoanut* is used in *The Home Cook Book.* Page references are to the 1878 facsimile edition, published by Whitecap Books, North Vancouver, 2002, with an introduction by Elizabeth Driver.
11. For example, Cocoanut Cones in *Evening Star,* May 4, 1895, using fresh coconut: 'Whisk three eggs till quite light, then add gradually 10 ounces of sifted sugar, and lastly six ounces of grated cocoanut; line some baking tins with white paper, and drop spoonfuls of the mixture in a cone shape on this, and bake in a rather cool oven until delicately colored. You will find it easier, if you have a forcing pipe with a wide pipe, to force the mixture out on to the paper with this, instead of a spoon'; and Cocoanut Pudding three days later, on May 7, in the same newspaper: 'For a cocoanut pudding take one and a half pints of milk, half a cupful of milk-cracker crumbs, half a cupful of sugar, heaped tablespoonful of butter, two eggs and half a cupful of cocoanut. Bake in a delicate crust, in small patty pans, for twenty minutes.'
12. The purpose is stated on the title page of the 1877 and 1878 editions, and in the preface to the 1877 edition.
13. See David Wright, *SickKids: The History of the Hospital for Sick Children* (University of Toronto Press, 2016), image 2.4, p. 43, 'Location of The Hospital for Sick Children Year 1875 1878 1892,' and pp. 26 and 34 (note 43). The hospital was at 31 Avenue Street, 1875–1876; 245 Elizabeth Street, 1878–1886; 67 College Street (at Elizabeth Street), 1892–1951, after which it moved to its current location at 555 University Avenue.
14. David Wright, *SickKids,* pp. 25, 45.
15. I am grateful to Daniel Panneton for his analysis of the censuses.

## DIGGING UP THE NORTH MARKET

1. D. B. Landon, 'Zooarchaeology and Historical Archaeology: Progress and Prospects,' *Journal of Archaeological Method and Theory,* Vol. 12, No. 1 (2005): 1–36.
2. A. Denison and R. Donald, *Report of Market Commission* (1898).
3. J. R. Robertson, *Robertson's Landmarks of Toronto, Fifth Series* (Toronto: J. Ross Robertson, 1908).
4. 'The St. Lawrence Market,' *Globe and Mail,* December 24, 1855.
5. 'Christmas Display in St. Lawrence Market,' *Globe and Mail,* December 23, 1858.

6.  'The Christmas Meat Market,' *Globe and Mail*, December 23, 1873.
7.  W. Canniff, 'Report of Medical Health Officer,' in Sessional Papers No. 14, Vol. 19, Part 3 of the First Session of the Sixth Legislature of the Province of Ontario, Session 1887 (Toronto: Warwick and Sons, 1887).

## THE CIVIC ENGAGEMENT OF WARD CHILDREN
### Swat the Fly
Katie Daubs, 'Beatrice White, the Girl Who Killed Half a Million Flies for Toronto,' *Toronto Star*, August 8, 2015.
'Rules of Swat the Fly Competition,' *Toronto Star*, July 6, 1912.
### Just Kids Safety Club
Various articles, *Globe and Mail*, March 30, 1928; March 31, 1928; April 2, 1928; April 4, 1928; May 4, 1928.
'AD Carter, Creator of "Just Kids" Comics,' *New York Times*, June 26, 1957.
### CNH
A. Irving, H. Parsons, and D. F. Bellamy, *Neighbours: Three Social Settlements in Downtown Toronto* (Toronto: Canadian Scholars' Press, 1995).
P. J. O'Connor, *The Story of Central Neighbourhood House 1911–1986* (Toronto Association of Neighbourhood Services, 1986).
Central Neighbourhood House Historical Highlights Year by Year: 1912, http://www.virtualmuseum.ca/sgc-cms/histoires_de_chez_nous-community_memories/pm_v2.php?id=story_line&lg=English&fl=0&ex=00000818&sl=9530&pos=1.

## THE MILK BOTTLE BATTLE
1.  'Highland Dairy Issues New Stock,' *Globe*, January 24, 1930, 7.
2.  'Robert Balmer McGiffin,' Biographical Dictionary of Architects in Canada 1800–1950. http://dictionaryofarchitectsincanada.org/node/682.
3.  Cheryl Emily MacDonald, *Adelaide Hoodless: Domestic Crusader* (Dundurn Press, 1986), 18.
4.  Kevin Plummer, 'Historicist: "If It's City Dairy It's Clean and Pure. That's Sure. How Toronto's City Dairy Became One of the Largest Dairies in the British Empire,"' Torontoist, November 30, 2013. https://torontoist.com/2013/11/historicist-if-its-city-dairy-its-clean-and-pure-thats-sure/.
5.  'Milk for Ward Babies,' *Globe*, July 7, 1908, 12.
6.  'Second Pure Milk Depot,' *Globe*. July 8, 1908, 12.
7.  'The Clean Milk Problem,' *Globe*, November 4, 1908, 12.
8.  'For Toronto's Babies: Depot Will Be Established to Pasteurize Milk,' *Globe*, May 20, 1909, 1.
9.  David Wencer, 'How John Ross Robertson Improved the Lives of Toronto's Children,' Heritage Toronto, October 21, 2009. http://heritagetoronto.org/milk-pasteurization-at-sick-kids/.
10. 'Toronto's Milk Supply,' *Globe*, November 22, 1909, 14.
11. Valerie Hauch, 'Once Upon a City: Dentonia Park Born of Massey's Dairy Dream,' *Toronto Star*, March 17, 2016. https://www.thestar.com/yourtoronto/once-upon-a-city-archives/2016/03/17/once-upon-a-city-dentonia-park-borne-of-masseys-dairy-dream.html.
12. 'Will Enforce Law for Clean Food,' *Globe*, May 20, 1911, 12.
13. 'Campaign Regarding Milk,' *Toronto Daily Star*, March 7, 1921, 3.
14. 'Drink More Milk,' *Toronto Daily Star*, April 4, 1921, 2.
15. 'Milk as Food Boomed All Over City To-Day,' *Toronto Daily Star*, April 5, 1921, 10.
16. Wencer, 'How John Ross Robertson Improved the Lives of Toronto's Children.'

## THE SELTZER BOTTLE'S JOURNEY

1. Bartmann is the original German name for the bottle. The English, and today's English scholars, often referred to it as a Bellarmine.
2. Germany is still known for its tall, stoneware beer steins.
3. A process to artificially carbonate water was discovered by Joseph Priestley in 1767 and he published his findings in 1772. Priestley believed carbonated water would cure scurvy. It doesn't.
4. Using Priestley's discovery, Jacob Schweppe established a commercial carbonated water business in Geneva in 1783. Schweppe moved the business to London, England, in 1792.

## ADDING SPARKLE TO EVERYDAY LIFE

1. Might Directory Company of Toronto Ltd. *The Toronto City Directory 1895*, Vol. 19. http://static.torontopubliclibrary.ca/da/pdfs/tcd1895.pdf.
2. Robert F. Barratt, 'Soft-Drink Industry,' *The Canadian Encyclopedia*. December 16, 2013. http://www.thecanadianencyclopedia.ca/en/article/soft-drink-industry/.
3. Ellen Scheinberg, 'Public Baths: Schvitzing on Centre Avenue,' in John Lorinc, Michael McClelland, Ellen Scheinberg, Tatum Taylor (eds.), *The Ward: The Life and Loss of Toronto's First Immigrant Neighbourhood* (Toronto: Coach House Books, 2015), 253.
4. Michael C. Bonasera and Leslie Raymer, 'Good for What Ails You: Medicinal Use at Five Points,' *Historical Archaeology*, Vol. 35, No. 3 (2001): 49–64. http://www.jstor.org/stable/25616938.
5. Dan Nosowitz, 'Germans Are the World's Most Discerning Seltzer Connoisseurs. Don't Mess with Mineralwasser,' Atlas Obscura. May 15, 2017. https://www.atlasobscura.com/articles/seltzer-germany-mineral-water.
6. Meredith B. Linn, 'Elixir of Emigration: Soda Water and the Making of Irish Americans in Nineteenth-Century New York City,' *Historical Archaeology*, Vol. 44, No. 4 (2010): 69–109.
7. Might Directory Company of Toronto Ltd., *The Toronto City Directory 1895*.
8. John Goodyer and David Dobing, 'The Unabridged James Eves Story,' Canadian Bottle Collectors. http://www.canadianbottlecollectors.com/the_unabridged_james_eves_story.pdf
9. Ibid.
10. Ellen Scheinberg, 'Taking Care of Business in the Ward,' in John Lorinc, Michael McClelland, Ellen Scheinberg, Tatum Taylor (eds.), *The Ward: The Life and Loss of Toronto's First Immigrant Neighbourhood* (Toronto: Coach House Books, 2015), 168–169.
11. Might Directories Ltd. *The Toronto City Directory 1923*. Vol. 48. https://archive.org/details/torontocitydirectory1923.
12. *The Toronto Jewish City & Information Directory* (1925), 218. http://www.ontariojewisharchives.org/Research/Toronto-Jewish-City-Directories.
13. Ben Teichman (as told to Norton Taichman), 'The House at 211 Beverly Street, a Memoir.' *The Ivansk Project* (e-newsletter), Issue 38, September–October 2009. http://www.ivanskproject.org/Newsletters/38.pdf.
14. *Canadian Druggist*, Vol. 15, January–December 1903. https://archive.org/stream/canadiandruggist15torouoft/canadiandruggist15torouoft_djvu.txt.
15. Howard Slepkof, 'Really Dysfunctional Family,' *Roots and Branches – Genealogical Explorations of Family and Community* (blog). December 28, 2015. http://exploringfamilyandcommunity.blogspot.ca/2015/.
16. Personal communication with Allen Rosenberg, November 2017.
17. Sarah Elton, 'The Last Seltzerman in Canada.' *Maclean's*. Vol. 123, No. 22, June 14, 2010.

## THE MULTIPLE LIVES OF ORDINARY BUILDINGS

1. Report of the Civic Improvement Committee of the City of Toronto, 1911. https://archive.org/details/reportofcivicimpootoro.

## FREEDOM ABOUNDS

1. *Globe*, August 5, 1852, 374.
2. An Emancipation Day celebration took place in Montreal on August 1, 1834, the day the Slavery Abolition Act took effect. See Natasha Henry, *Emancipation Day: Celebrating Freedom in Canada* (Toronto: Dundurn Press, 2010), 168.
3. Christine Mosser, *York, Upper Canada: Minutes of Town Meetings and Lists of Inhabitants, 1797–1823* (Toronto: Metropolitan Library Board, 1984); Natasha Henry, 'Black Enslavement in Canada,' *Canadian Encyclopedia*, 2015, accessed December 18, 2017, http://www.thecanadianencyclopedia.ca/en/m/article/black-enslavement/.
4. Mosser, *York, Upper Canada*.
5. 'Proceedings for the North American Convention held in Toronto, Canada, 1851,' ColoredConventions.org, accessed December 27, 2017, http://coloredconventions.org/items/show/324.
6. *Provincial Freeman*, August 5, 1854, 2.
7. Ibid; *Provincial Freeman*, July 29, 1854, 3; *Provincial Freeman*, August 12, 1854, 3; Adrienne Shadd, *The Journey from Tollgate to Parkway: African Canadians in Hamilton* (Toronto: Dundurn Press, 2010), 127.
8. Natasha Henry, *Talking about Freedom: Celebrating Emancipation Day in Canada*, 50.
9. *Globe*, August 3, 1858, 2.
10. Ibid.

## RESISTING STEREOTYPES

1. My sincere thanks to scholar Dr. Cheryl Thompson for her commentary on this paper. For Jim Crow and the Louisville connection, see George H. Yater, *Two Hundred Years at the Falls of the Ohio: A History of Louisville and Jefferson County* (Louisville: Filson Club, 1987), 59, and illustration. C. Vann Woodward, *The Strange Career of Jim Crow* (New York: Oxford University Press, 1955), gives 1832 as the date of the first performance. The song as first published is in the Lester S. Levy Collection of Sheet Music, Special Collections, at the Milton S. Eisenhower Library of the Johns Hopkins University.
2. The classic work on segregation is Woodward's *The Strange Career of Jim Crow*, which was revised and republished in multiple editions.
3. The largest collection of Foster's work is contained in the Foster Hall Collection, Number CAM.FHC.2011.0. See *Guide to Archives and Manuscript Collections at the University of Pittsburgh Library System*, University of Pittsburgh, Center for American Music; 'Christy's Minstrels,' *New York Times*, September 14, 1855.
4. Wilson R. Abbott to his Worship the Mayor and the Corporation of Toronto, July 20, 1841; To His Worship, the Mayor of Toronto, October 14, 1841; Wilson R. Abbott, to the Mayor and the Common Council of Toronto, May 9, 1842; Wilson R. Abbott et al. to His Honor the Mayor, the Aldermen and Councilmen of the City of Toronto, April 21, 1843, City of Toronto Archives.
5. The show was mounted in June and July at the Royal Lyceum Theatre by its manager, John Nickinson, with his daughter Virginia in blackface makeup in the role of Topsy. In 1857, a production with his elder daughter, Charlotte Nickinson, in the role of Eliza, was a sellout hit. The first was a serious play, but minstrel-show performers were included in the second, with songs specially written for performance by the Canadian Ethiopian Serenaders. See surviving playbills including Royal Lyceum (Toronto). *Uncle Tom's Cabin, or slave life*: printed advertisement, Toronto, February 6, 1857. Directed by John Nickinson; Eliza played by Miss C. Nickinson, Harvard Theater Collection, Houghton Library, Harvard University.
6. The authority on minstrelsy in Canada is Cheryl Thompson, whose groundbreaking post-doctoral project is entitled 'Visualizing Blackface Minstrelsy in Canada: Seeing Race, Negotiating Identities, 1890–1959.' This article is substantively informed by

her excellent "'Come One, Come All": Blackface Minstrelsy as a Canadian Tradition and Early Form of Popular Culture,' in *Towards an African Canadian Art History: Art, Memory, and Resistance*, Charmaine Nelson, ed. (Concord, Ontario: Captus Press, forthcoming), unpaginated. I am grateful to Dr. Thompson for sharing her unpublished work with me.

7. David Gardner, 'Burgess, Colin,' in *Dictionary of Canadian Biography*, vol. 13, University of Toronto/Université Laval, 2003 (accessed January 10, 2018), http://www.biographi.ca/en/bio/burgess_colin_13E.html. Garner attributes to Burgess the song 'Shoo, Fly! Don't Bother Me.' See also 'Cool Burgess, Minstrel Dead: As "Nicodemus Johnsing" the Toronto Comedian Long Reigned Supreme in Black Face Here and Abroad,' *Boston Herald*, October 25, 1905, 5.

8. As Thompson points out, long before the turn of the twentieth century, *Uncle Tom's Cabin* had lost its good influence, in part because of the popularity of minstrel shows mocking its earnest abolitionism.

9. *Globe*, June 14, 1909. See also Robin W. Winks, *The Blacks in Canada: A History*, 2nd ed. (Montreal: McGill-Queen's Press, 1997), 291.

10. For further reading, consult the website and bibliography compiled for *The Juba Project*, directed by Stephen Johnson, University of Toronto (accessed January 3, 2018), http://www.utm.utoronto.ca/~w3minstr/burntcork/conf_bibliography.html.

## REMEMBERING UNCLE TOM'S CABIN

1. Jo-Ann Morgan, *Uncle Tom's Cabin as Visual Culture* (University of Missouri Press: Columbia and London, 2007), 3.

2. Robin Bernstein, *Racial Innocence: Performing American Childhood from Slavery to Civil Rights* (New York: New York University Press, 2011), 13.

3. Sarah Meer, *Uncle Tom Mania: Slavery, Minstrelsy & Transatlantic Culture in the 1850s* (Athens, Georgia: University of Georgia Press, 2005), 2.

4. Ibid., 9–10.

5. David Gardner, 'Burgess, Colin (Cool).' *Dictionary of Canadian Biography*, http://www.biographi.ca/en/bio/burgess_colin_13E.html.

6. Hilary Russell, *Loew's Yonge Street and Winter Garden Theatres: A Structural, Architectural and Social History* (Toronto: Historical Research Division, Canadian Parks Service, 1990), 3.

7. Robert Brockhouse, *The Royal Alexandra Theatre: A Celebration of 100 Years* (Toronto: McArthur & Company, 2007), 8, 32.

8. *Evening Star*, December 20, 1898, 5.

9. *Toronto Globe*, April 9, 1901, 12.

10. John W. Frick, *Uncle Tom's Cabin on the American Stage and Screen* (New York: Palgrave MacMillan, 2012), 142.

11. Morgan, *Uncle Tom's Cabin*, 2.

12. Ibid., 42.

13. Morgan, *Uncle Tom's Cabin*, 181.

14. Yuval Taylor and Jake Austen, *Darkest America: Black Minstrelsy from Slavery to Hip-Hop* (New York: W. W. Norton & Company, 2012), 56.

15. Morgan, *Uncle Tom's Cabin*, 3.

16. Jill Weitzman Fenichell, 'Fragile Lessons: Ceramic and Porcelain Representations of Uncle Tom's Cabin,' see http://www.chipstone.org/article.php/280/Ceramics-in-America-2006/Fragile-Lessons:-Ceramic-and-Porcelain-Representations-of-Uncle-Tom%E2%80%99s-Cabin.

17. Ibid.

18. Marcus Wood, *Blind Memory: Visual Representations of Slavery in England and America, 1780–1865* (Manchester: Manchester University Press, 2000), 152.

19. Morgan, *Uncle Tom's Cabin*, 24.

20. Stephen Johnson, 'Uncle Tom and the Minstrels: Seeing Black and White on Stage in Canada West prior to the American Civil War,' in *(Post)Colonial Stages: Critical & Creative Views on Drama, Theatre & Performance*, ed. Helen Gilbert (Coventry: Dangaroo Press, 1999), 57.

21. Ibid., 62.

22. Meer, *Uncle Tom Mania*, 14.

23. 'Church Bulletins,' *Canadian Observer*, December 12, 1914, 3.

24. Jared Toney, 'Locating Disapora: Afro-Caribbean Narratives of Migration and Settlement in Toronto, 1914–1929,' *Urban History Review/Revue d'histoire urbaine*, Vol 38, No. 2 (Spring 2010): 80.

25. 'Toronto Jamaica Folk Attend Smart Wedding,' *Toronto Daily Star*, July 29, 1926, 25.

26. Noliwe Rooks, *Ladies' Pages: African American Women's Magazines and the Culture that Made Them* (New Brunswick, NJ: Rutgers University Press, 2004), 99.

## A BLACK LITERARY SOCIETY

1. Caverhill's *Toronto City Directory for 1859–60: Containing a Complete Alphabetical Directory of the Householders, and a Classified Business Director of the Subscribers* (Toronto: W. C. F. Caverhill, 1859), 292. This group is named elsewhere in the same directory (listing for G. W. Cary) as the 'Colored People's Moral and Mental Improvement Society.'

2. Phyllis M. Belt-Beyan, *The Emergence of African American Literacy Traditions: Family and Community Efforts in the Nineteenth Century* (Westport, Conn.: Praeger, 2004), 116.

3. Other groups in Canada West (Ontario) were the mixed-sex Wilberforce Lyceum Educating Society (Cannonsburg), the mixed-sex Dumas Literary Society (Chatham), the Ladies Literary Society (Chatham), and the Windsor Ladies Club. The Provincial Union Association, a mixed-sex political and benevolent organization, based in Toronto but with other branches, also had a literary mandate. See Heather Murray, *Come, Bright Improvement: The Literary Societies of Nineteenth-Century Ontario* (Toronto: University of Toronto Press, 2002), 200–3, 249, 261. The Excelsior group is mentioned in the *Provincial Freeman*, March 24, 1855. While the Freeman surely would have noted the launch of the Moral and Mental Improvement Society (African), issues from the relevant time period no longer exist.

4. Primarily, the city directories for 1856 (Brown's), 1859–60 (Caverhill's), 1861 (Brown's), 1862–63 (Hutchinson's), and 1866 (Mitchell's).

5. John Lorinc, 'The Black Community in St. John's Ward: An Essay Marking Black History Month in the City of Toronto,' City of Toronto website (February 2017), https://www.toronto.ca/explore-enjoy/history-art-culture/black-history-month/the-black-community-in-st-johns-ward/.

## THE SYNAGOGUE ON CENTRE AVENUE

1. Shaarei Tzedec, translated as 'Gates of Righteousness,' has several spelling variations: Shaarei Zedeck, Shaarei Tsedeck and Shaarei Tzedek being among the most common. The congregation's Markham Street shul and the shul on Centre Avenue were also widely known as the Russian or Russisher shul within the downtown Toronto Jewish community. The spelling used for this article is consistent with the congregation's current website.

**Works Consulted**

Dr. Zvi Cohen, ed. *Canadian Jewry: Prominent Jews of Canada.* Toronto: Canadian Jewish Historical Publishing Co., 1933.

Benjamin Kayfetz and Stephen A. Speisman. *Only Yesterday: Collected Pieces on the Jews of Toronto.* Toronto: Now & Then Books, 2013.

John Lorinc, Michael McClelland, Ellen Scheinberg, and Tatum Taylor, eds. *The Ward.* Toronto: Coach House Books, 2015.

Shmuel Mayer Shapiro. *The Rise of the Toronto Jewish Community*. Toronto: Now & Then Books, 2010.

Stephen A. Speisman. *The Jews of Toronto: A History to 1937*. Toronto: McClelland & Stewart, 1979.

Lawrence F. Tapper. *A Biographical Dictionary of Canadian Jewry, 1909–1914: From the Canadian Jewish Times*. Teaneck, NJ: Avotaynu Inc., 1992.

## WRITING HOME

1.  Still's book is available in full at http://www.gutenberg.org/files/15263/15263-h/15263-h.htm.

## CORRESPONDENT: CECELIA HOLMES

1.  John Merriwether Tinsley was born in Virginia in 1783, the son of a white Irish Revolutionary War soldier and an African American woman. His uncle was the law clerk in Richmond, Virginia, under whom statesman and future presidential hopeful Henry Clay apprenticed. Tinsley came to Canada with his wife, Douglass, and his married daughter's family, the Custaloes, in 1842 and established a small grocery store. After Douglass's death, Tinsley opened a carpentry business and began constructing homes in Macaulaytown (the southern end of St. John's Ward). A complex and outspoken man, Tinsley appeared often in newspaper articles regarding political protest against discrimination, antislavery activism, and African Canadian community events. He was also engaged in receiving fugitive slaves on behalf of William Still, secretary of the Pennsylvania Antislavery Society, and is mentioned in letters to Still as the most reliable local employer for African American immigrants. Tinsley was the only businessman of African descent with a biography in the first volume of C. Blackett Robinson's *History of Toronto and County of York* (Toronto: C. Blackett Robinson, 1885), 162, where Tinsley's ethnicity was not mentioned. This fascinating man would live to be 109, dying October 5, 1892. His passing elicited long obituaries in Toronto papers and even garnered mention under 'Telegraphic Brevities,' in the *New York Times* of October 7, 1892. The Tinsleys are buried in the Toronto Necropolis, although only Douglass Tinsley's gravestone is now legible.
2.  The Nat Turner Revolt was initiated by the literate and deeply religious Nat Turner, who was enslaved in Southampton County, Virginia. Months in the making, the rebellion was launched on August 21–22, 1831, and resulted in the deaths of more than fifty European-Americans. Although the revolt was rapidly put down, and the ringleaders executed, the resulting hysteria resulted in the violent deaths of uncounted numbers of innocent African Americans accused of conspiracy. Virginia considered abolishing slavery but chose instead to impose harsh new laws limiting the activities of African Americans, both enslaved and free, and requiring all freed Black people to leave the state within a year of their manumission. As a result, Toronto and other Canadian centres received substantial numbers of hard-working, entrepreneurial, and often moneyed Black American immigrants who established fine businesses and homes in their adopted homeland. Turner dictated his own account to a white attorney before his death. See Thomas R. Gray, *The Confessions of Nat Turner, the Leader of the Late Insurrection in Southampton, VA* (Richmond, VA: Thomas R. Gray, 1832).
3.  The early history of Benjamin and Ann Eliza Holmes, along with that of their two sons, is detailed in the pages of Cecelia's biography, Karolyn Smardz Frost's *Steal Away Home* (Toronto: HarperCollins Canada, 2017), esp. 30–46; Cecelia's rescue is described on pages 20–29 of the same volume.
4.  Hiram Wilson to Joshua Leavitt, *Emancipator,* August 28, 1840, reprinted in the *Colored American*, September 9, 1840.
5.  R. Macpherson, 'Dick, Thomas,' in *Dictionary of Canadian Biography*, vol. 10 (University of Toronto/Université Laval, 2003), accessed February 21, 2018, http://

www.biographi.ca/en/bio/dick_thomas_10E.html; Frederick H. Armstrong, 'Richardson, Hugh (1784-1870),' in *Dictionary of Canadian Biography*, vol. 9 (University of Toronto/ Université Laval, 2003), accessed February 21, 2018, http://www.biographi.ca/en/ bio/richardson_hugh_1784_1870_9E.html. Richardson told British traveller Harriet Martineau that 'the sublimest sight in North America is the leap of a slave from a boat to the Canadian shore. That "leap" transforms him from a marketable chattel to a free man.' See speech by Samuel Ringgold Ward delivered at Freemasons' Hall, London, England, June 21, 1853, in C. Peter Ripley et al., eds., *The Black Abolitionist Papers*, vol. 1, *Canada* (Chapel Hill, NC: University of North Carolina Press, 1985), 362-5.

6. The Abbotts had come to Toronto from Mobile, Alabama, by way of New York City during the winter of 1835-36, after their successful business was burned by a white mob. Robin W. Winks, 'Abbott, Wilson Ruffin,' in *Dictionary of Canadian Biography*, vol. 10 (University of Toronto/Université Laval, 2003), accessed February 21, 2018, http://www.biographi.ca/en/bio/abbott_wilson_ruffin_10E.html; Catherine Slaney, *Family Secrets: Crossing the Colour Line* (Toronto: Dundurn Group, 2003), esp. 13-18.

7. Archives of Ontario, RG 61-64, County of York Land Registry Office. Abstract index for Plan 147. GSU 197293. This gives a full record of transactions, including mortgages, on Lot 7, east side of Centre Street (now Centre Avenue), in Plan 147, City of Toronto.

MORE THAN A SHOEMAKER

1. 1861 Census of Canada, Toronto, St. John's Ward; *Brown's Toronto General Directory 1861* (Toronto: Brown, 1861), 37.

2. Fraternal orders of the nineteenth century characteristically refused membership to people of African descent, so separate African American organizations grew up paralleling the white-dominated orders. Lodges were founded in Canadian cities – including Toronto – by immigrating African Americans. The Grand United Order of Oddfellows was founded in New York in 1843, and incorporated through the British rather than American lodge. See Donald G. Simpson, Paul E. Lovejoy, eds., *Under the North Star: Black Communities in Upper Canada Before Confederation* (Trenton, NJ: Africa World Press, 2005), 122. There was a Grand United Order of Oddfellows lodge established in 1854 in Hamilton. This article suggests the founding of the Victoria Lodge at Toronto was at least slightly earlier. 'Grand United Order of Odd Fellows Soiree,' *Globe*, October 10, 1854.

3. Toronto was the only place in Canada West (Ontario) where the schools, churches, and institutions of higher learning were never segregated. The Toronto Normal School opened on Gould Street in 1847, and provided higher education for several very successful African Canadian graduates. For primary documentation regarding the life of Emeline Shadd, see her entry in *Breaking the Chains*, Harriet Tubman Institute, York University: http://tubman.info.yorku.ca/educational-resources/ breaking-the-chains/toronto/emeline-shadd/

4. Testimony of F. G. Simpson (shoemaker), Toronto, September 5, 1863, File No. 10 Canadian Testimony, MSS of the American Freedmen's Inquiry Commission, U.S. Department of War, Letters received by the Office of the Adjutant General, Main Series, 1861-70, National Archives, Washington (NARA). My gratitude to genealogist extraordinaire Guylaine Pétrin and Toronto attorney Matthew Furrow for kindly providing me with access to transcripts of these documents.

5. See, for instance, 'City Election: Influential Meeting of Coloured Electors,' *Globe*, December 19, 1857, for which Simpson was listed as Secretary in a meeting garnering African Canadian community support for city councillor Robert Moodie; 'Meeting of Coloured Electors,' December 19, 1857, which was to promote the election of George Brown, publisher of the *Globe*. On August 11, 1860, the *Globe* reported F. G. Simpson as chair for a 'Meeting of Coloured People to take into consideration questions of vital

importance to the coloured inhabitants of this Province.' For his union affiliation, see 'Address of the Hon. Alexander Mackenzie to the Toronto Working Men on the "National Policy"' (Toronto: Globe Printing Office, 1878), accessed February 10, 2016, http://qspace.library.queensu.ca/bitstream/1974/10300/1/addressofhonalexoomack.pdf.

6. 'Meeting of Coloured Citizens to Investigate,' *Globe*, May 25, 1882.

7. I am indebted to Guylaine Pétrin for bringing this article to my attention. According to her findings, Lewis later moved with his family to Vulcan, Alberta, where his daughter Mildred became the wife of famous African Canadian cowboy John Ware. For Ware's life, see David H. Breen, 'Ware, John,' in *Dictionary of Canadian Biography*, vol. 13 (University of Toronto/Université Laval, 2003), accessed February 17, 2018, http://www.biographi.ca/en/bio/ware_john_13E.html.

8. Laura Scott Simpson's maternal grandfather was noted Toronto barber Elisha Edmunds, who had arrived with three brothers in 1832, in the wake of Nat Turner's slave rebellion. He narrated his own story to an unnamed journalist, who published the account in 'Our Colored Citizens: Interviews with Some of Them on Important Subjects,' *Globe*, February 5, 1886, 6. The article erroneously gives the date of the Nat Turner events as 1829, instead of August 1831. Frank and Laura Simpson lived at 155 Richmond Street West, and he was employed seasonally as a waiter at Niagara Falls and then the Rossin House at King and York Streets in Toronto.

9. Re: Benjamin Pollard Holmes: Statutory Declaration of Francis Griffin Simpson: Death of client's first husband [sent via] John Rawn, Solicitor, Washington, DC, Postal Stamp: Jan. 27, 1897, Case of Cecelia J. Larrison, Louisville, Kentucky, service of William H. Larrison (Under-cook, Co. 'H'. 14th New York Heavy Artillery, Civil War): Civil War and Later Pension Files; Department of Veterans Affairs, Record Group 15: National Archives and Records Administration (NARA), Washington DC

10. The life of William Hubbard is detailed in Catherine Slaney, *Family Secrets: Crossing the Colour Line* (Toronto: Dundurn Group, 2003), esp. pages 207-8, and Stephen L. Hubbard, *Against All Odds: The Story of William Peyton Hubbard: Black Leader and Municipal Reformer* (Toronto: Dundurn, 1997).

## FRANCIS SIMPSON ON BEING BLACK IN 1860S TORONTO

1. The documents with the testimony provided to Howe are in the National Archives, Washington, DC. They were transcribed by Toronto lawyer Matthew Furrow as part of his research for a 2010 journal article, 'Samuel Gridley Howe, the Black Population of Canada West, and the Racial Ideology of the "Blueprint for Radical Reconstruction,"' *The Journal of American History* (September 2010): 344.

## THE LAYERED CITY

1. Rebecca Yamin, Pam Crabtree, and Claudia Milne, 'New York's Mythic Slum,' *Archaeology*, Vol. 50, No. 2 (March/April 1997): 44-53.

2. Edward Rothstein, 'A Burial Ground and Its Dead Are Given Life,' *New York Times*, February 25, 2010. http://www.nytimes.com/2010/02/26/arts/design/26burial.html (accessed February 24, 2018).

3. The museum site is available here: https://archaeology.crossrail.co.uk/.

4. Ivor Noël Hume, 'Preservation of the English and Colonial American Sites,' Archaeology, Vol. 14, No. 4, (December 1961): 250-56.

5. Maev Kennedy, 'Reconstructed Roman Temple of Mithras Opens to Public in London,' *Guardian*, November 8, 2017. https://www.theguardian.com/science/2017/nov/08/reconstructed-roman-temple-mithras-opens-public-bloomberg-hq (accessed February 26, 2018).

6. Ann-Eliza H. Lewis, ed., *Highway to the Past: The Archaeology of Boston's Big Dig* (Massachusetts Historical Commission: 2001). https://www.sec.state.ma.us/mhc/mhcpdf/Big_Dig_book.pdf (Accessed February 26, 2018).

7. Massachusetts Historical Commission, http://www.sec.state.ma.us/mhc/mhcarchexhibitsonline/index.htm.

8. Diane Sabourin, 'Pointe-à-Callière, the Montréal Museum of Archaeology and History,' The Canadian Encyclopedia. http://www.thecanadianencyclopedia.ca/en/article/musee-pointe-a-calliere/ (accessed February 26, 2018).

9. Jacques Guimont, 'Saint Louis Forts and Châteaux Archaeological Site,' The Canadian Encyclopedia. http://www.thecanadianencyclopedia.ca/en/article/saint-louis-forts-and-chateaux-archaeological-site/ (accessed February. 26, 2018).

10. 'The Auberbe Saint-Antoine Story,' https://www.saint-antoine.com/hotel/our-story.

11. William Moss, 'Quebec City's Archaeological Programme and Provincial Cultural Heritage Legislation,' in *Urban Archaeology, Municipal Government and Local Planning: Preserving Heritage within the Commonwealth of Nations and the United States,* Sherene Baugher, Douglas R. Appler, and William Moss (eds.) (Switzerland: Springer, 2017), 115–132.

12. Ann Hui, 'Archeologists Dig Up 19th Century Ship in Toronto's Downtown CityPlace,' *Globe and Mail,* May 7, 2015. https://www.theglobeandmail.com/news/toronto/archeologists-dig-up-19th-century-ship-in-torontos-downtown-cityplace/article24323618/ (accessed February 26, 2018).

13. 'Stage 4 Salvage Excavation of the Queen's Wharf Station Site,' Archaeological Services Inc., prepared for Context Developments, the City of Toronto and the Ontario Ministry of Tourism, Culture and Sport, December 2012. http://asiheritage.ca/wp-content/uploads/2016/04/09TE-016-stage-4-final-report.pdf (accessed February 28, 2018).

14. For further details, see: http://www.eraarch.ca/project/stanley-barracks/.

15. 'Remnants of Upper Canada's First Parliament Site Buried under a Toronto Car Wash,' CBC Radio. June 30, 2017. http://www.cbc.ca/radio/day6/episode-344-tomson-highway-the-hidden-site-of-canada-s-first-parliament-top-albums-for-canada-150-and-more-1.4178586/remnants-of-upper-canada-s-first-parliament-site-buried-under-a-toronto-car-wash-1.4178589. For further reading, see also: Frank Dieterman and Ron Williamson, *Government on Fire: The History and Archaeology of Upper Canada's First Parliament Buildings.* (Toronto: eastendbooks, 2001).

# IMAGE CREDITS

p. 1. University of Toronto Map and Data Library, from an original image at Library and Archives Canada; pp. 2–3, 4–5, 14, 15, 25, 38–39, 43, 46–47, 51, 54–55, 58–59, 65, 70, 75, 78, 79, 94–95, 99, 103, 109, 115, 125, 134–135, 138–139, 151, 159, 178–179, 198, 203, 210, 211, 219, 226–227, 231, 238–239, 254, 255, 258, 259, 262–263, Generously provided by Infrastructure Ontario; pp. 8–9. City of Toronto Archives, Fonds 2032, Series 841, File 1, Item 4; pp. 10–11. Courtesy of Holly Martelle; pp. 16–17. City of Toronto Archives, Fonds 200, Series 372, Subseries 32, Item 323; p. 19. City of Toronto Archives, Fonds 2043, Series 1587, Subseries 1, File 51; p. 29. Courtesy of the Toronto Public Library; p. 31. RG 1-58, MS 658 reel 480, p. 1644, Archives of Ontario; p. 33. RG 1-58, MS 658 reel 480, p. 1643, Archives of Ontario; p. 35. Generously provided by Infrastructure Ontario; p. 37. City of Toronto Archives, Fonds 2, Series 958, File 109, Item 2; p. 40. City of Toronto Archives, Fonds 200, Series 372, Subseries 32, Item 251; p. 49. Courtesy of Holly Martelle; p. 63. Courtesy of the Toronto Public Library; pp. 82–83. City of Toronto Archives, Fonds 1231, Item 1846; p. 85. City of Toronto Archives, Fonds, 1244, Item 1039; p. 89. City of Toronto Archives, Fonds 1244, Series 2119, Item 39.24; pp. 106–107. Courtesy of Joyce Zweig; p. 117. City of Toronto Archives, Fonds 200, Series 372, Subseries 32, Item 591; p. 119. William James, photographer. City of Toronto Archives, Fonds 1244, Item 0751L; pp. 120–23. Photographer unknown. Toronto Public Library, 982.17; p. 127. City of Toronto Archives, Fonds 2043, Series 1587, Subseries 1, File 46, Pearl Furniture on Centre Avenue; p. 131. City of Toronto Archives, Fonds 200, Series 410, File 1587; p. 137. *Globe and Mail*, April 20, 1895 (public domain); p. 145. *Provincial Freeman*, July 29, 1854, p. 3 (ink.ourdigitalworld.org); pp. 148–149. York University Libraries, Clara Thomas Archives & Special Collections, *Toronto Telegram* fonds, ASC06124; p. 154. City of Toronto Archives, Fonds 200, Series 372, Subseries 52, Item 794; p. 163. Caverhill's Toronto city directory for 1859-60, p. 292. Courtesy of the Toronto Public Library; pp. 168–169. City of Toronto Archives, Globe and Mail fonds, Fonds 1266, Item 8380; p. 175. Ontario Jewish Archives, Blankenstein Family Heritage Centre, accession 2008-6-4; p. 176. Ontario Jewish Archives, Blankenstein Family Heritage Centre, accession 1977-5-8; p. 181. City of Toronto Archives, Fonds 200, Series 372, Subseries 33, Item 140; p. 185. Ontario Jewish Archives, Blankenstein Family Heritage Centre, accession 2008-1-8; p. 187. City of Toronto Archives, Fonds 1118, Series 377, Item 308; pp. 189, 194–195. Courtesy of the Toronto Public Library, with thanks to Mary-Esther Lee for her donation; p. 196. William Still, from *The Underground Railroad from Slavery to Freedom* by Albert Bushnell Hart and Wilbur Henry Siebert, ed. 2. Macmillan: 1898, p. 74; p. 207. Courtesy of Holly Martelle; p. 209. From *Makers of History* by Helen McWorter Simpson, 1981; p. 213. Public domain, (www.wvculture.org/history/jbexhibit/bbsph05-0028.html); p. 221. City of Toronto Archives, Fonds 200, Series 372, Subseries 33, Item 137; p. 225. From 'Work Bike and Eat,' courtesy of Keith Lock; p. 229. Courtesy of the Toronto Public Library; p. 235. From *The Jew in Canada*, Arthur Daniel Hart, ed. (Toronto: Hunter-Rose, 1926).; p. 237. Ontario Jewish Archives, Blankenstein Family Heritage Centre, accession 1975-4/1; p. 243. Courtesy of Holly Martelle; p. 245. City of Toronto Archives, Fonds 1244, Item 766; pp. 246–247, 248, 249, 250–251. Courtesy of Timmins Martelle Heritage Consultants; p. 266. *Five Points, 1827*, George Catlin; p. 273. Queen's Wharf (goadstoronto.blogspot.ca); pp. 274–275. University of Toronto Map and Data Library, from an original image at Library and Archives Canada; p. 304. City of Toronto Archives, Fonds 200, Series 372, Subseries 33, Item 136.

Front cover: City of Toronto Archives, Globe and Mail fonds, Fonds 1266, Item 8380; 1891 Census, Image No.: 30953_148173-00331, Library and Archives Canada website: http://www.bac-lac.gc.ca; 1884 and 1893 fire insurance maps, Goad's Atlas of the City of Toronto, http://goadstoronto.blogspot.ca Back and spine: Generously provided by Infrastructure Ontario

# THE CONTRIBUTORS

MATTHEW BEAUDOIN is currently the manager of Archaeological Assessments at Timmins Martelle Heritage Consultants Inc. Matthew
completed his PhD at Western University studying nineteenth-century
colonial categories in Ontario. This work built off his previous research
working with the Labrador Métis at Memorial University.

NICOLE BRANDON, MA, is an archaeologist and material culture analyst who
specializes in the colonial period. Her graduate thesis was an analysis of
stoneware excavated from a seventeenth-century site in Ferryland,
Newfoundland. Currently based in London, Ontario, at Timmins
Martelle Heritage Consultants, Inc. Nicole's varied career spans twenty
years across four provinces.

ARLENE CHAN, who grew up in Toronto's Chinatown, is the author of seven
books about the history, culture, and traditions of the Chinese in
Canada, including *The Chinese in Toronto from 1878* (Dundurn, 2011).
She layers in her family stories and childhood memories when she
writes and lectures, and as she leads tours of Chinatown.

GORDON CHONG was born in Toronto in 1943 at the Toronto General
Hospital. He attended dental school on Elm Street. After ten years of practice, he was elected as senior alderman in Ward 6, serving on both Toronto
and Metro councils simultaneously. He is proud to have signed the application for the first Pride parade despite opposition from some older
Chinese and non-Chinese constituents, and is delighted that Toronto is
one of most diverse and welcoming metropolitan areas in North America.

ELIZABETH DRIVER is the Director/Curator of Campbell House Museum, adjacent to The Ward. Her ground-breaking study, *Culinary Landmarks: A Bibliography of Canadian Cookbooks, 1825–1949* (University of Toronto Press, 2008), won the Bibliographical Society of Canada's Tremaine Medal, and she has lectured and published widely about food history. She is a past president of the Culinary Historians of Canada.

ABBEY FLOWER fell in love with history while listening to her great-grandmother (who lived to be 110) tell stories around the kitchen table. After discovering archaeology, there was no turning back. Abbey has a BA in archaeology and anthropology from Memorial University in Newfoundland, and an MA in medieval archaeology from the University of York in the UK. Abbey worked for several years in consulting archaeology, with public archaeology programs, and at the provincial Ministry of Tourism, Culture and Sport, before taking on her current role as heritage specialist at Infrastructure Ontario.

BETHANY GOOD is a social worker and PhD candidate at the University of Toronto. She became familiar with The Ward as research coordinator on a project focused on the representation of children in early twentieth-century Toronto. Her doctoral research explores how digital media use among youth is understood and addressed by mental health practitioners.

KATHY GRANT is a public historian. Since making a promise to her ailing father, a World War II veteran, to highlight the stories of Black veterans, she has collaborated with the Canadian War Museum, Library and Archives Canada, and Veteran Affairs Canada. Her efforts were formally acknowledged in 2012, when Kathy received a Queen's Diamond Jubilee medal. Her Black Canadian Veterans web page receives over a half-million views a year.

NATASHA HENRY, president of the Ontario Black History Society, is an historian, educator, curriculum developer, and award-winning author focusing on Black Canadian experiences. She has developed the educational resources for exhibits and web-based projects on the Black experience in Canada, including the CBC miniseries *The Book of Negroes*. Natasha is completing a PhD in history at York University, researching Black enslavement in early Ontario.

CRAIG HERON is professor emeritus at York University, where he taught in the history and labour studies programs for thirty-five years. He is the author of numerous articles and books on Canadian social history, including *Booze: A Distilled History* (2003), *The Worker's Festival: A History of Labour Day* (2005), and *Lunch-Bucket Lives: The Remaking of the Worker's City* (2015). He has been co-chair of the Workers Arts and Heritage Centre, vice-chair of the Ontario Heritage Foundation, and president of the Canadian Historical Association.

SARAH B. HOOD serves on the board of the Culinary Historians of Canada and often writes about local food. Her next book, to be published by Reaktion Books in the UK, will be *Jam, Jelly & Marmalade: A Global History*.

VID INGELEVICS is a visual artist, independent curator, and occasional writer. He currently holds the position of Program Director, Photography, at the School of Image Arts, Ryerson University. He has exhibited his artwork in Canada, the United States, Europe, and Australia. He was recently involved in coordinating an exhibition at the City of Toronto Archives that explored the use of photography by social activists in early-twentieth-century Toronto as a tool of advocacy for the improvement of the lives of children in The Ward.

HEATHER MURRAY is a professor in the Department of English at the University of Toronto. She is the author of *Come, Bright Improvement: The Literary Societies of Nineteenth-Century* and other works on Canadian cultural organizations and print history. She is currently writing a history of The Ward's Gerrard Street Village, Toronto's first bohemia.

The REV. GREER ANNE WENH-IN NG 伍 吳 詠 嫣 is a retired professor at Emmanuel College, Victoria University, at the University of Toronto, who previously taught at Vancouver School of Theology and Trinity Theological College, Singapore. An ordained minister of the United Church of Canada, she continues to guest preach in various congregations around the Greater Toronto Area and to co-chair Emmanuel College's Committee on Asian/North American Asian Theologies (CANAAT) in its Centre for Religion and Its Contexts.

GUYLAINE PÉTRIN, BA, MLS, is a graduate of the University of Toronto. She is a part-time reference librarian at Glendon College, York University. Guylaine is also a genealogist, historian, and author who specializes in Upper Canada and Toronto. She is currently researching the Black community in Toronto before 1850.

PETER POPKIN, PHD, CAHP, MCIFA, has over seventeen years of professional experience in both consulting and academic archaeology in Canada and internationally. Peter was nominated for a 2017 Heritage Toronto Public History Award for his archaeological contribution to the St. Lawrence Market North redevelopment project in the City of Toronto.

TOM PORAWSKI currently works as an archaeologist with Timmins Martelle Heritage Consultants Inc. He completed his MA at Western University in 2008. Tom helped supervise the Armoury Street Dig and is analyzing the animal bone recovered there. His interest in zooarchaeology began early on, due to its potential to identify hidden details about past human populations.

WAYNE REEVES is chief curator for City of Toronto Museums & Heritage Services. This is his fourth writing project with Coach House, and the first without an aqueous theme. In 2008, he co-edited *HTO: Toronto's Water from Lake Iroquois to Lost Rivers to Low-flow Toilets* with Christina Palassio.

DAVID ROBERTSON is a partner at Archaeological Services Inc. and director of the firm's Planning Assessment Division. He is project archaeologist for many of ASI's projects in complex urban settings, as well as for specialty planning studies related to cultural heritage.

SIMON PATRICK ROGERS is the special collections archivist for the John M. Kelly Library at the University of St. Michael's College in the University of Toronto. He has written on a variety of archival and local history topics, including photography, music, architecture, and Jewish history.

ROSEMARY SADLIER, OONT, led the Ontario Black History Society from 1993 to 2015. As president, she contributed to the recognition of Black history though education, research, and outreach, and pressed the Canadian government to make Black History Month a national annual event, beginning in 1995. Born and raised in Toronto, she has degrees in teaching and social work, with family roots in Canada reaching back to 1793. Rosemary has received numerous honours for her work, including the Order of Ontario and the William Peyton Hubbard Race Relations Award.

DR. ELLEN SCHEINBERG is a historian, writer, and seasoned information professional. She is the president of Heritage Professionals, a firm specializing in archival, museum, and information management initiatives. She is also a proud Torontonian who promotes and celebrates the history of the city through her writing, tours, and presentations.

KAROLYN SMARDZ FROST is an archaeologist, historian, and award-winning author. Her biography of freedom-seekers Lucie and Thornton Blackburn, *I've Got a Home in Glory Land* (Thomas Allen, 2007), won the Governor General's Literary Award in 2007. Her newest book, *Steal Away Home* (HarperCollins Canada, 2017), tells the story of Cecelia Jane Reynolds. Cecelia's Toronto home was excavated during the 2015 dig in St. John's Ward. Karolyn is adjunct professor at Acadia University, and Senior Research Fellow for African Canadian History at the Tubman Institute, York University.

DR. CHERYL THOMPSON is assistant professor, Creative Industries, at Ryerson University. She was a Banting Postdoctoral fellow (2016–18) at the University of Toronto and the University of Toronto Mississauga in drama, theatre, and performance studies. Her first book, *Beauty in a Box: Detangling the Roots of Black Beauty Culture in Canada*, will be published with Wilfrid Laurier Press in 2018.

RONALD F. WILLIAMSON is founder of Archaeological Services Inc. He has a PhD from McGill University in anthropology and is an associate member of the Anthropology Graduate Faculty at the University of Toronto. He has published extensively on both Indigenous and early colonial Great Lakes history.

# THE EDITORS

HOLLY MARTELLE earned a PhD from the University of Toronto based on her research on Iroquoian populations in southern Ontario. In addition to sixteen years of experience in the road-building and aggregate industries, Holly has worked as a heritage planner at the Ministry of Tourism, Culture and Sport and taught at several universities throughout the province. Holly is a past president of the Ontario Archaeological Society.

Her research interests include nineteenth-century institutions, urban archaeology, the archaeology of gender and marginalized groups, women in archaeology, and archaeological ceramics. In 2003, she founded Timmins Martelle Heritage Consultants Inc. with Dr. Peter Timmins. In 2013, the firm was honoured with the Ontario Archaeological Society's award for Excellence in Cultural Resource Management.

MICHAEL McCLELLAND (CAHP OAA FRAIC), registered architect and founding partner of ERA Architects, specializes in heritage conservation, heritage planning, and urban design. Having begun his career at the Toronto Historical Board, Michael works with a wide range of public and private stakeholders. He is the coordinating architect for the Distillery District and the heritage architect for several significant Toronto projects, including the Royal Ontario Museum, and has recently won awards for projects including the Broadview Hotel and the heritage conservation work for Casey House.

Michael frequently contributes to the discourse surrounding heritage architecture and landscape architecture in Canada. He has taught at the University of Toronto and Ryerson University, published many articles, and served as an editor for several publications and books, including the

Coach House anthologies *The Ward: The Life and Loss of Toronto's First Immigrant Neighbourhood* (2015) and *Concrete Toronto* (2007). He has received numerous awards and honours, including recognition from the Ontario Association of Architects and the Toronto Society of Architects, for his contribution to the built environment and architecture.

TATUM TAYLOR is a writer, heritage planner, and Texan transplant, currently based in Toronto. She holds a master's degree in historic preservation from Columbia University, where she wrote her thesis on interpreting the heritage of marginalized communities in a museum environment.

As part of her work at ERA Architects, Tatum authored the Preliminary Heritage Interpretation Plan for the New Toronto Courthouse, and led the content development for a number of displays in Toronto City Hall, highlighting artifacts from the Armoury Street Dig. She co-edited the Coach House anthologies *The Ward: The Life and Loss of Toronto's First Immigrant Neighbourhood* (2015) and *Any Other Way: How Toronto Got Queer* (2017). Both were shortlisted for the Toronto Book Award; *The Ward* was also shortlisted for the Ontario Speaker's Book Award and won the Heritage Toronto Book Award.

JOHN LORINC is a Toronto journalist and editor. He writes about urban affairs, politics, business, the environment, and local history for a range of publications, including the *Globe and Mail*, the *Toronto Star*, *Walrus Magazine*, and *Spacing*, where he is a senior editor. He has won numerous magazine awards for his feature writing. John has been reporting about municipal government in Toronto since 1995, and began writing about local history in 2004, initially with profiles of R. C. Harris and Charles Hastings.

He is also the author of three books, including *The New City* (Penguin, 2006), and a co-editor of three previous Coach House anthologies: *The Ward: The Life and Loss of Toronto's First Immigrant Neighbourhood* (2015), *Subdivided: City-building in the Era of Hyper-Diversity* (2016), and *Any Other Way: How Toronto Got Queer* (2017). John is currently the Toronto non-fiction editor for Coach House.

# ACKNOWLEDGEMENTS

THE EDITORS WOULD like to express their thanks to many people who supported this anthology in various ways, both direct and indirect. They include Cary Mignault, Ainsley Davidson, and Geoff Woods of Infrastructure Ontario, which generously provided all of the artifact photographs found in this anthology; the office of ERA Architects; the staff and crew of Timmins Martelle Heritage Consultants Inc.; Greg Henkenhaf and Joanna Bell; Matthew Furrow; Susan Hughes, City of Toronto; the staff of the City of Toronto Archives, especially Gillian Reddyhoff and John Huzil; Michael Freisan at the Ontario Jewish Archives; Mayor John Tory, Premier Kathleen Wynne, and city council-lor Kristyn Wong-Tam; Ranbir Singh and Keerthana Kamalavasan, Toronto mayor's office; Shauna Brail, University of Toronto; Anthony Collins and Scott Colby, *Toronto Star*; Matt Blackett, *Spacing*; and the members of the New Toronto Courthouse Heritage Interpretation Working Group, several of whom contributed to this volume.

We would also like to offer our deep gratitude to the wonderful people at Coach House Books, who have provided amazing support for this and other local history projects. They include Crystal Sikma, Jessica Rattray, Ricky Lima, Rick/Simon, designer Ingrid Paulson, copy editor Stuart Ross, and of course Alana Wilcox, who said yes.

Typeset in Leo and Gotham
Printed on Rolland Enviro Satin paper,
 100% post-consumer recycled, FSC certified,
 milled in Canada

Edited by Holly Martelle, Michael McClelland,
 Tatum Taylor, and John Lorinc
Designed by Ingrid Paulson

Coach House Books
80 bpNichol Lane
Toronto ON M5S 3J4
Canada

416 979 2217
800 367 6360

mail@chbooks.com
www.chbooks.com